MEN *of* CHARACTER

MEN *of* CHARACTER

PROFILES OF 100 PROMINENT LDS MEN

LLOYD D. NEWELL, SUSAN EASTON BLACK,
AND MARY JANE WOODGER

Covenant Communications, Inc.

Cover image: *Glasses, Paper and Books on a Desk* © Photodisc, courtesy gettyimages.com.

Cover design copyright © 2015 by Covenant Communications, Inc.

Published by Covenant Communications, Inc.
American Fork, Utah

Printed in the United States of America
First Printing: April 2015

21 20 19 18 17 16 15   10 9 8 7 6 5 4 3 2 1

ISBN 978-1-62108-711-3

Acknowledgments

We express appreciation to Richard E. Bennett and the Religious Studies Center at Brigham Young University for research support. We are particularly grateful to student editors and research assistants—Ruth Covington, Sarah Miller, Alyson June Fulmer, Charlotte Carol Searle, Carli Hanson, Shaina Robbins, Leah Welker, Lisa Moncur, and Kayley Byers—for sharing their scholastic talents. We are also grateful for library and archival personnel for their kindness and expertise. We are indebted to Kathryn Jenkins Gordon of Covenant Communications, Inc., for her encouragement and confidence that a book about the lives of prominent Latter-day Saint men would inspire generations of readers.

INTRODUCTION

IT IS NOBLE MEN OF The Church of Jesus Christ of Latter-day Saints whose impressive accomplishments and quiet acts of benevolence we feature in *Men of Character*. In so doing, we recognize that there are thousands, if not millions, of Latter-day Saint men whose lives and characters witness that Jesus is the Christ. Choosing only a hundred of these to feature in this book has been difficult. After all, each outstanding man makes a contribution and is worthy of recognition. And we know we could compile countless volumes profiling prominent LDS men of character who have made a positive difference in the world. In an effort to limit our choices, we looked at a broad range of men who have accomplished something extraordinary—those who left an indelible mark. The men we selected stood out in a crowd, whether the crowd was a sports arena or a boardroom, a Church or an academic setting, a concert hall or a political debate. These men have made a difference.

Of course, first among Latter-day Saint men is the Prophet Joseph Smith, who has "done more save Jesus only, for the salvation of men in this world, than any other man that ever lived" (D&C 135:3). Likewise, each of the Presidents of The Church of Jesus Christ of Latter-day Saints has left a permanent influence for good. Other Church leaders who exemplified characteristics of love, devotion, and true discipleship were also included—such as Matthew Cowley, who loved the Maori people, and Neal A. Maxwell, whose devoted discipleship provided an example for all to follow.

Many of the Latter-day Saint men featured in this book excelled in a particular talent. Arnold Friberg painted unforgettable images of the Book of Mormon and at same time shared his gifts internationally as the art designer of the 1956 film *The Ten Commandments*. Ernest L. Wilkinson, who grew up in "Hell's Half Acre," became the seventh president of Brigham Young University and advanced the institution from an enrollment of four thousand to twenty-five thousand students and from a campus of six buildings to more than two hundred. Then there is Glenn Beck, who has known addiction and sobriety, marital decay and familial harmony, and who has authored seven *New York Times* bestsellers and received national recognition for his multimedia influence. Also recounted is the athletic prowess of Steve Young, named MVP of Super Bowl XXIX and inducted into the Football Hall of Fame, as well as the talent of Donny Osmond, whose recordings have sold more than one hundred million records. We present and celebrate the business acumen of J. Willard Marriott, which captivated the hospitality industry; the political power of Reed Smoot, who helped create the laws of the land; and the philanthropic outreach of Jon Huntsman Sr., which touches and helps the lives of thousands of people in need of medical care at the Huntsman Cancer Institute.

Each of these men has an inspirational story to tell. Their stories are about life, love, and a unique determination to succeed. We hope you will find within these pages biographical vignettes that may make a difference in how you live your life. Learn how and why some Latter-day Saint men made contributions in the professional world while others reached out to strengthen government, education, the arts, and families. Discover why many chose to hone their talents through long hours of patient practice while others were simply thrust onto the center stage of life. For many of these prominent men, balancing Church, family, and career came easily. For others, juggling personal life and fame was difficult while they shared the message of the restored gospel at home and abroad.

We have learned much while researching and writing about the lives of these eminent men. We resonate with their victories and empathize with their sorrows and defeats. To stand back and view another is to learn volumes about one's self. The messages of these men, both thunderous and gentle, reveal that true happiness and greatness are never found in compromising one's self. They are found in reaching beyond one's self to a higher source and for higher purposes. By reaching up, these men reached out to make a difference in the world. Some learned the hard way that keeping the commandments of God brings inner peace and happiness. Digression from or neglecting God-given roles or talents led others to sorrow and disappointment. We discovered that the path through life was smoother for the men who dedicated their lives to God at an early age. For each of their lives and the lessons and examples herein, we give thanks.

Why a book featuring LDS men? It is our hope that *Men of Character* will help readers realize that they too can develop talents and share their gifts; serve their families, the Church, and the broader community; and leave a lasting legacy for future generations to follow.

—Lloyd Newell
—Susan Easton Black
—Mary Jane Woodger

TABLE *of* CONTENTS

DANNY AINGE

Drive

Courtesy of *Deseret News*.

FEW LATTER-DAY SAINTS HAVE HAD a longer or more celebrated athletic career than Danny Ainge. As a high school student he was named to the all-American first team in football, basketball, and baseball—the only high school student to date to be so recognized for his athletic prowess. While attending Brigham Young University, Danny was again an all-American in basketball and was named national collegiate player of the year. Danny played major league baseball with the Toronto Blue Jays for three seasons and basketball in the National Basketball Association (NBA) for fourteen seasons. He coached the Phoenix Suns for four seasons before becoming executive director of Basketball Operations for the Boston Celtics. He is currently president of Basketball Operations for the Celtics.

Daniel Ray Ainge, son of Don and Kay Ainge, was born on March 17, 1959, in Eugene, Oregon. As a star athlete at North Eugene High School, Danny led his basketball team to back-to-back state championships. While enrolled at Brigham Young University, he met and courted Michelle Toolson; they married in March 1979 and became the parents of six children. Of Michelle, Danny said, "Truly an angel from heaven, my wife, Michelle, has been my greatest motivator. She is such a model of consistency and obedience. Her toughness, her unwavering faith, and her ability to endure me and my career, with our six children, have been remarkable. She knows everything about me and still loves me. That's not easy."[1]

Danny became a legendary basketball star at Brigham Young University. He is probably most remembered for his March Madness coast-to-coast drive and game-winning, last-second shot against Notre Dame in 1981, which advanced the Cougars to the Elite Eight. His 2,467 scored points at BYU remain in the top-twenty career list for the NCAA. In 1981 Danny was selected as the College Basketball Player of the Year after receiving the Joe Lapchick, Eastman, and John Wooden awards for his athletic ability on the basketball court. Danny set nine Western Athletic Conference records, ten BYU records, and at one time held the NCAA record for scoring in double figures in 112 straight games. He also excelled in scholastics, being voted twice to the academic all-American team by the College Sports Information Directors of America. Danny was inducted into the BYU Hall of Fame in 1991.[2]

The Boston Celtics selected Danny in the second round of the NBA draft. He played for the Celtics (1981–1989), Sacramento Kings (1989–1990), Portland Trail Blazers (1990–1992), and the Phoenix Suns (1992–1995). Danny won NBA Championship rings with the Celtics in 1984 and 1986 and helped his team to final appearances in 1985 and 1987. During his years in the NBA, Danny refused to party with his teammates. When Boston Celtics star Kevin McHale accused him of not having any fun, Danny recalled, "I just looked at him like he was crazy." Danny then replied, "You've got to be kidding me. I'm having the fun of my life. I'm living a dream. I have a beautiful young family. I'm playing in the NBA with the Boston Celtics. I mean, what could be more fun than that?"

In 1984 after the Celtics won the NBA championship game, Danny had as much fun as anyone when the corks popped. "They were all spraying champagne, and I had a can of orange soda and was drinking it and spraying it," he remembered. "The lifestyle of the NBA has done nothing but strengthen my testimony of principles of the gospel, such as that 'wickedness never was happiness.' I witnessed firsthand that living in an almost Hollywood- or rock-star-type of atmosphere is the last thing that brings happiness. There's no joy in the fun. As time went on, I think even my teammates recognized that I was having all the fun in the world."[3]

Danny retired from professional basketball in 1995 to coach the Phoenix Suns. In 1999 he resigned from his coaching position to spend more time with his family. Of that decision, he said, "My treasures were at home, yet my thoughts were constantly on the court. I would read good books and listen to inspired words and then apply them, not to my personal life but to coaching and my team. My true treasures, my beautiful wife and children, were often neglected," he added. "I finally decided to resign as head coach of the Suns, and it was one of the best decisions I've made in my life."[4]

During his years in professional sports, Danny maintained his passion and drive in his devotion to The Church of Jesus Christ of Latter-day Saints. While serving as first counselor in a bishopric, Danny anticipated a change, as the bishop had served for five years. "But, honestly, there was no way they were going to call me, with my schedule, to be a bishop," he said. To his surprise, he was then called to be a bishop. Danny recalled, "I had my doubts when they called me to be bishop, but I think that it will just compel me to find balance even more." Danny's youngest daughter, Taylor, wrote of her father's call: "My dad was called to be the new bishop of our ward yesterday. He is such a busy man and is about to become much, much busier. And my poor mom has been looking forward to having her husband home again after the NBA Finals. I guess that is not going to be happening anymore. But despite the time and effort they are about to start putting into this ward, they are excited and eager to serve. It has been a great reminder of what great people my parents are and how blessed I am to have such great examples."[5]

Danny remains in the athletic trenches, but his deeper and broader perspective of the things that matter most shapes his life today. "The person I am most grateful to, and to whom I owe the most, is my Savior, Jesus Christ," said Danny. "I am thankful for His life, thankful that even as a mortal, He lived perfectly. His unwavering love inspires me daily. His atonement is the source of hope in my life. Without it, I would be lost. The knowledge of His life puts my life in perspective. I can link the past, present, and future together, knowing that I, with my family, can be reconciled with God forever."[6]

1   *Why I Believe* (Salt Lake City: Deseret Book, 2001), 9–10.
2   "Danny Ainge," The Official Home of the BYU Cougars, http://byucougars. com/athlete/m-basketball/danny-ainge.
3   Michael R. Walker, "The Many Names of Danny Ainge," *BYU Magazine*, Winter 2009, http://magazine.byu.edu/?act=view&a=2357.
4   *Why I Believe*, 10.
5   Walker.
6   *Why I Believe*, 11.

Truman O. Angell
Faithfulness

Courtesy of Religious Education
Image Project, Brigham Young
University.

TRUMAN ANGELL'S LIFE IS A TESTIMONY to the fact that life never goes according to plan. His obedience and faithfulness to the Church and its leaders led him to building projects that he could never have imagined. In an April 21, 1868, journal entry, Truman wrote of his work as the architect of the Church: "If the President and my brethren feel to sustain a poor worm of the dust like me to be Architect of the Church, let me strive to serve them and not disgrace myself. . . . May the Lord help me so to do."[1] Truman's statement of obedience is just one example of his commitment to prophetic leaders.

Truman O. Angell, son of James W. and Phebe Angell, was born on June 5, 1810, in North Providence, Rhode Island. Truman's father deserted the family when Truman was five years old. By age nine, Truman had attended school for only two winters due to his heavy responsibilities on the family farm. At age seventeen, he became an apprentice to a carpenter and joiner. Near the same time, Truman felt "an earnest desire to become a subject of Christianity."[2] This desire prepared him to receive the gospel message presented by Latter-day Saint missionaries a few years later.

In 1833 Truman embraced Mormonism. Following his baptism, he fulfilled a short mission to the Eastern states, traveling more than five hundred miles to share the good news of Jesus Christ.[3] In 1835, Truman moved to Kirtland, Ohio, where the Prophet Joseph Smith assigned him to design and work on buildings in the community. Truman spent long hours working on the walls, priesthood pulpits, and windows of the Kirtland Temple. In the rooms of the temple, Truman recorded, "The power of God was made manifest to encourage us wonderfully."[4] It was there that Truman received an endowment from God and a blessing from Joseph Smith Sr. telling of his future role as a builder in the kingdom of God: "Yea thou shalt be mighty as Enoch who built a city unto God."[5]

After Truman was ordained a Seventy, he anticipated serving another mission. When Joseph Smith asked him to build a store, Truman told Joseph that he was "about to go out into the vineyard to preach." Joseph said, "Well, go ahead." However, Truman did not serve that mission. He recalled, "The next day I looked up and saw the First Presidency of the Church together; distant about forty rods: I dropped my head, and continued on my work. At this time a voice seemed to whisper to me, 'It is your duty to build that house for President Smith,' and while I was meditating, I looked up, and Bro. Joseph Smith Jr., was close to me. He said, 'It is your duty to build that house.' I answered, 'I know it.' Accordingly I changed my determination and yielded obedience."[6]

After enduring religious persecution in Ohio, Missouri, and Illinois, Truman and his family trekked across the plains to the Salt Lake Valley. In the valley, Brigham Young, like Joseph Smith before him, appointed Truman to design "homes, schools, churches, a sugar factory, forts, stores, a penitentiary, a theater, a governor's mansion, and, most importantly, temples."[7] To prepare him for designing these structures, Brigham sent Truman on a thirteen-month mission to Europe to learn the architectural styles of the past and present.

By 1852 Truman was clearly the most prominent architect in Salt Lake City, having worked on twenty-two projects in the community.[8] From 1853 until his death in 1887, Truman continually worked on the most important project of his career—the Salt Lake Temple.[9]

In spite of poor health and personal heartaches, for thirty-four years Truman served the Lord through his architectural designs. Many other talented and equally trained men worked as Church architects for a time, but it was Truman who endured "years of frustration and friction . . .

receiving little recognition and inadequate compensation." He was an "uncommonly loyal and devoted servant of the Church . . . [achieving] more than he aspired to do simply by doing what he regarded as his duty." In announcing Truman's death on October 16, 1887, the editor of the *Deseret News* epitomized him as a "staunch and true Latter-day Saint."[10]

1   Dean R. Zimmerman, "The Salt Lake Temple," *New Era*, June 1978, 34.

2   Shannon W. Ostler, "Truman O. Angell: Builder of the Kingdom," *Friend*, June 1987, 43.

3   Ibid.

4   Paul L. Anderson, "Truman O. Angell: Architect and Saint," in *Supporting Saints: Life Stories of Nineteenth-Century Mormons,* ed. Donald Q. Cannon and David J. Whittaker (Provo, Utah: BYU Religious Studies Center, 1985), 137.

5   Anderson, 139.

6   Truman O. Angell, *Autobiography*, L. Tom Perry Special Collections, Harold B. Lee Library, Brigham Young University, 3–4.

7   Ostler, 44.

8   Anderson, 146, 148.

9   Anderson, 149; John L. Hart, "A Will to Carry On," *Church News*, June 13, 1992, 16.

10 Anderson, 167–168.

DAVID ARCHULETA

Faithfulness

Courtesy of Jyle Dupuis.

AT AGE SIX, DAVID ARCHULETA listened to a recording of a *Les Misérables* concert. After a few hours, his parents noticed that he sang along with nearly every song and had even memorized some of the lyrics. As he recalled that experience, David wrote, "Though I couldn't possibly understand then what all the songs were about, I understood very clearly that it had struck me deep in the heart. . . . I had never felt so much passion for anything like that before."[1] Within a decade, David's passion for music had led him to perform before millions of people worldwide on the famed television show *American Idol*.

David James Archuleta, son of Jeff Archuleta and Lupe Maria Mayorga, was born on December 28, 1990, in North Miami, Florida, and raised in Utah. His is a musically gifted family: his father comes from a long line of singers, musicians, and performers, and his mother is a singer and a dancer.[2] As a child, David was a guest soloist in his parents' band at a local restaurant.[3]

In 2001, although lacking confidence and feeling uncomfortable on stage, David entered the Utah Talent Competition. Before his solo performance, David was "such a nervous, slobbering mess that [he] could barely get a sentence out."[4] After offering a prayer to God, he relaxed and sang "I Will Always Love You" by Whitney Houston before the competition, judges, and audience. The audience's enthusiastic response surprised David. He was even more surprised when he won first place in the children's division.[5]

Following this award, David was invited to sing on the *Jenny Jones Show*, which aired in Chicago. When the Chicago-based audience applauded, David internalized the fact that he had an unusual ability to sing and to sing well. His appearance on the *Jenny Jones Show* was followed by several opportunities to sing for nationally known artists and singers such as Natalie Cole and Kelly Clarkson. In 2003 he competed in the *Star Search 2* competition, finishing as the Junior Vocal Champion. During the interview that followed, David was asked why he enjoyed singing before large audiences. "I love singing because it makes people feel good and it makes me feel good inside," he said. "Everyone loves music."[6]

Just as David was launching his career in the music industry, his ability to be a vocal performer was threatened. An illness had left him struggling to breathe, and singing strained his voice. Physicians diagnosed David with partial vocal paralysis, the treatment options being either a high-risk surgery or hours of vocal therapy. David opted for therapy, which tended to be more frustrating than successful. By the time David entered high school, he assumed all plans for a musical career were out of reach.[7] Yet, after seeing little improvement for years, David finally began to breathe freely and his voice felt less strained. Of his recovery, David said, "I definitely believe some kind of miracle was at play when my voice, for no understandable or explainable reason, started to gradually feel better."[8]

David's dream of a musical career was again ignited, and he performed as opportunities were presented. Of the many singing opportunities that came his way, an audition to perform on the seventh season of *American Idol* was the biggest. "At first I felt a bit silly to be praying about something as unimportant as a TV show," David said. "[But] I felt strongly that I had to go. Even if I failed, I thought to myself that maybe there is something that I need to learn from going."[9]

After several grueling audition sessions, David was invited to be a contestant on *American Idol*. To the television audience, he appeared the judges' favorite from the beginning of his six-month performance schedule.[10] As a contestant, his time was consumed with rehearsals, performances, interviews, and press and media events. Though he focused most of his time and energy on his music, David kept up with schoolwork and other responsibilities. But for him, "it [was] a very real challenge to stay grounded spiritually. . . . Though I wasn't in touch with too many people outside of the *Idol* world during those six months, my relationship with God was the one I worked on the most. . . . I would be a contestant on *Idol* just for a short time, but I would be a son of my Heavenly Father forever."[11] During his months on *American Idol*, thousands of fans cast their votes for him. At the end of the season, David was named runner-up, garnering about 44 percent of the fan-based votes.

David signed with Jive Records and released his first single on August 1, 2008. The single debuted at number two on the Billboard Hot 100 and sold 166,000 downloads the first week. He has since released several successful albums and singles. In 2010, he released a *New York Times* bestselling autobiography.[12] That same year, he was the featured vocal performer in the Christmas concert of the Mormon Tabernacle Choir. Between concert rehearsals, he completed his Eagle Scout Award.[13] The down-to-earth and humble attitude of young David led a journalist from *Billboard* magazine to praise him for his "innocence and humility" and for filling a humble "void" for fans.[14]

During a Salt Lake City Christmas concert in 2011, David announced that he had accepted a mission call to serve in Chile. *Rolling Stone* and *USA Today* found his announcement newsworthy yet wondered why such a gifted young man would leave stardom to serve a two-year LDS mission. David explained, "It's not because someone told me I was supposed to do it and not because I no longer want to do music anymore. It's what I feel I need to do next in my life."[15] He told fans, "I'm going to be trying my best to focus on the people over there [in Chile]. . . . It's time for me to work on my relationship with [God] and the time that I need to give him."[16] David reported to the Missionary Training Center in March 2012 and served an honorable mission in Chile.

1   David Archuleta, *Chords of Strength: A Memoir of Soul, Song, and the Power of Perseverance* (New York: Celebra, Penguin Group, 2010), 31–32.

2   Archuleta, 12–13, 16–18; "David Archuleta Biography," The Ace in Entertainment, AceShoebiz.com, http://www.aceshowbiz.com/celebrity/david_archuleta/biography.html.

3   Archuleta, 33.

4 Ibid., 38–40.

5 Ibid., 40–42.

6 Ibid., 52–54, 60, 64, 74, 76–77, 202.

7 Ibid., 80–84.

8 Ibid., 89.

9 Ibid., 95–96.

10 Bill Lamb, "David Archuleta," About.com, Top40/Pop," http://top40.about.com/od/a/p/davidarchuleta.htm.

11 Archuleta, 119–126, 131, 187–188.

12 Ibid., 148; Jonathan Cohen, "Rihanna Fends Off Archuleta Atop Hot 100," *Billboard*, Aug. 21, 2008, http://www.billboard.com/articles/news/1044392/rihanna-fends-off-archuleta-atop-hot-100.

13 Trent Toone, "David Archuleta: the Eagle, the Temple and the Music," *Deseret News*, Nov. 28, 2011.

14 Jamie Lawson, "Rising Stars," *LDS Living Magazine*, June 4, 2008, http://www.ldsliving.com/story/4780-rising-stars.

15 Hillary Bowler, "Reaction to David Archuleta's Announcement of Serving an LDS Mission," *Deseret News*, Dec. 21, 2011, http://www.deseretnews.com/article/705396212/Reaction-to-David-Archuletas-announcement-of-serving-an-LDS-mission.html.

16 Josh Furlong, "David Archuleta Begins 2-Year Missionary Service," *Deseret News*, March 28, 2012, http://www.deseretnews.com/article/865553076/Pop-star-David-Archuleta-begins-2-year-Mormon-mission.html.

LEONARD J. ARRINGTON

Questioning

Courtesy of L. Tom Perry Special
Collections, Harold B. Lee Library,
Brigham Young University.

"I HAVE POSSESSED A QUESTIONING spirit all my life and have never found it to conflict with my Mormonism," said Leonard J. Arrington.[1] "I firmly believe that a person may be a converted Latter-day Saint *and* a competent and honest historian of the religion."[2] Leonard was the first Church Historian to be called to that position after being academically trained.

Leonard James Arrington, son of Noah Arrington and Edna Corn, was born on July 2, 1917, near Twin Falls, Idaho. Leonard recalled that the focus of his childhood was work. "Our primary responsibility was to work—school was secondary—even church," he said. "I do not remember that church played an important part of our life."[3] In his youth Leonard raised chickens, competed in local and state fairs, and became the Idaho president and national first vice-president of the Future Farmers of America.

Leonard's interest in Church history began at age fifteen when he read *Joseph Smith, An American Prophet* by John Henry Evans. Of this book, Leonard said, "The book portrays Joseph Smith as a person with an open mind, a questioning mind, a person in pursuit of education and knowledge. I accepted this as representing the spirit of Mormonism."[4]

In 1935 Leonard enrolled in the University of Idaho with an agricultural emphasis. By the end of his freshman year, he had changed his major to economics. Leonard described his college experience as an intellectual crisis, for he was "puzzled by the conflicting theories of evolution, behaviorism and theodicy. Although he never fully answered the questions raised by these issues, he emerged with an open-minded faith tempered by . . . liberalism."[5] Leonard graduated with honors in 1939 and continued his education at the University of North Carolina at Chapel Hill. As to serving a mission, Leonard said, "I felt a strong sense of mission in my schoolwork and felt the need to continue it."[6]

At Chapel Hill, Leonard met and courted Grace Fort, a Presbyterian. They were married in 1943, the same year Leonard tried to enlist in the U. S. Navy and then as an Air Force officer but was denied due to being shorter than five feet six inches, the minimum height requirement for an officer. In March 1943, he was drafted into the U. S. Army. Of his military service, Leonard said, "I served for fourteen months as a prisoner-of-war processor in Morocco, Algeria, and Tunisia, followed by fifteen months with the Allied Commission in Italy."[7]

While serving in Italy, Leonard wrote to John A. Widtsoe, a member of the Quorum of the Twelve Apostles, asking him for "suggestions for a dissertation on some phase of Mormon economic history." Widtsoe replied, "If you desire to write a thesis dealing with some phase of the economics of the Latter-day Saint Church, you have a field at your command." This was the beginning of what became an eleven-year writing project that culminated in his dissertation and the acclaimed publication *Great Basin Kingdom*. Reviewers hailed *Great Basin Kingdom* as "one of the most important books ever produced about the Mormons and Mormonism," "a significant and definitive contribution," and "easily the most informative single volume yet published on the Mormons in Utah."[8]

After graduating with his PhD in economics, Leonard was employed as a professor at Utah State University from 1946 to 1972. During one sabbatical leave, he was a fellow at the Henry E. Huntington Library and Art Gallery in San Marino, California. From 1958 to 1959, he was a Fulbright Professor of American Economics at the University of Genoa in Italy, and from 1966 to 1967 he was a visiting professor of history at the University of California, Los Angeles. From 1972 to 1987 he was Lemuel H. Redd Jr. Professor of Western American History at Brigham Young University. During these years, he had a "voluminous publication schedule" that is partially explained as a prodigious team effort.[9] "None of those [team] projects, however, had the power to propel [Leonard's] scholarly career in the creative, original direction toward which his great first book had pointed."[10]

On April 6, 1972, following three decades of preparation, Leonard was sustained as Church Historian at a general conference. After two years of service in this capacity, Leonard wrote, "I would not change places with any historian in America; nor, as a Mormon, would I change places with any church official with a different assignment. I am proud that all my work in the documents has increased my love for the church and my faith in its divine mission." One of Leonard's most treasured moments as Church Historian was when President Spencer W. Kimball said to him, "I want you to know that I love you very much, and that the Lord is pleased that you are the historian of His Church." Of this comment, Leonard said, "Kimball's loving blessing was a treasure to me and an affirmation of our work."[11]

After ten years as Church Historian, Leonard was released in 1982 and asked to take his team of historians to BYU and create an institute for studying Mormon history. "I interpreted our move to BYU as a way to preserve our scholarly integrity," Leonard wrote. "Under university administration, we could continue our scholarly work in an atmosphere of academic freedom." Although Leonard served as the director of the Joseph Fielding Smith Institute at BYU, "it was little more than a nominal appointment, for he retained his home in Salt Lake City and traveled to BYU only when necessary for a meeting or a class."[12]

Leonard wrote, "On July 2, 1987, I reached seventy years of age, and BYU administrators decided I should be terminated."[13] Although retired, Leonard continued to be active in historical associations such as the Mormon History Association, which he helped found in 1965, and the Western History Association. "If I had an extra $100 I went to an [economics] convention; or a trip to a historic site," he said.[14]

Leonard died on February 11, 1999, of heart complications. In his autobiography, he wrote, "Speaking for myself and, I think, for most of the historians who have worked with me, some tension between our professional training and our religious commitments seems inevitable. . . . My experience was a holy, never-to-be-forgotten encounter—one that inspired me to live up to the promises held out for those who receive the gift of the Holy Ghost."[15]

1   Gary Topping, *Leonard J. Arrington: A Historian's Life* (Norman, OK: The Arthur H. Clark Company, 2008), 208.

2   Leonard J. Arrington, *Adventures of a Church Historian* (Chicago: University of Illinois Press, 1998), 237.

3   Topping, 22.

4   Ibid., 208.

5   David J. Whittaker, "Leonard James Arrington: His Life and Work," *Dialogue: A Journal of Mormon Thought* 11 (Winter 1978): 25.

6   Topping, 24.

7   Arrington, 2.

8   Whittaker, 26, 23.

9   Ibid., 31.

10 Topping, 97.

11 Arrington, 112, 107.

12 Topping, 126, 127.

13 Arrington, 229.

14 Topping, 20.

15 Arrington, 236, 29.

ALAN ASHTON

Conviction

BECAUSE PRESIDENT DAVID O. MCKAY was his grandfather, some might suppose that Alan Ashton—CEO and cofounder of WordPerfect—never had to study to gain a strong personal testimony of the gospel of Jesus Christ. However, Alan said, "Even with that close connection to the leader of the Church, my testimony did not come from him, nor did it come from my parents. They were certainly influential in my attending Church meetings in my youth, but my conviction of the truth came from my individual study and obedience to the gospel principles."[1]

Alan Conway Ashton, son of Conway A. Ashton and Emma Rose McKay, was born in 1942 in Salt Lake City, Utah. "In middle school and high school I became interested in the stories and teachings in the scriptures," he said. "I loved the teaching of my 9th grade seminary teacher so much that during the summer when school was out I rode my bike three miles to his home early in the morning three times a week to hear him teach and explain the New Testament parables of Jesus."

After graduating from high school in Salt Lake City, Alan joined the 23rd Army Band and played the trumpet for the Utah National Guard. For basic military training, Alan was sent to Fort Ord near Monterey, California. During basic training, he said, "I read the Book of Mormon during the hourly ten-minute smoking breaks. I had a pocket-sized copy of the Book of Mormon that I had with me as we had classes and as we marched from place to place. . . . One night shortly after I had finished reading the Book of Mormon I climbed down from my top bunk and went alone into a large classroom in an adjacent room and knelt down on the hard, cold tile floor in the far corner of the room and offered a sincere prayer to my Heavenly Father in the Name of Jesus Christ asking if the Book of Mormon was true. I received a wonderful, powerful, warm, tingling sensation which enveloped me from head to foot. I rejoiced at receiving this confirmation of the Holy Ghost."[2]

Following this confirmation, Alan served an honorable mission to Germany. After returning to the United States, he pursued his educational goals at the University of Utah, where he graduated magna cum laude in mathematics in 1966. That same year, he went on a blind date with Karen Jackman. They courted and were married in 1968 in the Salt Lake Temple. Two years later, Alan earned a PhD in computer science from the University of Utah. While working toward his PhD, Alan "submitted two computer projects for possible research—one involving music and the other word processing. His professors opted for the first idea."[3]

In 1972 Alan became a professor of computer science at Brigham Young University, where he taught for the next fourteen years. During his tenure at the university, Alan met Bruce Bastian and in 1978 began working with Bruce on "what eventually became the world's premiere word processing software"—first named Satellite Software International and later WordPerfect Corporation. Before Alan left BYU to become the president and cofounder of WordPerfect Corporation, the graduating computer science class of 1986 nominated him "Outstanding Professor of the Year."[4] One year later, as president and CEO of WordPerfect, Alan was named "Entrepreneur of the Year" by the Small Business Association of Utah.[5]

Under Alan's presidency, WordPerfect software was designed to be easy to use and powerful, with the first version of the software being a word processor that operated on Data General minicomputers. As other versions of the software were added, WordPerfect became the world's top-selling DOS word processor.[6] By 1993, WordPerfect Corporation had more than five thousand employees worldwide and $700 million in revenue. In 1994 Novell, Inc., purchased WordPerfect and invited Alan to serve on its board of directors.[7]

Since then Alan has founded ASH Capital, an investment company. More relevant to the state of Utah, Alan and his wife, Karen, cofounded Thanksgiving Point in Lehi, Utah, in 1995 as a "permanent expression of their thanks."[8] Thanksgiving Point includes a "fifty-two-acre garden, the largest dinosaur museum in the world, a working farm, shops, restaurants, fifteen theme areas, nearly five miles of walking trails, a championship-caliber golf course, and a multi-screen movie theater."[9] Nearly 1.5 million people visit Thanksgiving Point each year. As to why Alan and Karen wanted to create such a beautiful expression of their gratitude, Alan said, "We wanted to create something for the people around us. . . . We've been blessed financially and with a large family. We wanted to give something back to the community and the families in our area."[10]

From 2004 to 2007 Alan served as president of the Toronto Canada West Mission. He currently serves on the BYU President's Leadership Council and as president of the Provo Utah Temple. Of his concept of life, Alan said, "To me success and happiness are not necessarily having a flourishing business, making life easy and comfortable, but having close and intimate relationships."[11] Alan enjoys being with his wife, Karen, their eleven children, and a host of grandchildren, knowing that his family will be together forever because of his testimony of the sacred covenants they have made in holy temples.

1   "Testimony of Alan C. Ashton," Mormon Scholars Testify, July 2010, http://mormonscholarstestify.org/1368/alan-c-ashton.

2   Ibid.

3   "Entrepreneurship Founders: Alan Ashton," BYU Marriott School: Center for Entrepreneurship and Technology, 2013, http://marriottschool.byu.edu/advisoryboard/detail.cfm?mem=1045&group=3.

4   "Thanksgiving Point Founders," Biographical Sketch, www.thanksgivingpoint.org/document.doc?id=127.

5   Alan C. Ashton, "'A "Perfect" Journey': WordPerfect Helping the World Communicate," William R. and Erlyn J. Gould Distinguished Lecture on Technology and the Quality of Life, Third Annual Address, J. Willard Marriott Library, University of Utah, Oct. 5, 1994.

6   See Jeanette Borzo, "Ashton: We Have Information at Your Fingertips," 15, no. 13 InfoWorld (March 29, 1993):102.

7   "Thanksgiving Point Founders."

8   Ibid.

9   Susan Easton Black and Mary Jane Woodger, eds., "Karen Ashton," *Women of Character* (American Fork, Utah: Covenant, 2011), 7.

10 "Testimony of Alan C. Ashton," Mormon Scholars Testify.

11 "Entrepreneurship Founders: Alan Ashton."

Richard Ballantyne

Selflessness

Courtesy of the Church History
Library, The Church of Jesus
Christ of Latter-day Saints.

IN A ROOM TWENTY FEET LONG and eighteen feet wide, Richard Ballantyne held the first Sunday School meeting for children in the Rocky Mountains. Neighborhood children sat on wooden slabs and listened as Richard dedicated the room for instructing the young. During the first year Sunday School was held in 1849, about fifty children attended. Today, children attending Sunday School number in the millions. As to why Richard built an extra room onto his house for instructing the young, he said, "I felt . . . that the Gospel was too precious to myself to be withheld from the children."[1]

Richard Ballantyne, son of David Ballantyne and Ann Bannerman, was born on August 26, 1817, in Whitridgebog, Scotland. As a youth, Richard helped contribute to the financial well-being of his family by working as a gardener, farm laborer, and cow herder until age fourteen, when he was apprenticed to a baker. Richard quickly learned the baker's technique, was promoted to foreman, and made plans to one day have his own bakery shop.

While serving as an officer of the Relief Presbyterian Church in Scotland, Richard organized a Sunday School for children to receive religious instruction. Yet he was concerned over certain doctrines of his faith and spent long hours in prayer and meditation. In 1842, Richard's religious struggle over doctrine ended when he was baptized a member of The Church of Jesus Christ of Latter-day Saints near Leith, Scotland. The following year, he and his extended family immigrated to the United States and settled in Nauvoo, Illinois, where Richard managed several businesses. Despite Richard's having suffered persecution, being kidnapped, and being held hostage by a mob, his faith did not waiver.

In 1846, after helping build wagons and carriages for the Mormon westward trek, Richard fled from persecution in Nauvoo to safety in Iowa Territory and then on to Winter Quarters, Nebraska. In Winter Quarters, he met and was married to Huldah Meriah Clark on February 18, 1847, by Heber C. Kimball. By 1848, Richard, Huldah, and their firstborn son entered the Salt Lake Valley.

Soon after entering the valley, Richard considered the possibility of schooling children. Approaching his bishop about the matter, Richard was given permission to start a Sunday School for children. On December 9, 1849, the first Sunday School meeting of The Church of Jesus Christ of Latter-day Saints was held in his home. During the meeting, children sang, prayed, listened to scripture, and heard the story of Jesus.

As time passed, the children's Sunday School moved from Richard's home to the Salt Lake 14th Ward meetinghouse. Richard formed Sunday Schools in other areas of the Salt Lake Valley and in Juab and Weber counties. He also organized the Eden School District, became a Weber County Commissioner, and served on the Ogden City Council. Wherever he resided, his work centered on helping children. "Under his direction, more schools were built, educational standards were improved, and public health facilities were expanded."[2]

In 1852, Richard interrupted his school and business ventures to accept a mission call to India. Of his twelve-month service in Madras, India, Richard wrote, "When I left Madras we had baptized 12 persons; ordained one Elder; preached the Gospel in almost every nook and corner of that large city, and several of the adjacent villages and cantonments; established a monthly paper of 8 pages; printed 1000 numbers of the 'Only Way to be Saved;' 1000 of the 'Proclamation of the Gospel;' 400 of a 'First,' and the same number of a 'Second Reply' to the Rev. T. Richards, of the English Church." After three years in India, however, Richard said of his labors, "We saw little fruit as the result of our toils."[3]

After returning to the United States in 1855, Richard enjoyed financial success as a manager of merchandising companies, two railroads, and a newspaper, but the Panic of 1893 wiped out his enterprises and left him a poor man. Richard maintained notoriety, however, for being the founder of the first Sunday School in the Church. He also took special pride in having founded a Sunday School for the Utah School for the Deaf and Blind. On Richard's eightieth birthday, "three thousand Sunday School children and teachers and four brass bands marched in a parade to honor him."[4] Richard died on November 8, 1898, in Ogden, Utah, while serving as a senior member of the high council of the Ogden Utah Stake.

When Richard was asked why he was so anxious for children to be taught the gospel of Jesus Christ, he said, "I was early called to this work by the voice of the Spirit, and I have felt many times that I have been ordained to this work before I was born, for even before I joined the Church, I was moved upon to work for the young. Surely no more joyful nor profitable labor can be performed by an Elder."[5]

1   *Jubilee History of the Latter-day Saints Sunday Schools, 1849–1899* (Salt Lake City: Deseret Sunday School Union, 1900), 12.

2   Jane McBride Choate, "Heroes and Heroines: Richard Ballantyne," *Friend*, March 1989, 49.

3   *Millennial Star* 2, vol. 17 (Jan. 13, 1855): 28.

4   Choate, 49.

5   Andrew Jenson, *Latter-day Saint Biographical Encyclopedia*, 4 vols. (Salt Lake City: Publishers Press, 1901–1936), 1:705.

MELVIN J. BALLARD

Fervor

Courtesy of L. Tom Perry
Special Collections, Harold B.
Lee Library, Brigham Young
University.

MELVIN BALLARD'S BIRTH WAS AN answer to his mother's prayer. Margaret Ballard, who knew much sorrow due to the deaths of her small babies, pleaded with the Lord that her next child would live to adulthood. "She saw no person, but a voice spoke plainly to her saying, 'Be of good cheer. Your life is acceptable, and you will bear a son who will become an apostle of the Lord Jesus Christ.'" Greatly comforted by this sacred experience, Margaret was confident that her son Melvin would live to be an Apostle of the Lord.[1]

Melvin Joseph Ballard, son of Henry Ballard and Margaret McNeil, was born on February 9, 1873, in Logan, Utah. His sister Myrtle recalled that as a child, "Melvin loved life, and he enjoyed humor and mischief. Time was precious to him and from his birth he seemed always to be grasping at every moment to learn and prepare himself for the future. Whatever task was his to do, he did it with all his might and all his strength." At a young age, Melvin learned the importance of hard work. Whether working, studying, or serving the Lord, he was devoted to the task. "He was a hard worker, in logging and farming," Myrtle remembered. "When noontime came, all hands laid down for a nap after lunch. Not Melvin! He always carried a precious book with him, and instead of sleeping he would sit down to read and study."[2]

While studying music at Brigham Young College in Logan, Utah, Melvin met and courted Martha "Mattie" Annabelle Jones. Melvin and Martha were married on June 17, 1896. Of their marriage, Bryant S. Hinckley remarked, "For more than forty-three years [Martha] walked by his side, always doing heroically her part as wife and mother. . . . She was constant and steadfast in her efforts to promote [Melvin's] welfare. Her loyalty and encouragement contributed much to his success."[3]

Melvin received a degree in music from Brigham Young College. Although he wanted to further his education at Harvard, the Lord had other plans for him.[4] When Martha was expecting their first child, Melvin was called to serve a mission in the Eastern states. Though it was a sacrifice for him and his wife, Melvin put aside family cares and temporal interests to serve the Lord.

On his mission, Melvin struggled to overcome fears of rejection. Having spent his whole life surrounded by those who shared his values, he was unnerved by the negative sentiment expressed to him, other missionaries, and the Church. While it was difficult for him to face opposition, as time went by he conquered his fears. Melvin recorded the following in a journal entry: "In the evening we decided to hold a street meeting. Never shall I forget the feeling I had in contemplating this effort. I would grow sick, then chill. . . . I stepped into the ring feeling very weak, but with the determination to do my best. After I had said a few words a man commenced heckling. This aroused me, and I broke forth speaking at the top of my voice. All fear left me. . . . I had great liberty in bearing testimony to the message I love and in crying repentance to the people of this generation."[5]

After Melvin completed an honorable mission, he returned to Logan to be with Martha and their young son. Melvin supported his family through founding the Logan Knitting Factory and other successful enterprises. In 1902 he was again called to serve a mission, this time to Boise, Idaho. From 1909 to 1919 he served as president of the Northwestern States Mission.

In 1919 Melvin was called to the Quorum of the Twelve Apostles. As an Apostle, he touched the hearts of many with his beautiful singing voice and his powerful conference addresses. In 1925 he dedicated South America for the preaching of the gospel of Jesus Christ. In his dedicatory prayer, Melvin prophesied that "thousands will join the

Church here. . . . The day will come when the Lamanites in this land will be given a chance. The South American Mission will be a power in the Church."[6] Melvin also served on the General Music Committee and was instrumental in compiling an LDS hymnal. He also helped initiate and integrate the Boy Scout and welfare programs into the Church.[7]

Before leukemia took his life in 1939, Melvin told of seeing a vision in which he met the Savior Jesus Christ. "The feeling that I had in the presence of him who hath all things in his hands," recalled Melvin, "to have his love, his affection, and his blessing was such that if I ever can receive that of which I had but a foretaste, I would give all that I am, all that I ever hope to be, to feel what I then felt!"[8]

1   M. Russell Ballard, ed., *Melvin J. Ballard: . . . Crusader for Righteousness* (Salt Lake City: Bookcraft, 1966), 26–27.

2   Ibid., 31.

3   Bryant S. Hinckley, *Sermons and Missionary Services of Melvin Joseph Ballard* (Salt Lake City: Deseret Book, 1949), 29; Ballard, 32–33.

4   Lawrence R. Flake, *Prophets and Apostles of the Last Dispensation* (Salt Lake City: Deseret Book, 2001), 448; Ballard, 32.

5   Ibid., 33, 37–39.

6   Ibid., 84.

7   Flake, 449; Ballard, 31, 85–87.

8   Lewis J. Harmer, *Revelation* (Salt Lake City: Bookcraft, 1957), 165–67; Flake, 450.

DEE JAY BAWDEN

Happiness

Courtesy of Dee Jay Bawden.

BY THE TIME DEE JAY BAWDEN was a senior in high school, he had completed the general education requirements for college and was looking forward to taking a year of advanced art classes in Salt Lake City before entering a university. His plans changed, however, when his bishop promised him, "If you take seminary, it will be the most important class you'll take." Following the counsel of his bishop, Dee Jay enrolled in seminary at Granger High School in Salt Lake City. While watching a short film on Joseph Smith's First Vision in his seminary class, Dee Jay began to wonder if Joseph really saw God the Father and His Son Jesus Christ. Searching for an answer, Dee Jay read the Book of Mormon and gained a testimony of the prophetic calling of Joseph Smith. When his seminary class asked him to sculpt a bust of Joseph Smith, Dee Jay studied the life of the Prophet and in that process had "an amazing experience" that fortified his testimony of Joseph's First Vision and the truthfulness of The Church of Jesus Christ of Latter-day Saints. Dee Jay still holds this testimony dear today.[1]

Dee Jay Bawden was born on January 12, 1951, in Salt Lake City, Utah. His mother, a talented artist, taught Dee Jay how to draw proportionate figures and faces while he was still in elementary school. His father, a fine woodcarver, taught him how to find potential for beauty in solid materials. Under his parents' tutelage, Dee Jay honed his unusual artistic talents and by age thirteen had constructed a "nine-foot-tall rearing mustang" as a mascot for his junior high school. "When I did that," Dee Jay explained, "[I thought it] was so fun that I said, 'This is what I want to do for my whole life!'"[2]

Dee Jay was not the only one excited about his artistic talent. His high school sculpture teacher, Jay Del Morris, told Dee Jay that he would "do many works" that would have a positive influence in the world.[3] After graduating from high school, Dee Jay served a mission to Japan from 1970 to 1972. On that mission, his testimony of Jesus Christ was strengthened.

After completing an honorable mission, Dee Jay enrolled in the University of Utah on an art scholarship. At the university, he chose not to draw or create nude statues except those required for his classes. In their place, Dee Jay drew and created models that gave expression to his testimony, for he very much desired to be "ready to do the likenesses of Christ"[4] like the *Christus* statue displayed on Temple Square in Salt Lake City.

While attending the University of Utah, Dee Jay met and courted his beautiful future wife, JoAnn Giles. They were married on September 7, 1973, in the Salt Lake Temple and became the parents of fourteen children. After JoAnn's death in 1997, Dee Jay married Deana Johansen, his former high school sweetheart. Together, Dee Jay and Deana are the parents of eighteen children. Paraphrasing the words of Ezra Taft Benson, Dee Jay said, "Happy is a man who has found his God, his eternal companion, and a work that he loves. That's me."[5]

From 1975 to 1979, Dee Jay worked part time as a professional sculptor and full time as a laborer at Kennecott Copper Mine. While working with a jackhammer at the mine, Dee Jay thought, "Ooh, Michelangelo would have loved one of these." It was at that moment that Dee Jay received the inspiration that he had been searching for to finish a statue of Christ. He quit his full-time job and, with the full support and faith of his wife, became a full-time sculptor. "If a person receives those kinds of experiences [the kind that prepared him to become a full-time sculptor] . . . it's easy to make the right decisions," said Dee Jay.[6] After working on the image of Christ's visage for seven years, Dee Jay said of his final product, "Not that this is the most accurate likeness of Christ, but that's not important; it has the right feeling, the right spirit."[7]

In 1980 when he finished his famed sculpture of Christ, Dee Jay presented the sculpture to President Spencer W. Kimball. At that time, President Kimball told Dee Jay that he would yet "do many things for the church."[8] During President Kimball's administration, Dee Jay was commissioned five times by the Church to create statues. Collaborating with Ed Fraughton and Florence Hansen, he constructed a more forensically accurate model of the faces of Joseph and Hyrum Smith based on their death masks, skull measurements, and early Nauvoo paintings.

Dee Jay continues to build his testimony through sculpting religious works of art. For him, the importance of his statues is the good that they do for others and the emotions that they communicate. "The most challenging and most fulfilling statues to do are of the Savior," he admits. "Then everything else after that is just wonderful too." Dee Jay has been commissioned to work on religious statues for many Christian denominations and enjoys sharing his testimony and happiness through his work. He says, "I couldn't have more blessings than that. Do what you love. Have a family who loves you. . . . The art is all secondary to that."[9]

When one meets Dee Jay, it is evident that he has found his God, family companionship, and a work that he loves, for he is happy. He hopes to work "for twenty more years." Of his future plans for increasing his talent and faith, Dee Jay said, "I'll continue to do, until I die, the things that the Lord wants me to do."[10]

1   Interview with Dee Jay Bawden by Carli Hanson, July 15, 2013, Provo, Utah; transcription in author's possession.

2   Ibid.

3   Ibid.

4   Ibid.

5   Ibid.; Ezra Taft Benson said, "Happy is the man who has found his worship, his wife, and his work—and loves all three" ("In His Steps," March 4, 1979, transcript, *BYU Speeches Archive*, Brigham Young University).

6   Interview with Dee Jay Bawden.

7   Ibid.

8   Ibid.

9   Ibid.

10   Ibid.

GLENN BECK

Inquiry

Courtesy of Gage Skidmore.

"GOD AND I HAVE A UNIQUE RELATIONSHIP," said popular broadcaster and businessman Glenn Beck. "I believe that I am one of his most impertinent children." Though Glenn considers himself impertinent, he professes that God has never given up on him. Through the ups and downs of his life—including cycles of sobriety, addiction, familial love, and marital decay—Glenn has never stopped searching for truth. He asks honest questions and claims that "your only agenda for any question should be 'I want the truth. I don't care what the truth is; I want the truth.'"[1]

Glenn Edward Beck, son of William Beck and Mary Janssen, was born on February 10, 1964, in Everett, Washington. At age eight, he developed an interest in broadcasting when his mother gave him *The Golden Years of Radio*, a collection of comedic and dramatic productions from the 1930s and 1940s. As he listened to the words of the collection, "pictures" were created in his mind.[2]

Glenn made his debut at age thirteen as a disc jockey on the radio. To many of his young friends, Glenn was on his way to stardom. However, his mother's struggle with alcohol and drug addiction, his parents' divorce, and his mother's suicide left Glenn devastated and confused. "Everything I had become was, in part, because of my mother, and I had never been able to get over losing her that way," he said. "It had tied me up in so many emotional knots that I had no idea how to get free."[3]

After graduating from high school, Glenn worked for small and then large broadcasting networks in Utah, Texas, Maryland, Connecticut, and Washington, DC, garnering national attention. Though his career skyrocketed, happiness evaded him.

"The more successful I had become," he said, "the more miserable I had become. I was empty inside."[4] His understanding of God and what he had been taught about God in Catholic schools stopped making sense to him, and he turned from religion.

Glenn married Claire McCabe in 1983, and they became the parents of two daughters.[5] Their marriage was compromised when Glenn turned to alcohol and drugs. A separation and divorce followed. The lowest point of his life, however, was when a doctor told him that with the way he was poisoning himself with alcohol, he would be dead within six months.[6] It was then—when he realized that he was missing his daughters' childhood because of alcoholism—that he determined to get control of himself.

As he struggled with sobriety, Glenn searched for answers to his questions about life. Hoping to find those answers, he enrolled at Yale University and studied philosophy and theology. "I had an open book in every room," recalled Glenn. "I got rid of TV. I had a book in my pocket at all times and a different book in every single room of the house."[7]

While searching for answers, Glenn met and began dating Tania Colonna. When Glenn suggested marriage to Tania, she refused, insisting that if she agreed to marry him they would have to find a faith and attend a church regularly. Glenn was resistant to her idea, but realized that by joining a church he could put God back into his life. Glenn, Tania, and Glenn's daughters soon began what they affectionately called their "church tour," attending a variety of churches listed in the phone book.

Friend and colleague Pat Gray, a member of The Church of Jesus Christ of Latter-day Saints, suggested that if Glenn wanted to honestly look for answers he should give the Mormon Church a chance. Glenn's admiration for Pat's happy and stable family life led him to attend a worship service of The Church of Jesus Christ of Latter-day Saints. When Tania and his children began attending a local Mormon church each week, Glenn agreed to meet with LDS missionaries. "I put those missionaries through the ringer," he said. "I did all of my investigation. My wife did hers. We weren't married yet, but we searched as a couple and as individuals. I was not going to accept something that wasn't true. I was not going to live a lie."[8] Glenn and Tania were married and baptized members of The Church of Jesus Christ of Latter-day Saints. Glenn is now a father of four and remains a devoted member of the Church.

Through the years Glenn has become the host of many popular talk radio and television programs. From 2006 to 2008 he hosted his own show on *CNN Headline News.* His success on CNN led to a remarkably successful show that ran for two and half years on the FOX News channel. He is the author of seven number-one *New York Times* bestsellers, and he has received national recognition for his multimedia influence. He is also a successful businessman and public speaker.

Glenn attributes the miraculous change in his life to the healing power of Jesus Christ and his willingness to search for answers. The personal slogan that guides his life comes from a letter written by Thomas Jefferson in 1787: "Question with boldness."[9] His personal quest for answers has been an inspiration to thousands, if not millions, throughout the world. Glenn is a man "armed with quick wit, an informed opinion and a unique ability to inspire others to rise to their full potential with an open heart."[10]

1   Glenn Beck, *An Unlikely Mormon: The Conversion Story of Glenn Beck* (Salt Lake City: Deseret Book, 2008), DVD.
2   Glenn Beck and Keith Ablow, MD, *The 7: Seven Wonders That Will Change Your Life* (New York: Threshold Editions, 2011), 23.
3   Beck and Ablow, 23.
4   Beck.
5   Sheri and Bob Stritof, "The Tania and Glenn Beck Marriage Profile," About. com: People and Relationships, http://marriage.about.com/od/politics/p/Tania-And-Glenn-Beck-Marriage-Profile.htm.
6   Beck and Ablow, 26.
7   Ibid., 19, 26, 28–30, 34; Beck.
8   Beck.
9   Beck and Ablow, 55; and Beck.
10 James Davis, "'The Leader We Need Is You,' Beck Tells 17,000 at BYU," *Deseret News,* June 30, 2008.

LOWELL L. BENNION

Community Activist

Courtesy of *Deseret News*.

NOTED EDUCATOR AND HUMANITARIAN LOWELL BENNION was known as the "Patriarch of Volunteerism"[1] in Utah. As a devoted disciple of Jesus Christ, Lowell lived by the self-professed creed:

> Learn to like what doesn't cost much.
> Learn to like reading, conversation, music.
> Learn to like plain food, plain service, plain cooking.
> Learn to like fields, trees, brooks, hiking, rowing, climbing hills.
> Learn to like people, even though some of them may be different from you. . . .
> Learn to like to work and enjoy the satisfaction of doing your job as well as it can be done.
> Learn to like the song of birds, the companionship of dogs.
> Learn to like gardening, puttering around the house and fixing things.
> Learn to like the sunrise and sunset, the beating of rain on the roof and windows and the gentle fall of snow on a winter day.
> Learn to keep your wants simple and refuse to be controlled by the likes and dislikes of others.[2]

Lowell L. Bennion, son of Milton Bennion and Cora Lindsay, was born on July 26, 1908, in Salt Lake City, Utah. In 1928 Lowell graduated from the University of Utah, married Merle Colton, and accepted a mission call to serve in the Swiss-German Mission. After Lowell's mission, his wife, Merle, joined him in Europe as Lowell studied to complete a PhD in sociology at the University of Strasbourg. After earning his PhD, Lowell, Merle, and their family (which eventually numbered six children) returned to America and settled in Salt Lake City.

In 1934 Lowell decided to accept a call to be the first director of the University of Utah's LDS Institute of Religion instead of continuing on in a scholarly career in the sociology of religion. He not only founded the institute but created the Lambda Delta Sigma fraternity with the hope of helping college students integrate learning with service. Thereafter, nearly every Saturday for the next thirty years Lowell accompanied a Lambda Delta Sigma chapter or two as they cleaned a yard, painted a house, or delivered food donated from his or others' gardens to help those in need.[3]

For ten years, beginning in 1962, Lowell was a professor of sociology and associate dean of students at the U of U. At age sixty-four, Lowell left academia to become the director of the Salt Lake Community Services Council. For the next sixteen years, he directed community services for those residing in the Salt Lake Valley. Lowell organized hands-on volunteer service programs, which included founding a homeless shelter, providing a food bank for thousands of needy households, and coordinating hundreds of volunteers to help the elderly and handicapped with chores. Lowell then founded and served as the director of the Teton Valley Boys Ranch in Driggs, Idaho. The ranch provided urban youth with summer opportunities for outdoor work and recreation. Lowell—or "Doc," as they called him at the ranch—derived great satisfaction from supervising the summer work and recreation of more than two thousand teenagers. Today, the Birch Creek Ranch carries on the Teton Valley Ranch tradition of community service, hard work, and simple living.[4]

In addition to organizing these volunteer outreach programs, Lowell authored dozens of books and essays and gave scores of lectures placing Latter-day Saint thought and practice in the realm of social morality— service and volunteerism. Although humble and reserved in his personal life, Lowell was a courageous, outspoken, and effective foe in his speeches against religious prejudice, racism, sexism, and materialism. He demonstrated his philosophy and teachings through community service and inspired thousands of others to offer devoted, effective, and practical humanitarian efforts in their communities and beyond. Lowell wrote curricula for the Sunday School organization and priesthood quorums of the Church and served as a bishop in the East Millcreek 12th Ward.[5]

Lowell liked to listen as others told him their problems. He would frequently interrupt any conversation with the question, "How can I help?" He painted houses, weeded gardens, served food, and did whatever needed to be done to assist others. As one volunteer director said of him, "[Lowell is] not particular about whom he helps. Religion and race didn't matter to him. He's one of a kind."[6]

Lowell received many honors for his humanitarian outreach efforts, including an honorary doctorate from the University of Utah (1982); the establishment of the Lowell L. Bennion Center for Community Service (1986); and the Caring Award (1989), given to ten Americans at the nation's capital who best exemplify compassionate service. In 1985 when Lowell received the Good Samaritan Award from Utahns Against Hunger, the executive director of United Way said, "[Lowell is] a combination of an Old Testament prophet, who wants to give you his vision of what should be, and a New Testament good Samaritan, who doesn't stand back and talk, but steps in to do the good work himself." Lowell and his wife, Merle, received the Presidential Citation from Brigham Young University at the August 1991 commencement.[7]

After a ten-year struggle with Parkinson's disease, Lowell died on February 21, 1996. To the question "What does it mean to follow Christ?" Lowell answered,

> Everything in the gospel depends on love. The most important thing a Latter-day Saint can do is love his neighbor—all of God's children, the poor, the sinner, the rich, the black, the Caucasian, the old, the young, the enemy, the widow, the orphan. A disciple of Christ is not caught up in material things. He does not lay up for himself "treasures on earth," living in luxury while half the world goes to bed hungry. He uses his means and wealth to give employment, education, opportunity, even food to those in need. A disciple of Christ is

humble, meek, and lowly. He does not have all the answers; he asks, seeks, and knocks. He is not self-righteous. He is characterized by discontent over his own ignorance and sins and over the suffering of his fellowman.

1   "Bennion Center Honors Namesake with Community Service, U New Center, University of Utah, http://unews.utah.edu/news_releases/bennion-center-honors-namesake-with-community-service/.

2   Eugene England, "The Achievement of Lowell Bennion," *Sunstone*, July 1988, 29.

3   "Lowell L. Bennion," Lowell Bennion Community Center, University of Utah, http://bennioncenter.org/documents/LowellBio.pdf.

4   Ibid.; Birch Creek Ranch, www.birchcreekserviceranch.org.

5   "Lowell L. Bennion"; "Death: Lowell L. Bennion," *Deseret News*, Feb. 23, 1996, http://www.deseretnews.com/article/473312/DEATH-LOWELL-L-BENNION.html?pg=all; see also Donald Q. Cannon, Richard W. Cowan, and Arnold K. Garr, *Encyclopedia of Latter-day Saint History* (Salt Lake City: Deseret Book, 2001), 90–91.

6   Jack Fenton, "Volunteer, 83, Moves Slowly But Covers a Lot of Ground," Utah Educational Network, http://www.uen.org/Centennial/17PhilanB.shtml.

7   Eugene England, "Bennion, Lowell L.," http://www.uen.org/utah_history_encyclopedia/b/BENNION_LOWELL.html.

Ezra Taft Benson

Steadfast

Courtesy of the Church
Archives, The Church of Jesus
Christ of Latter-day Saints.

FROM 1985 TO 1994, Ezra Taft Benson served as the thirteenth President
of The Church of Jesus Christ of Latter-day Saints. As President, he was
tireless in exhorting Latter-day Saints to beware of pride and to read
the Book of Mormon, the keystone of their religion. Ezra was known
worldwide as a family man, leader, patriot, and a devoted disciple of Jesus
Christ. On Ezra's nineteenth birthday, United States President George Bush
presented him the Presidential Medal, citing his service to three great
loyalties—God, family, and country.

Ezra Taft Benson, son of George Taft Benson Jr. and Sarah Dunkley,
was born on August 4, 1899, in Whitney, Idaho, the eldest of eleven
children. Ezra was named for his great-grandfather Ezra Taft Benson, the
first man to be called to the Apostleship after the martyrdom of Joseph
Smith. At Ezra's birth, when the attending doctor concluded the baby had
not survived, his grandmothers took him and dipped his body in cold
and then warm water until they heard Ezra cry. Both grandmothers bore
testimony that Ezra's life was spared by God.[1]

Ezra Taft—or Ezra "T," as he liked to be called—grew up on a family
farm in Whitney, Idaho, where he learned the practical purposes of hard
work. He attended the Oneida Stake Academy, a Church-run school in
Preston, Idaho, and later Utah State Agriculture College (now Utah State
University). During World War I, he served in the military. At the end of

the war, Ezra accepted a mission call to Great Britain, where he presided over the Newcastle area in 1923.

After his mission, Ezra enrolled in Brigham Young University, where he was designated in the yearbook as "the most popular man." After graduating from BYU, Ezra married his eternal sweetheart, Flora Smith Amussen, on September 23, 1926, in the Salt Lake Temple.[2] Ezra and Flora became the parents of six children, two sons and four daughters.

After his marriage, Ezra continued his education at Iowa State College, graduating in agricultural science with a master's degree in 1927. Ezra was then employed as a county farm agent and as an extension specialist for the University of Idaho while serving concurrently as stake president in Boise, Idaho. He pursued additional graduate work at the University of California at Berkeley until he became the executive secretary of the National Council of Farmer Cooperatives in Washington, DC. While working in the nation's capital, Ezra also served as president of the Washington DC stake.

On October 7, 1943, Ezra was called to be an Apostle of the Lord Jesus Christ. As a member of the Quorum of the Twelve Apostles, he served as president of the European Mission, reopened missionary work on that continent, and supervised the distribution of welfare supplies and aid to Europeans following World War II. With the permission of President David O. McKay, Ezra served as the Secretary of Agriculture in the cabinet of United States President Dwight D. Eisenhower from 1953 to 1961. In this position, he was recognized for his leadership in advocating prayer in cabinet meetings and for making the higher choice when it came to moral decisions affecting the nation, no matter the opposition.

Ezra traversed the nation many times as Secretary of Agriculture, holding hundreds of press conferences and delivering countless speeches. He was featured on the covers of *US News and World Report*, *Newsweek*, *Business Week*, and twice on the cover of *Time* magazine. He wrote more than a dozen books, including *Crossfire: The Eight Years with Eisenhower*, *The Constitution: A Heavenly Banner*, and *God, Family, Country: Our Three Great Loyalties*. Universities from Maine to Hawaii awarded him honorary doctoral degrees. Of Ezra's contributions to the Eisenhower cabinet, President David O. McKay said that they will "stand for all time—as a credit to the Church and the nation."[3]

In 1973 Ezra became President of the Quorum of the Twelve Apostles and, on November 10, 1985, President of The Church of Jesus Christ of Latter-day Saints. During his administration, the Church continued to expand as temples were dedicated in North and South America, Europe, and Asia. The Brigham Young University Jerusalem Center for Near Eastern Studies was also dedicated and missionary work was extended to fifty additional countries throughout the world.[4]

Ezra delivered eight major addresses on the stages or cycles of life that were compiled in *Come, Listen to a Prophet's Voice*. His addresses "Beware of Pride" and "Cleansing the Inner Vessel" warned Latter-day Saints against the evils of pride. In his other addresses, Ezra's consistent themes were love of country, freedom, home, family, and the Lord and His gospel; however, few of his addresses are better remembered than his words about the Book of Mormon. Ezra believed that Latter-day Saints should not only read daily from the Book of Mormon but that they should flood the earth with this powerful scripture. A little-known personal hallmark of his administration was that Ezra and his wife, Flora, attended the temple every Friday morning when able.

Like his predecessor, President Spencer W. Kimball, Ezra faced great health challenges incident to old age. For example, at age eighty-nine Ezra had a mild heart attack that greatly impaired his health. Adding to his woes, on August 14, 1992, Flora, his beloved wife of nearly sixty-six years, died. Ezra's health continued to decline until his death in Salt Lake City from heart failure on Memorial Day, May 30, 1994, at the age of ninety-four.[5]

Ezra Taft Benson left a legacy of devotion to God, family, and country that few men could equal. He blessed the lives of millions through his service to the Church and his leadership talents in the field of agriculture. He also blessed his family through a lifetime of devotion to them and their needs, which included performing each of the marriage ceremonies of his children in the Salt Lake Temple. Truly, it can be said that Ezra's life is one worthy of emulation.

1   Sheri Dew, *Ezra Taft Benson: A Biography* (Salt Lake City: Deseret Book, 1987), 13–14.

2   Arnold K. Garr, Donald Q. Cannon, and Richard W. Cowan, *Encyclopedia of Latter-day Saint History* (Salt Lake City: Deseret Book, 2001), 94, 96.

3   Ibid., 95.

4   Ibid., 96.

6   "Death: Flora Amussen Benson," *Deseret News*, Aug. 17, 1992, http://www.deseretnews.com/article/242804/DEATH-FLORA-AMUSSEN-BENSON.html; "Ezra Taft Benson: 13th President of the Church," *Church History, The Church of Jesus Christ of Latter-day Saints*, http://www.lds.org/churchhistory/presidents/controllers/potcController.jsp?leader=13&topic=facts.

ALEX BOYÉ

Believing in Self

Courtesy of Alex Boyé.

FOUR OR FIVE TIMES A WEEK, young Alex Boyé had the same dream about dying. It was really "scary stuff for a young kid," he remembered. As disturbing as the dreams were, he never mentioned his nightmares to anyone, until at the age of sixteen he was talking with some Mormon missionaries. As he shared his frightening dreams with the missionaries, their message brought him peace for the first time, and there "was a total transformation inside of [his] heart."[1]

In 1970, while pregnant with Alex, his mother, Caroline Boyé, immigrated to London while his father, whom he never met, remained in Nigeria. Alex was born October 5, 1970, in London's rough Tottenham neighborhood.[2] When Alex was just eleven years old, his mother told him she was going on a trip to Nigeria for three weeks. She was gone for the next eight years; Alex spent much of his youth in foster homes with Caucasian parents. Alex remembers that being abandoned left him with "pent up resentment for everything," especially for being poor. At one point Alex was even eating food out of trash cans.[3] The only relief he had was through dancing to the music of Motown, starting with Stevie Wonder and Kool and the Gang.[4]

Alex was working at a McDonald's when his LDS manager invited him to hear a presentation by Mormon sister missionaries. Because Alex wanted the chance to talk to some American girls, he agreed. He found a message that moved him and a community ready to take him in. "I felt like I was back in a functional family in some way," he recalls.[5] He was baptized soon after.

The first time Alex sang in public was while serving a mission for The Church of Jesus Christ of Latter-day Saints in Bristol, England. "His knack for connecting with audiences became obvious as he performed LDS hymns and other music for church groups. At the conclusion of his service, his mission president's final advice was to do something with his musical talent."[6]

After he returned from his mission, Alex became a backing dancer for performers like George Michael. Then in 1995 he formed the boy band Awesome, which toured across Europe. The band became a success, selling half a million CDs in Europe, but Alex became disenchanted with "the raunchiness of life as a touring musician." As a fully committed Latter-day Saint keeping the Word of Wisdom and the law of chastity, it was difficult to be a pop star. Alex kept his scriptures with him every single day to ward off "the temptation everywhere."[7] "I had this dream of being a musician, but it was taking me down a road that led somewhere I didn't want to go," he says.[8]

Looking back on being a member of a pop band Alex recalls, "It really was a great experience. . . . It got to the point where I had all the things I ever thought would make me happy. I had fun and money—but then it really went pear-shaped." Despite the fame, glory, and fortune, Alex felt emptiness in his life that none of these worldly accolades could sufficiently fill. "I was climbing the ladder of success," he explains, "but when I got to the top, I found myself leaning on the wrong side of the wall."[9]

"On my mission, the spirit was there when I sang," Alex shares. "In the band it wasn't ever like that, and even though I was now on my own, it still didn't feel like I was where the Lord wanted me to be. One day I was reading the scriptures and it said to forsake this world and seek for something better and how the song of the righteous is a prayer unto Him. I realized I wanted to do music that was more uplifting—that could do something for someone."[10] So Alex followed his motto: "Just believe, then let the Lord do the work He promised He would!"[11]

When Alex left the band in 1999 to pursue a solo career, he lost everything. The record company took his apartment, clothes, phone, and money.[12] Alex had been praying to know what to do when one night in 2000, he received an answer: "I had a dream I was running away from something, and there was someone who pointed me to a place and said, 'Hide here.' So I hid underneath some bushes, in a lake, and then I remember . . . the water tasted salty. I woke up the next day just thinking, 'Salt Lake! That's where I'm supposed to be.'" A few days later, Alex received the confirmation he needed for his decision to move to Utah when he received an invitation to attend the Mormon Arts Festival.[13]

Alex shares, "I think that those who make the greatest change in this world are those who believe in themselves first, then the miracles follow."[14] Since immigrating to Utah, Alex has experienced many things he considers miraculous, including crossing over from a pop artist to a Christian singer; giving a Book of Mormon to Prince Charles; joining the Mormon Tabernacle Choir; and marrying his wonderful wife, Julie Jeppson, in the Salt Lake Temple. Alex's music has been featured on several movie soundtracks, and two solo songs are featured on Mormon Tabernacle Choir albums.[15] Alex declares:

> We as human beings tend to spend a lot of our time with negative self-talk and not believing in ourselves, which in turn gives power to the adversary. . . . I believe the way we please God is to have ultimate confidence in our abilities to accomplish GREAT things. . . . Once we are in this frame of mind, then the Lord steps in and makes up for what we lack and brings about amazing things in our individual lives. It has taken me a while to apply this, but now that I have, I am seeing incredible things happen in my life with my music and other areas of my life![16]

1   Joe Shute, "British Mormons Take on the Book of Mormon," *The Telegraph*, Apr. 10, 2013.

2   Celia R. Baker, "Former British Pop Sensation Alex Boyé Finds His Voice in Mormon Tabernacle Choir," *The Salt Lake Tribune*, July 19, 2009.

3   Alex Boyé, Frontman: The Alex Boyé Story, http://deseretbook.com/Front-Man-Alex-Boye-Story-Deseret-Book-Company/i/5078003 (DVD).

4   Boyé.

5   Baker.

6   Ibid.

7   Shute.

8   Baker.

9   Ibid.

10   "Alex Boyé: Song of the Heart," ldsgenesisgroup.org.

11   Nicole Sheahan, "Alex Boyé: Being the Change—Inside Mormon Music," *Deseret News*, Dec. 11, 2009.

12   "Alex Boyé: Song of the Heart."

13   Emily McClure, "Alex Boyé's American Dream Comes True with U.S. Citizenship," *LDS Living*, Feb. 28, 2012.

14   Sheahan.

15   "Alex Boyé in Concert to Spread Message of Hope," *Deseret News*, May 6, 2012.

16   Sheahan.

HUGH B. BROWN
Confidence

Courtesy of the Church History
Library, The Church of Jesus
Christ of Latter-day Saints.

IN 1906, HEBER J. GRANT, the mission president of the Church in England, received a letter from a minister stating, "Send me the best man you have in your mission and I will debate with him and defeat him." President Grant knew that Hugh B. Brown was the missionary who could win the debate. "To be honest," said Hugh, "I was elated with the prospect of such an encounter, as I had considerable faith in my ability to meet with such a man. I can lick that fellow with the scriptures I now have at my command." After the debate, the minister told Hugh, "I have been opposing you Mormons all along, but I want you to know now that what I have heard tonight has convinced me that I was wrong and that you are right. I want to join your church."[1]

Hugh B. Brown, son of Homer and Lydia Jane Brown, was born on October 24, 1883, in Granger, Utah. Hugh's mother instilled self-confidence in him from an early age. "My angel mother . . . had faith in my destiny," wrote Hugh. "All through my life [she] helped me to believe and try to be worthy of it. . . . If I would 'behave myself' there was nothing I could not do, become, or have. She held that promise before me all my life."[2] His father, on the other hand, was somewhat difficult to live with. Hugh said, "Although I admired my father and loved him in a way, I never felt intimate or close to him."[3]

At age fifteen, Hugh moved with his family to Canada so that his father could fulfill an LDS mission by helping build a canal. While other youth in Canada spent free time playing ball, Hugh spent his time reading, for he was a "voracious reader" and longed for more education.[4] His desire to learn began to be fulfilled in 1903 when Hugh enrolled in Brigham Young College at Logan, Utah. At the college Hugh met Zina Young Card and told his mother, "I am going to marry that girl some day."[4] But education and marriage were put on hold when Hugh accepted a mission call to England. Hugh called his mission "the first love of my life,"[6] for it "strengthened [his] personal testimony and the sense of destiny."[7]

On his mission, Hugh often wrote to Zina Card but never expressed his intention to marry her. He did, however, confess his love for Zina to his missionary companion, George Webb. When Webb returned to Utah after his mission, he went to see Zina and told her that he had to meet the woman Hugh Brown was going to marry. Zina, who was engaged to another and knew nothing of Hugh's intentions, was shocked.[8]

When Hugh came home from England, he asked Zina to break off her engagement. When she told him that she would have to think about it, Hugh was heartbroken and went back to Canada. He discussed the issue with his stake president, who promised Hugh that if he would confess his love to Zina, she would marry him. Hugh followed his stake president's counsel and after Hugh professed his love to Zina, Hugh and Zina were married in the Salt Lake Temple on June 17, 1908.[9] Of Zina, Hugh said, "She believed in me. . . . At times when I lost faith in myself she would say, 'You must stay with it. We must see it through.'"[10]

Hugh and Zina made their home in Cardston, Canada, and were blessed to be the parents of eight children. Hugh supported his family by serving in the Canadian military. He is credited with organizing a Latter-day Saint military contingent in England during World War I. Hugh advanced to the rank of major in the military and felt that he would have reached a higher rank if his superiors had not been prejudiced against Latter-day Saints.

After the war, Hugh studied law and was admitted to the Canadian bar in 1921. That same year, at age thirty-seven, he was sustained as president of the Lethbridge Canada Stake. To best serve the needs of stake members, Hugh traveled two thousand miles on poor roads through snow and hailstorms to visit the five wards and seven branches in his stake.[11]

In 1937 Hugh was called to be the president of the British Mission, the first of many full-time Church positions he held. While serving as mission president, Hugh was contacted by a diplomatic correspondent representing *The People* periodical. Hugh made his personal library available to the correspondent, saying that his was "the best library in Europe on the Mormon question. . . . Everything that has ever been written against us is there—and all the things that have been written in favor of the church, all the works by church leaders are there." He encouraged the correspondent to spend thirty days in his library to learn about Mormonism before writing a series of articles against Mormonism. With typical confidence Hugh warned the correspondent that "if he spent thirty days in that library reading on Mormonism, he would ask for baptism." The correspondent found such a notion preposterous. Yet at the end of thirty days, he asked for baptism.[12]

Following a stint as LDS servicemen's coordinator and as a professor of religion at Brigham Young University, Hugh accepted employment as a general consultant for oil interests in Canada.[13] Hugh later recounted the prayer he gave to the Lord early one morning: "Although it looked like I was going to become wealthy as a result of my oil ventures, and if in His wisdom it would not be good for me or my family I hoped He would put an end to it."[14] Soon after offering this prayer, Hugh was called to be an Assistant to the Quorum of the Twelve Apostles. Hugh believed this calling was the fulfillment of his mother's confidence in him. Hugh was later called to the Quorum of the Twelve Apostles and as a counselor to President David O. McKay. Though some viewed these leadership callings as interfering with Hugh's professional goals, Hugh saw them as evidence that the Lord was pleased with his life. Through Church service, Hugh touched thousands of lives as he confidently gave of himself to others. Hugh died on December 2, 1975.

1   Edwin B. Firmage, ed., *An Abundant Life: The Memoirs of Hugh B. Brown* (Salt Lake City: Signature Books, 1988), 25.

2   Ibid., ix, 2.

3   Ibid., 2.

4   Edwin Brown Firmage, "Elder Hugh B. Brown, 1883–1975: In Memoriam," *Ensign*, Jan. 1976, 88.

5   Firmage, *An Abundant Life*, 8.
6   Hugh B. Brown, "A Missionary and His Message," *Ensign*, July 1972, 86.
7   Eugene E. Campbell and Richard D. Poll, *Hugh B. Brown: His Life and Thought* (Salt Lake City: Bookcraft, 1975), 36.
8   Firmage, *An Abundant Life*, 40.
9   Ibid., 40, 46.
10   Campbell and Poll, 80.
11   Firmage, "Elder Hugh B. Brown," 90.
12   Firmage, *An Abundant Life*, 108.
13   Ibid., 111–112.
14   Firmage, "Elder Hugh B. Brown," 90.

RICHARD BUSHMAN
Curiosity

Courtesy of Richard Bushman.

RICHARD BUSHMAN IS THE FOREMOST scholar on Joseph Smith and the early beginnings of Mormonism. He is a devout member of The Church of Jesus Christ of Latter-day Saints and has served as a bishop, a stake president, and a patriarch. Richard did not shy away from hard work to establish himself as a Mormon scholar. He "never faced overt discrimination as a Mormon in secular academia although he experienced insensitive comments and 'expressions of scorn.' Mainly, people show 'a great curiosity: How can you be a scholar and believe in all of these extravagant doctrines and happenings?' [Richard] said. His personal response and that of most Mormons is not to push back too aggressively."[1]

Richard Lyman Bushman was born on June 20, 1931, in Salt Lake City, Utah. His parents, like so many in Utah during the Great Depression, left Salt Lake City hoping for a better economic foothold elsewhere and settled their family in Portland, Oregon. As a youth, Richard "never felt the need to rebel." As to his youthful views of the LDS Church—based on his stake, which covered nearly half of the state of Oregon—Richard concluded, "I never thought that Mormonism was powerful. I thought it was weak. This little church just struggling to get a toehold."[2]

It was not until Richard's sophomore year at Harvard that doubts about the LDS faith crept into his thinking. His main issue was not with the history of the Church, but with the existence of a God—"Did he exist in any form or not?"[3] Of this query, Richard said, "I'm not someone who has a simple faith that just everything is absolutely true beyond any doubt."[4] As to his experience at Harvard, Richard said, "I loved everything about Harvard—the people, the studies, the atmosphere. I was more myself there than I had ever been in my whole life. Harvard helped redeem me, too, but it also eroded my faith in God."[5]

Nevertheless, Richard accepted a mission call to the New England states. "I couldn't say when I went on my mission that I knew the gospel was true," recalled Richard. "I was sort of in this limbo of uncertainty about everything."[6] In the first interview with his mission president, Richard was asked if he had "a testimony of the gospel. I said I did not. [The mission president] was not at all rattled. He asked if I would read a book, and, if I found a better explanation for it than the book itself gave, to report it to him. Then he handed me the Book of Mormon."[7]

On his mission, Richard worked "like crazy to figure out whether or not I could believe the Book of Mormon. Finally after some weighing everything I had at hand, which was limited, I just had this affirmation. . . . It was just an affirmation that yes this is *right*." In explaining his intellectual struggle, he said,

> I'm a person who lives in this divided world. . . . I always am hearing those questions and engage constantly in these internal debates where I try to make a point against [an] imaginary contestant of some kind. But what really comes around to me is a very simple thing. The big word for me is goodness. . . . I want to go where I find goodness . . . where I have brothers and sisters that I love and admire and want to work with, and where I live in a universe where I have an incentive to improve and grow better sometimes, and I just get that over and over with church.[8]

He added, "After I returned from the mission field, I no longer had doubts, but I did have questions."[9]

Richard returned to his studies at Harvard and changed his emphasis from science and math to history. The decision seemed strange at first, for, as he confessed, "the worst grades I got in college were in my American history course." Richard graduated from Harvard with a bachelor's degree in 1955, a master's degree in 1960, and a PhD in the history of American civilization in 1961. Of being a historian, he said, "In the process of doing history, I found it enjoyable. It wasn't reading history, I never have been [a] very great reader of history books, but of doing history, thinking about things, putting that evidence together."[10]

Richard taught history at Harvard, Brigham Young University, Boston University, and the University of Delaware before joining the faculty at Columbia. During the 2007–2008 academic year, he was the Howard W. Hunter Visiting Professor in Mormon Studies at Claremont Graduate University and held a Huntington Library Fellowship. His appointment to the Claremont faculty was viewed by "non-Mormon academics and Mormon church leaders" as "a significant advance in serious scholarship about the [LDS] religion."[11]

Today, Richard is the Gouverneur Morris Professor Emeritus of American History at Columbia. He is best known for his publications *From Puritan to Yankee: Character and the Social Order in Connecticut, 1690–1765* (1967); *King and People in Provincial Massachusetts* (1985); *The Refinement of America: Persons, Houses, Cities* (1992); and *Joseph Smith: Rough Stone Rolling* (2005). In 2007, he garnered "national attention as a media commentator about Mormonism's role in American life and the presidential candidacy of former Massachusetts Gov. Mitt Romney."[12]

As to Richard's feelings about his Church membership, he said, "I've prayed and paid tithing and gone on a mission and taken every Church call that's come and been quite willing to give my all and to consecrate myself in the temple. . . . I would just be foolish to give up on all these good things. I wouldn't give them away for the world."[13]

1 Larry Gordon, "Mormon-studies Professorship is California's First," *Los Angeles Times*, Oct. 30, 2007.

2 "Growing Up as Richard Bushman," Mormonheretic.org, May 29, 2012, John Dehlin interview with Richard Bushman, http://mormonheretic.org/2012/05/29/growing-up-as-richard-bushman/.

3 Richard Lyman Bushman, *Believing History: Latter-day Saint Essays*, ed. Reid L. Neilson and Jed Woodworth (New York: Columbia University Press, 2004), 21.

4   "Growing Up as Richard Bushman."
5   *Believing History*, 21.
6   "Growing Up as Richard Bushman."
7   *Believing History*, 22.
8   "Growing Up as Richard Bushman."
9   *Believing History*, 23.
10   "Why Bushman Became a Historian," Mormonheretic.org, June 1, 2012, John Dehlin interview with Richard Bushman, http://mormonheretic. org/2012/06/01/why-bushman-became-a-historian/.
11   "Mormon-studies Professorship is California's First."
12   Ibid.
13   "Bushman's Testimony of Joseph Smith," Mormonheretic.org, June 29, 2012, John Dehlin interview with Richard Bushman, http://mormonheretic. org/2012/06/29/bushmans-testimony-of-joseph-smith/.

GEORGE Q. CANNON

Optimism

Courtesy of the Church History
Library, The Church of Jesus
Christ of Latter-day Saints.

GEORGE Q. CANNON WAS A MISSIONARY, statesman, businessman, defender of
the faith, author, Apostle, and counselor to four Presidents of The Church of
Jesus Christ of Latter-day Saints. Following his death in 1901, he was eulogized
in newspapers across the nation as being second only to Brigham Young in
impacting the transformation of Utah from a desert prairie to a thriving state.[1]
President Joseph F. Smith said of George, "I know him to be a man of sterling
integrity, a man in whom the spirit of God dwelt, a man of great intelligence,
one of the wisest men I ever knew. And I know that the uppermost thought of
his life has ever been the building up of Zion, and the establishment of truth
and righteousness in the earth and the promulgation of the Gospel."[2]

George Quayle Cannon, son of George Cannon and Ann Quayle, was
born on January 11, 1827, in Liverpool, England. George first heard of
the restored gospel from his uncle, John Taylor, who came to his parents'
home in 1840. After reading the Book of Mormon, George's father said, "A
bad man could not have written it and a good man would be afraid to. It
is from God."[3] Two years after joining the Church, the Cannon family set
sail for America and the new Zion located on the banks of the Mississippi
River. Unfortunately, George's mother died at sea and his father died of
sunstroke shortly after arriving in the community of Nauvoo.

At age fifteen, George saw the Prophet Joseph Smith: "Without a
word from anyone to point him out or any reason to separate him from

others who stood around, he knew him instantly." George later said that he "would have known [Joseph] among ten thousand. There was that about him which to the Author's eyes, distinguished him from all the men he had ever seen."[4] Under the hands of John Smith, the Prophet's uncle, George received his patriarchal blessing. In the blessing George was promised that rulers and great men of the earth would listen to his teachings and that he would lead thousands to Zion. He was further promised the gift to speak any language and that his speech would be "powerful and persuasive." He was also blessed with the power to perform miracles and that he would have a companion and "a numerous posterity, who shall be esteemed as the excellent of the earth." By the end of George's life, each of these remarkable promises was fulfilled.[5]

In 1849 Brigham Young called George to accompany missionaries en route to California to obtain much-needed Church funds by digging for gold along stream beds. After fulfilling this assignment, George set sail from San Francisco to Hawaii to fulfill another missionary assignment. On his Hawaiian mission, George witnessed several missionaries become discouraged with their labors and return to the mainland. George prayed fervently to the Lord for the courage to fulfill his mission. "It was here that he talked with the Lord, heard His voice and felt His holy presence. This was such a sacred experience that he seldom made any public reference to it. It remained with him all his life. His dying testimony to his son who sat by his bedside in his last hours was that he knew that God lived, for he had heard His voice."[6]

On this same mission, George was able to overcome his fear of speaking before large groups. Believing that the Lord was with him, George never let an opportunity pass him by to talk to people and improve his understanding of the Hawaiian language. However, he did not overcome his loneliness until he "found the value of the Book of Mormon. It was a book which I had always loved. But I learned there to appreciate it as I had never done before. If I felt inclined to be lonely, to be low spirited, or homesick, I had only to turn to its sacred pages to receive consolation, new strength and a rich outpouring of the Spirit."[7] Knowing that the Book of Mormon was not available in the Hawaiian language, George began translating the book in 1851. He completed the translation on July 22, 1853, just two and a half years later.

Following his missionary labors, George gave great service to the Lord and His chosen servants. He served as a private secretary to Brigham Young, helped organize the Sunday School program of the Church, and presided over the Great Britain Mission. He published the *Millennial Star* and the *Juvenile Instructor* and edited the *Deseret News*. In addition, he authored several books, worked tirelessly for the statehood of Utah, served five terms in the state legislature, and is credited with building such entities as ZCMI, Union Pacific Railroad, Utah Power and Light, and George Q. Cannon & Sons (which later became Deseret Book).

In 1860, George was called to the Quorum of the Twelve Apostles. Thirteen years later, Brigham Young asked him to serve as a counselor in the First Presidency of the Church. From 1873 until his death in 1901, George served in the First Presidency as a counselor to four Church Presidents—Brigham Young, John Taylor, Wilford Woodruff, and Lorenzo Snow. At the death of each President, George felt deeply the loss of one of his best friends.

Throughout his life George was intensely loyal to the Lord and to leaders of the Church. Following George's death on April 12, 1901, President Lorenzo Snow stated, "In our councils, whatever might be the matter under consideration, although my decision was sometimes opposed to his views, he invariably yielded his point gracefully and gave me his most loyal support."[8] George was known for his unwavering faith in God and in the restored gospel of Jesus Christ. He was also known for his optimistic view that no matter how bleak circumstances might look at the moment, in the end God would overrule all things for good.

"We need not fear," George said. "God is with us; the angelic hosts are with us, the glorious army of martyrs who have died for the truth in the past ages of the world are looking down upon us, interested in this great work and in its success."[9]

1 Lawrence R. Flake, *Prophets and Apostles of the Last Dispensation* (Provo, Utah: BYU Religious Studies Center, 2001), 184.
2 *Millennial Star*, 63:312.
3 Davis Bitton, *George Q. Cannon* (Salt Lake City: Deseret Book, 1999), 34.
4 Flake, 182.
5 Bitton, 49.
6 Flake, 183.
7 Jane McBride Choate, "George Q. Cannon," *Liahona*, Feb. 1989.
8 Bitton, 450.
9 George Q. Cannon, "George Q. Cannon, Feb. 24, 1889: Destiny of the Church Prison Life," *Collected Discourses 1886–1889*, Vol. 1 (Salt Lake City: Deseret Book, 2013).

BILLY CASPER

Satisfaction

Courtesy of *Deseret News.*

By any standard Billy Casper's golf career ranks among the greatest in the history of the game. Yet golfer Johnny Miller described Billy as "the most underrated golfer of all time, hands down." His plaque at the World Golf Hall of Fame reads, "At the peak of his powers, he got more attention for his allergies, his conversion to Mormonism, his eleven children (six of them adopted) and his offbeat diet of buffalo meat and organically grown vegetables. The public would come to know very little of Billy Casper, making him arguably the best modern golfer who never received his due."[1]

William Earl Casper Jr., son of William Earl and Isabel Casper, was born June 24, 1931, in San Diego, California. By 1934 Billy and his parents had moved to New Mexico. "The first golf club I ever hit was a 5-iron in Silver City, New Mexico. I was four years old. I don't remember how far the ball went, but I remember for sure the club was a 5-iron. Because that's the club my dad hit," Billy said. The three-hole course in Silver City was a cow pasture on his family farm built by his father and his uncle.

By age six, Billy was living in a house—"a shack, really"—in the Sorrento Valley of Southern California. His father worked at a dairy and his mother worked at a telephone company. When Billy was nine the family moved to Chula Vista, a suburb south of San Diego. "I started hanging around the [San Diego Country Club] golf course when I was nine," he recalled. "Not doing much, just acting interested, making friends, hitting balls and putting on the greens when I could. When it got dark I had the greens all to myself and I just kept putting."[2]

By age eleven Billy was a caddy. Although he was at the country club nearly every day, his dream was to play baseball for the New York Yankees. As for school, Billy wasn't "book smart[.] I was street smart," he said. His golf game "took off" in high school, but his interest in school never did, with the exception of his interest in classmate Shirley Franklin. "I don't know what qualifies as love at first sight," recalled Billy. "But I went home knowing I'd met the girl of my dreams."[3]

Billy enrolled at Notre Dame in Indiana on a golf scholarship. Although his golf game showed promise, Billy was homesick. "One morning in December I got up, threw my stuff in a bag and left," said Billy. "I just couldn't take it any longer. I went to the train station and bought a one-way ticket back to California." Once in California, Billy enlisted in the Navy and was assigned to Special Services—"Navy talk for working at the base golf course, a nine-hole three-par facility called Sail Ho that was part of the San Diego Naval Training Center." Each day Billy played golf. He said of his tour with the Navy, "As it turned out, serving my country was very good for my golf game."[4]

On June 28, 1952, Billy married Shirley Franklin, the love of his life. Of Shirley, Billy said, "No golfer has had a better companion. Ever. Shirley never swung a club but she was behind every shot I hit. Of the more than three thousand rounds of golf I played as a professional on the regular and senior Tours, Shirley walked at least eighty-five percent of them, and that's a conservative estimate."[5] Although Billy and Shirley were broke and in debt after his stint with the Navy, Billy became a professional golfer.

"I won the San Diego County Open in my first tournament as a pro and added $150 to the family budget," Billy said. During those first years, he overheard another pro player say, "I don't know why [Billy] Casper's going on Tour. With his game, he'll starve to death. Why doesn't he go out and get a nice job selling insurance?" Billy never sold insurance, but always knew that he was "one step away from working the assembly line at the rivet factory."[6]

As Billy continued to play competitive golf, he caught the "start of the biggest wave in golf's history." Billy said, "In a decade, I watched as the golf Tour went from house trailers to jets." This golden age of golf put the Masters, the U.S. Open, and the PGA Championship on television sets in homes throughout the country. "Galleries were large and growing, new golf courses were being built all over the world, and an unprecedented number of people took to the links."[7]

From 1964 to 1970, Billy won twenty-seven tournaments. His record in the Ryder Cup remains the best in the game of golf. By 1970 Billy had become golf's second millionaire, right behind Arnold Palmer. Golfers Jack Nicklaus, Gary Player, and Arnold Palmer wrote of Billy, "Simply put, Billy Casper was a threat to win every golf tournament he entered. He beat us as many times as we beat him. You don't have to take our word for it. Look it up. Billy's fifty-one PGA career wins rank seventh all-time. He won two U.S. Opens and one Masters. He won at least one tournament a year for sixteen straight seasons, from 1956 through 1971, a record exceeded only by two of the undersigned (seventeen years each for Arnold and Jack)."

But as the years passed and Billy aged, he said, "Golf is a cruel mistress. Unlike team sports like baseball, football, and basketball, there is no front office man to inform you that your contract hasn't been picked up for next season, no general manager or coach to break the news to you that you're off the roster or you've been bumped from the starting lineup. You have to do it yourself, and after years of convincing yourself that you *can* do it, it's not an easy thing to convince yourself that you can't."[8]

For twenty-two years (1970 to 1992), Billy ran golf camps that involved about two hundred youths each summer. He appeared numerous times on *Shell's Wonderful World of Golf,* which featured televised golf matches in exotic locations. Billy designed twenty-five golf courses and started a golf management company that today manages more than 160 golf courses around the world.

Playing competitive golf on the Senior Tour kept Billy connected with old friends. "By 1987, the Senior Tour had expanded to thirty-two events and a purse of nearly $9 million (by 2012 it was over $50 million)." Of playing on the Senior Tour, Billy said, "I won nine times on the Senior Tour in less than a decade and collected more in official winnings than I did my entire career on the regular Tour."[9]

For all Billy's successes on and off the golf course, there are two areas in his life that trumped all others. The first began in the 1960s when two members of The Church of Jesus Christ of Latter-day Saints knocked on his front door and introduced themselves as holding the priesthood office of Seventy. Billy remembered, "My ears perked up. Seventy was an important number to me. I liked seventy! It was a good golf score. We invited the men in and called the kids to come into the living room." Billy and his family were baptized on January 1, 1966.

The second area that trumped all others for Billy was family. Billy said, "My greatest reward in life is, has been, and always will be, my family. Nothing has brought me more joy and satisfaction. At last count our eleven children had expanded to include thirty-four grandchildren and fifteen great-grandchildren. Family is indeed the gift that keeps on giving." In his eighties, Billy reflected on his life and sais, "When I look back, my vision keeps getting better. The longer I live the clearer I can see and appreciate where my life has taken me and all the wonderful things I've been able to experience."[10]

Billy Casper died on February 7, 2015, at the age of eighty-three at his home in Springville, Utah.

1   Billy Casper, James Parkinson, and Lee Benson, *The Big Three and Me* (Columbus, Missouri: Genesis Press, Inc., 2012), 16, 17; original italics omitted.
2   Ibid., 53, 55, 57.
3   Ibid., 65, 73, 79.
4   Ibid., 84, 85, 91.
5   Ibid., 275.
6   Ibid., 96, 101, 145.
7   Ibid., 28, vii.
8   Ibid., viii, 243.
9   Ibid., 257.
10 Ibid., 181, 273, 265.

CLAYTON CHRISTENSEN

Innovation

Courtesy of Evgenia Eliseeva
Photography.

CLAYTON CHRISTENSEN IS A PROFESSOR of business administration at the Harvard Business School and is regarded as one of the world's leading experts on innovation and growth. He has published bestselling books, started businesses, consulted with scores of companies and executives, and served The Church of Jesus Christ of Latter-day Saints in many callings, including as a bishop and an Area Seventy. Clayton believes that a good yardstick for measuring success is how much your life influences other people for the better.

Clayton Christensen, son of Robert and Verda Mae Christensen, was born on April 6, 1952, in Salt Lake City, Utah, and was reared in a loving and devout Latter-day Saint home. He graduated with highest honors in economics from Brigham Young University (1975) and received a master's of philosophy degree in applied econometrics from Oxford University (1977), where he studied as a Rhodes Scholar. While at Oxford, Clayton, who stands six feet eight inches tall, was the starting center for the men's basketball team. He made a difficult decision while at Oxford to not play basketball in a championship game held on a Sunday.[1]

Clayton received an MBA degree from the Harvard Business School in 1979. In 1982 he was named a White House Fellow and later an assistant to two secretaries of the United States Department of Transportation. In 1992, Clayton received a doctorate in business administration from the

Harvard Business School. He holds five honorary doctorate degrees and an honorary chaired professorship at the Tsinghua University in Taiwan.

Clayton is an experienced entrepreneur, having started three successful companies: CPS Technologies, which has become a leading developer and manufacturer of products using high-tech materials; Innosight, a consulting firm that uses Clayton's theories of innovation to help companies create new growth businesses; and Rose Park Advisors, a firm that identifies and invests in disruptive companies. Clayton is the bestselling author of eight books and more than a hundred articles. In 1997 his book *The Innovator's Dilemma* received the Global Business Book Award as the best business book of the year, and in 2011 *The Economist* named *The Innovator's Dilemma* one of the six most important business books ever written.

Clayton has been featured twice (in 1998 and 2011) as the cover story in *Forbes* magazine; in 2011 a poll of thousands of executives, consultants, and business school professors named Clayton the most influential business thinker in the world. In 2012, he published the bestselling *How Will You Measure Your Life?*, a book based on an article he wrote for the *Harvard Business Review*.[2]

As to why Clayton believes in the doctrines of the Church, he wrote,

> I had been given a Rhodes Scholarship to study at Oxford University in England. After I had lived there for a few weeks, far away from the supportive environment in which I had been raised, it became clear that adhering to Mormonism in that environment was going to be *very* inconvenient. . . . I decided, as a result, that the time had come for me to learn for certain and for *myself* whether Mormonism was true. . . . Accordingly, I reserved the time from 11:00 until midnight, every night, to read the Book of Mormon. . . . After I had done this for several weeks, one evening in October, 1975 . . . I felt a marvelous spirit come into the room and envelop my body. I had never before felt such an intense feeling of peace and love. I started to cry, and did not want to stop. I knew then, from a source of understanding more powerful than anything I had ever felt in my life, that the book I was holding in my hands was true.[3]

From that moment on, Clayton has made his family and the gospel of Jesus Christ his first priority. He served a mission in South Korea from 1971 to 1973, and served in the Boy Scouts of America for twenty-five years as a Scoutmaster, cub master, den leader, and a troop and pack committee chairman. He and his wife, Christine, live in Belmont, Massachusetts, and are the parents of five children.

After experiencing serious health challenges—including a heart attack, cancer, and a stroke—Clayton concludes, "The measure by which God will assess my life isn't dollars, but the individual people whose lives I've touched. . . . Don't worry about the level of individual prominence you have achieved. Worry about the individuals you have helped become better people."[4] Helping others has been and continues to be what Clayton Christensen's life is all about.

1   See Thomas S. Monson, "The Three Rs of Choice," *Ensign*, Nov. 2010, 87.
2   Clayton Christensen (blog), www.claytonchristensen.com.
3   *Why I Believe* (Salt Lake City: Deseret Book, 2001), 93–94.
4   Jamshid Ghazi Askar, "Y Grad's Life Advice Goes Viral on Web," *Deseret News*, Aug. 12, 2010, A6.

MAC CHRISTENSEN
Compassion

Courtesy of The Mormon
Tabernacle Choir, The Church of
Jesus Christ of Latter-day Saints.

WHEN IT COMES TO BUSINESS MATTERS, few can equal Mac Christensen—or Mr. Mac, as he is better known. The soft-spoken Mac is the founder of the successful Utah clothing chain Mr. Mac. The public recognizes him by his catchy phrases and hand gestures shown in his television commercials. But what Mac's public persona does not reveal is what motivates him and makes him happy—blessing the lives of others.

Those who know Mac best speak of his generosity. For example, President Thomas S. Monson said, "No one cares about others more than Mac. No one!" Then parodying the Mr. Mac television commercials, he added, "No one is a better friend than Mac. No one!" Senator Orrin Hatch described Mac as one of the "greatest institutions" in Utah, for "he goes about doing good things for people all the time. . . . He's always giving service to others."[1]

Fred Macray Christensen was born on May 11, 1934, in the small town of Ephraim, Utah. To Mac, family life has always been important; he and his wife, Joan, have eight children, thirty-seven grandchildren, and twenty-three great-grandchildren. To his ever-growing family, Mac is an example of hard work, integrity, and charity. He is a leader and righteous priesthood holder committed to the admonition of the Savior to go about life "doing good."

That admonition was tested by the tragic death of his son in 1985. President James E. Faust explained,

> Here in Salt Lake City in 1985, Bishop Steven Chris-
> tensen, through no fault of his own, was cruelly and
> senselessly killed by a bomb intended to take his life. He
> was the son of Mac and Joan Christensen, the husband
> of Terri, and the father of four children. With his parents'
> consent, I share what they learned from this experience.
> After this terrible deed, the news media followed mem-
> bers of the Christensen family around relentlessly. On
> one occasion this media intrusion offended one of the
> family members to the point that Steven's father, Mac,
> had to restrain him. Mac then thought, "This thing will
> destroy my family if we don't forgive. Venom and hatred
> will never end if we do not get it out of our system." Heal-
> ing and peace came as the family cleansed their hearts
> from anger and were able to forgive the man who took
> their son's life.[2]

Before opening Mr. Mac stores, Mac worked in clothing retail at ZCMI, a large downtown Salt Lake City department store. There Mac recognized a customer problem that was not being addressed in the menswear department—if a customer wanted to purchase a suit, he went to one department; for a pair of shoes he went to another department; for luggage, another; and so forth. Mac believed that better service mandated a "one-stop shop" so that customers would not be shuffled from one department to another. In Mac's mind, better service, quality of merchandise, and price point needed more attention than he saw in the men's department at ZCMI.

In 1966 Mac opened the first Mr. Mac, a thousand-square-foot store in Bountiful, Utah. His "one-stop shop" proved an immediate success. For more than four decades, the reputation of Mr. Mac as a trusted source for men's suits and clothing needs has grown to include nine locations in the Intermountain West.[3] Although his sons and others now manage the day-to-day affairs of the business, Mac still plays a significant leadership role.

On a regular basis, Mac devotes more time to giving service than to dressing businessmen and missionaries in Mr. Mac's signature two-pant suit. For example, Mac served as the director of the Washington DC Temple Visitors' Center, where he welcomed guests and explained the Church and its programs to thousands of visitors.

In 2011 Mac was recognized for his support of the Cystic Fibrosis Foundation and presented with the Breath of Life Award, an award that is given "to caring, generous, selfless people who are driven by the desire to make the community and the lives of others better." That same year, he was awarded the Days of 47 Pioneers of Progress Award for his business and community service. Mac's most notable service, however, came at the request of President Gordon B. Hinckley, who invited him to be president of the Mormon Tabernacle Choir. Mac's response was, "I'm tone deaf." President Hinckley quickly replied, "Oh, we don't want you to sing."[4]

Stepping into the role of Mormon Tabernacle Choir president seemed an unlikely transition, but for Mac it was an easy fit. His skill as a businessman, negotiator, and financial expert made it possible for him to successfully manage the operations, staff, and marketing of the choir, the Orchestra at Temple Square, and the Bells on Temple Square. Mac oversaw the administrative components, financial operations, and a myriad of details associated with the choir and orchestra.

Mac served as president of the Mormon Tabernacle Choir and Orchestra at Temple Square from November 2000 to July 2012, saying of the choir, "I would like more people to know more about the Mormon Tabernacle Choir, because the more they know about the Choir the more they will know about the Church. . . . I want every single person in the world to hear the Choir. The music the Choir makes will bring spirituality and goodness to the whole world—we can bring people together through song." Mac's goal was nearly reached when the Mormon Tabernacle Choir performed for 3.5 billion people during the opening ceremonies of the 2002 Winter Olympics in Salt Lake City.[5]

Mac has lived a remarkable life, built a successful business, rubbed shoulders with some of the great leaders of our time, and yet remains a humble boy from Ephraim. "I think sometimes that I'll wake up one day standing next to a haystack in Ephraim," he said, "and realize this has all been a dream." His hard work has made his dream come true.

1   "Mr. Mac, Mac Christensen, Honored for Charity Work," *Deseret News*, Nov. 21, 2011, http://www.deseretnews.com/article/705394728/Mr-Mac-Mac-Christensen-honored-for-charity-work.html?pg=all.

2   James E. Faust, "The Healing Power of Forgiveness," *Ensign*, May 2007, 68–69.

3   "Mr. Mac History," Mr. Mac, Nov. 9, 2010, http://www.mrmac.com/blog/category/mr-mac-history/.

4   Lee Benson, "Leading the Choir Suits This Mac Very Well," *Deseret News*, Jan. 13, 2011, www.deseretnews.com/article/700100591/Leading-the-choir-suits-this-Mac-very-well.html.

5   Information provided by the Mormon Tabernacle Choir.

J. REUBEN CLARK JR.
Dutiful Service

Courtesy of the Church History
Library, The Church of Jesus
Christ of Latter-day Saints.

WHEN THE UNITED STATES ENTERED World War I, J. Reuben Clark felt duty-bound to serve his country. Although forty-six years old and the father of four children, Reuben joined the army as a commissioned major in the Judge Advocate General's Officers' Reserve Corps. For Reuben, being in the military meant a dramatic cut in pay—he made a tenth of his civilian salary—but patriotism and a sense of duty to his country were the greater good. Reuben received the Distinguished Service Medal for his military service. Throughout the rest of his life, as with his stint in the military, Reuben put religion, family, and country above worldly ambitions.[1]

Joshua Reuben Clark Jr., son of Joshua R. Clark and Mary Woolley, was born September 1, 1871, in Grantsville, Utah. His father was a Civil War veteran who was baptized into The Church of Jesus Christ of Latter-day Saints one month after attending his first Sunday service.[2] His maternal grandfather was a prominent bishop in Salt Lake City. Bishop Woolley had such a strong sense of duty that people said if he were to die by drowning, they should "look for his body upstream, for he would never go along with the current."[3]

Reuben grew to manhood in relative poverty, learning the meaning of hard work as he did daily chores on a family farm. Although his formal education did not begin until he was ten, Reuben loved learning and would often pour over books in his father's library after a day of farm work. "Reuben would 'rather miss his meals than to miss a day from school,'" his father recalled.[4]

At age nineteen, Reuben attended the Latter-day Saints' College in Salt Lake City and later the University of Utah.[5] During his college years, Reuben worked as a secretary for Dr. James E. Talmage, a future member of the Quorum of the Twelve Apostles. When Dr. Talmage was appointed curator of the Deseret Museum, the First Presidency of the Church indicated that if Reuben would serve as the assistant curator, his service would "be credited to him the same" as a full-time proselyting mission. The opportunity to work closely with Dr. Talmage gave Reuben many religious and educational experiences. For example, Reuben played a key role in editing Talmage's manuscript *The Articles of Faith*.[6]

While attending the University of Utah, Reuben regularly walked past the home of Luacine Annetta Savage. When Reuben saw Luacine through a window, he immediately resolved to marry her. She, however, needed convincing. In 1898, after a long courtship, Reuben and Luacine were married in the Salt Lake Temple by James E. Talmage.

After graduating as class valedictorian from the University of Utah, Reuben taught school in Salt Lake City before being accepted into law school at Columbia University in 1903. Before departing for New York, Reuben received a priesthood blessing from President Joseph F. Smith, who set him apart to be "an exemplary Latter-day Saint among the gentiles of the world." Many law students recognized Reuben as bright and hardworking. Nevertheless, his daughter recalled that during her father's study sessions, "a knock at his open study door would get [his children] his complete and affectionate attention."[7] Reuben excelled above other students, including classmate and future United States President Franklin D. Roosevelt, who failed a difficult class.

After graduating from Columbia, Reuben and his family moved to Washington, DC, where Reuben served as an assistant solicitor of the United States State Department. Although he had little experience, Reuben found himself directing much of United States foreign policy. He was later appointed solicitor of the State Department, where he played a significant a role in implementing U.S. foreign policies with Mexico. In 1913 Reuben resigned from the State Department and opened a private law practice. Although he prospered in his legal practice, Reuben closed his practice to join the Army and serve in World War I.

After the war, Reuben served in various government positions from 1918 to 1930, making significant contributions to U.S. foreign policy. In October 1930 President Herbert Hoover appointed Reuben as the U.S. ambassador to Mexico. Reuben found great satisfaction as an ambassador and learned to love the Mexican people. After serving less than three years as an ambassador, however, he sacrificed his career to serve in the First Presidency of the Church.

On April 6, 1933, Reuben was sustained as second counselor to President Heber J. Grant. He was the last man to be called to the First Presidency without first being ordained a member of the Quorum of the Twelve Apostles. Having never served in a bishopric, stake presidency, or any leadership position in the Church, Reuben felt inadequate to be in the First Presidency. Yet he humbly accepted the call, stating, "It is for the Lord to say how and where I shall serve. . . . I appreciate the honor the call brings to me."[8]

Reuben adapted quickly to his new calling and worked hard to relieve President Grant of undue stress. For example, one day President Grant arrived at his office and found his desk cleared of mail and stacks of paperwork. He also found a note saying, "Brother Grant, this is your desk, J. R. C."[9]

Reuben was later sustained as First Counselor in the First Presidency and as a member of the Quorum of the Twelve Apostles. Reuben is remembered for his key role in leading the Latter-day Saints through the Great Depression and World War II, and encouraging them to stay out of debt. His conference addresses are legendary, especially his address entitled "To Them of the Last Wagon."

In 1951, after serving for more than fifteen years as First Counselor in the First Presidency, Reuben was called to be the second counselor to President David O. McKay. "An audible gasp filled the Tabernacle" at the announcement, as many believed that Reuben had been demoted. His reaction on that April morning has become the hallmark of Reuben's service. He said, "In the service of the Lord, it is not where you serve but how. In the Church of Jesus Christ of Latter-day Saints, one takes the place to which one is duly called, which place one neither seeks nor declines. I pledge . . . devoted service to the tasks that may come to me to the full measure of my strength and my abilities."[10]

On October 6, 1961, after almost thirty years of service in the First Presidency of the Church, Reuben was reunited with his dear Luacine, who had preceded him in death seventeen years earlier. Not long after Reuben's death, Brigham Young University honored his memory by announcing that a law school bearing the name J. Reuben Clark would be built on campus.[11]

1   Ethan Vincent, *The Legacy of J. Reuben Clark* (Provo, Utah: Brigham Young University, 2007), DVD.

2   *Counselors to the Prophets*, comp. Michael K. Winder (Roy, Utah: Eborn Books, 2001), 348.

3   Ibid.

4   Ibid.

5   Ibid., 348–349.

6   David H. Yarn Jr., *Young Reuben: The Early Life of J. Reuben Clark, Jr.* (Provo, Utah: Brigham Young University Press, 1973), 60; Frank W. Fox, *J. Reuben Clark: The Public Years* (Provo, UT: Brigham Young University Press, 1980), 15; *Counselors*, 349.

7   D. Michael Quinn, *J. Reuben Clark: The Church Years* (Provo, Utah: Brigham Young University Press, 1983), 13, 19–20; Fox, 36; *Counselors*, 349–350.

8   *Counselors*, 354–355; Gene A. Sessions, *Prophesying upon the Bones: J. Reuben Clark and the Foreign Debt Crisis, 1933–1939* (Urbana, IL: University of Illinois Press, 1992), 45–50.

9   Quinn, 73; *Counselors*, 354–355.

10   J. Reuben Clark, Jr., *Conference Report*, April 1951, 154; *Counselors*, 359–360.

11   Vincent.

KIM B. CLARK

Family Balance

Courtesy of Kim Clark.

PROFESSORS AND SCHOLARS ALIKE QUESTIONED why Kim Clark would leave the prestigious levels of scholarship at Harvard University in 2005 to become the president of a small university in rural Idaho. Kim's reason had everything to do with his desire to follow a prophet and an experience in his youth that shaped that desire. Kim recalls,

> When I was a little boy, about eleven years old, I had a defining experience that has influenced my whole life. It was 1960, I was living in Salt Lake City, and our ward . . . had built a new chapel. . . . President David O. McKay came to dedicate our chapel. I remember feeling a compelling desire to be at that dedication that day. Somehow I got permission from my mom and dad to walk to the chapel, about three blocks from my house, two hours before the dedication. One of the reasons I went was to see the prophet in person. When I arrived, hardly any people were there. I was early enough to get a seat right up front in the chapel. I still remember what David O. McKay looked like and what I felt as an eleven-year-old when he walked into that chapel. In my little-boy heart, I knew this was the prophet of God. I knew it, and I felt it. It was a powerful experience that has stayed with me my whole life.[1]

Kim B. Clark, son of Merlin Clark and Helen Mar Hickman, was born on March 20, 1949, in Salt Lake City, Utah. Kim was eleven years old when his family moved to Spokane, Washington, where he enjoyed a happy childhood playing sports and filling adolescent years with music and friends. At age eighteen, Kim was accepted as a premed major to Harvard University. After a dismal freshman year at Harvard, Kim withdrew to accept a mission call to the South German Mission. After completing an honorable mission, he enrolled for a year at Brigham Young University, where he excelled in academics and, more importantly, met the love of his life, Sue Lorraine Hunt of Waterflow, New Mexico. They were married in the Salt Lake Temple.

Kim and Sue moved to Massachusetts, intending to stay for only a few years until Kim completed his schooling at Harvard, but Massachusetts became their home for nearly thirty-five years. After receiving a bachelor's degree in 1974, a master's degree in 1977, and a PhD in economics from Harvard in 1978, Kim joined the faculty of the Harvard Business School. As a professor and then a dean at Harvard, Kim's scholarly research focus was on the interaction of technological innovation and competition in industry evolution.

Although his was a highly technical field, when interviewed by the media or while interacting with students and faculty, Kim preferred to speak of ethics, moral integrity, values, and priorities more than the impact of technology on society. Kim taught his students that no success in the business world could compensate for failure in their families. He incorporated this teaching in his own family and added an additional rule—no business work at night or on the weekends. Kim said, "I decided that when 5:30–6 P.M. comes, I would drop what I was doing and go home. We've lived by it pretty well. Occasionally, I run into situations where I can't do that. I discovered that the work I am involved in is so engrossing that it entices me to work way past the time I should be home. Many people find that in their professions. But I believe that no matter how enticing the work is, there's no more important place for a husband and father to be in the evening than at home." Becoming first a family man and then a scholar, educator, and business expert has been a learning process for Kim. "It's not like I woke up one day, was married and had it all figured out," he said. "Over the years, I've learned that my family and church are the most important things in my life."[2]

For Kim's family of seven children, his presence in the home has brought a sense of security and stability. Weekly family home evenings, regular scripture study, and consistent family prayer have proved a blessing to each family member. Yet Kim willingly has accepted time-consuming Church callings such as bishop, Gospel Doctrine teacher, Scoutmaster, and counselor in a stake mission presidency.[3] When President Gordon B. Hinckley asked Kim to accept the presidency of Brigham Young University–Idaho in 2005, Kim said, "I had no question in my mind about what I would do. It was not a hard decision because I love God's prophets—and that love is one of the reasons I'm a Mormon."[4]

As president of BYU–Idaho, Kim had daily opportunities to sustain Church leaders and move forward the visionary objectives of the university to "create a wholesome learning environment in which students can strengthen their commitment to their faith and receive a quality education that prepares them for leadership in the home, the community, and the workplace."[5] Kim is a sterling example of obedience to the prophet and of learning how to balance and prioritize life.

1   Joseph A. Cannon, *Why I'm a Mormon* (Salt Lake City: Ensign Peak, 2012), 73.
2   Gerry Avant, "New Harvard Dean Flowered in Academics after His Mission," *LDS Church News*, Feb. 24, 1996, http://www.ldschurchnews.com/articles/print/28516/New-Harvard-dean-flowered-in-academics-after-his-mission.html.
3   "Dr. Kim B. Clark," Inaugural Program, BYU–Idaho, http://www2.byui.edu/President/inauguration/kimbclark.htm.
4   Cannon, 74.
5   http://www.byui.edu/about?cid=hli:115.

KRESIMIR COSIC

Enthusiasm

Courtesy of the Church History
Library, The Church of Jesus
Christ of Latter-day Saints.

A HERO ON AND OFF the basketball court, Kresimir Cosic—also known
as the "Gentle Giant"—played basketball and lived the gospel of Jesus
Christ with passion and enthusiasm. Many were surprised when Kresimir
joined The Church of Jesus Christ of Latter-day Saints in 1971. Of
his conversion, he said, "In Yugoslavia most of the young people are
completely atheistic, and that's the way I lived. When I came to Provo
I didn't change. I was an atheist for two years while I was in Provo.
Nobody was farther from becoming a Mormon than I was. . . . When I
was a junior, I decided to figure out a few things. I had things I wanted
to know."[1] After his baptism, Kresimir committed his life to two great
passions: basketball and the Church.[2]

   Kresimir Cosic, son of Ante and Danita Cosic, was born on
November 26, 1948, in Zagreb, Croatia. He grew to manhood in Zadar,
Yugoslavia, and on the nearby Dalmatia Island. Due to his extraordinary
height (six feet eleven inches) and shoe size (seventeen), Kresimir was a
natural choice for any youth basketball team. He was recruited to play
basketball at Brigham Young University in the 1960s. After leading
Yugoslavia to an Olympic Silver Medal in 1968, he enrolled at BYU in
1970 and quickly became one of the most popular players in the history
of Cougar athletics. Fans were drawn to him because of his excitement,

good humor, and on-court antics and because he played the game with gusto and emotional intensity. Whether it was leading a fast break with guard-like play, dribbling between his legs, or shooting an impressive skyhook, Kresimir's infectious enthusiasm endeared him to all who saw him play. BYU Marriott Center attendance numbers testify to his popularity and skill. It was said that "[Coach] Stan Watts built the Marriott Center, Marriott paid for it, and Kresimir Cosic filled it."[3]

Kresimir's decision to attend Brigham Young University was historic in terms of paving the way for international basketball players to come to the United States to improve their basketball skills at the collegiate level. He was the first foreign player to earn all-American honors after leading BYU to two WAC titles and two NCAA appearances in the early 1970s. During the 2005 NCAA Men's Basketball Tournament, CBS Television analyst Billy Packer singled out Kresimir in a discussion of the quality of international players playing college basketball. Packer said, "Kresimir Cosic, who played at BYU, was really the first great international player to play college basketball in the United States."[4]

While at BYU, Kresimir learned English and read the Book of Mormon, gaining a testimony of the restored gospel in the process. When asked what impressed him about the Book of Mormon, Kresimir said, "Well, it's certainly the best book I have ever read. There's no question about that. The book applies to today's people much more than in the days when Joseph Smith translated it, because it speaks about the way it is now. I was traveling all over the world, and I saw many places, and I saw most of the prophecies being fulfilled; it's amazing. That really is a good book. There are many things in it that are coming true now."[5]

Following his success at BYU, Kresimir was offered two NBA contracts but declined both in favor of returning to Croatia to help the Church get a foothold in his country and to participate with and coach the Yugoslavian Olympic team. His Yugoslavian team won the silver medal in 1976 and the gold in 1980 at the Olympics.[6] As a member of the Yugoslavian National Team, Kresimir participated in four world championships and eight European championships. Professionally, Kresimir played with and later coached Olimpia Milano and Cibona Zagreb, winning five Yugoslavian league titles.[7]

Before his untimely death due to cancer on May 25, 1995, Kresimir was working tirelessly for peace in his troubled homeland as deputy ambassador for Croatia to the United States. On May 6, 1996, Kresimir was posthumously inducted into the Basketball Hall of Fame in Springfield, Massachusetts—the second BYU Cougar and only BYU player to receive the prestigious honor (BYU basketball coach Stan Watts was inducted in 1986). In 2001 Kresimir was inducted into the Utah Basketball Hall of Fame and on March 4, 2006, his No. 11 jersey was retired by BYU in a halftime ceremony with more than twenty thousand fans in attendance. Kresimir was only the second BYU basketball player to have his jersey retired (the first being Danny Ainge). On June 1–3, 2012, a three-day celebration in Croatia was held in remembrance of Kresimir and the establishment of the Church in that country.[8]

Never one to hold back on the basketball floor, Kresimir also stood tall for the Church in Europe and across the world. He shared the gospel with so many people in eastern Europe that it is said that the history of the Church in former Yugoslavia (now Croatia, Slovenia, Bosnia, Serbia, and Montenegro) started with Kresimir.

1   Dick Davis and Duane Hiatt, "Kresimir Cosic—Basketball and Baptism," *New Era*, Feb. 1974.

2   See Donald Q. Cannon, Richard O. Cowan, and Arnold K. Garr, *Encyclopedia of Latter-day Saint History* (Salt Lake City: Deseret Book, 2001), 252–253.

3   Ralph R. Zobell, "Top Ten Athletes of All Time," KSL News, Nov. 3, 2011, http://www.ksl.com/?nid=272&sid=17917602.

5   "Kresimir Cosic: BYU Hall of Fame Inductee," Official Home of the BYU Cougars, http://byucougars.com/node/83959?ajax=1.

5   Davis and Hiatt.

6   "Kresimir Cosic: #11," Official Home of the BYU Cougars, http://byucougars.com/athlete/m-basketball/kresimir-cosic; see also "Retired Jersey," *BYU Basketball 2010–2011 Info Guide*, http://byucougars.com/files/media_guides/m-basketball/2011/tradition/retired.html.

7   "Hall of Famers: Kresimir Cosic," Naismith Memorial Basketball Hall of Fame, http://www.hoophall.com/hall-of-famers/tag/kresimir-cosic.

8   "Anniversary Observed: Church's Beginnings in Former Yugoslavia Observed," *LDS Church News*, July 21, 2012, http://www.ldschurchnews.com/articles/62558/Anniversary-observance-Churchs-beginnings-in-former-Yugoslavia-observed.html; see also "Retired Jersey," *BYU Basketball 2010–2011 Info Guide*.

STEPHEN R. COVEY

Principle-Centered

STEPHEN COVEY WAS AN AUTHOR, speaker, educator, entrepreneur, and businessman. He inspired millions of people with the power of universal principles of leadership in his number-one *New York Times* bestseller *The 7 Habits of Highly Effective People*, which sold more than twenty-five million copies and was printed in forty languages. Around the world, his name is synonymous with principles and practices of personal and organizational effectiveness. As Stephen spoke to standing-room-only audiences throughout the world, his message was simple—true success means being "principle-centered" in all areas of life. A teacher at heart, Stephen enjoyed saying, "There are three constants in life: change, choice and principles."[1]

Stephen Richards Covey, son of Stephen Glenn Covey and Irene Louise Richards, was born on October 24, 1932, in Salt Lake City, Utah. He was a grandson of Stephen L Richards, an Apostle and counselor to President David O. McKay, and a grandson of Stephen Mack Covey, founder of Little America Hotels, which began near Granger, Wyoming. As a young boy, Stephen showed promise of becoming a gifted athlete, but when a medical condition limited his athletic ability, he turned to academics and debate. Stephen excelled in school, earning a bachelor's degree in business administration from the University of Utah, a master's degree in business administration from Harvard University, and a PhD in religious education from Brigham Young University.[2]

Although Stephen was widely popular during the last decades of his life, his greatest joys were his wife of more than fifty-five years, Sandra Merrill, and his posterity of nine children and numerous grandchildren and great-grandchildren. He also received much joy from his vibrant testimony of the gospel of Jesus Christ. On his mission to England, while speaking in small meetinghouses throughout Great Britain and on a square in Hyde Park, Stephen discovered his talent for teaching. After completing an honorable mission in 1954, he knew exactly what he wanted to do with his life—teach and inspire others to enjoy greater success in their lives.

Stephen turned down an offer to take over the Little America Hotel family business to begin his career in teaching at the Brigham Young University School of Management and as an assistant to President Ernest L. Wilkinson. When national business school rankings were released and BYU landed the twenty-fifth spot, Merrill J. Bateman, dean of the School of Management, said, "It was the first time and maybe the last that a school has been ranked because of its organizational behavior department. Steve was a key person in the group that helped develop a reputation for Brigham Young University. And we've been building on it ever since."[3]

At the core of Stephen's influence at the School of Management was his individual approach to teaching. Even though he taught large sections filled with students, he took time to teach each student as though he or she was his personal friend. Before leaving the university to pursue his dream of owning a leadership consulting company, writing books, and traveling the world, he was recognized as one of the most popular professors on the BYU campus.[4]

Stephen became recognized as one of the world's foremost leadership authorities, organizational experts, and thought leaders with the publication of *The 7 Habits of Highly Effective People*. In 2002 *Forbes* magazine named *The 7 Habits of Highly Effective People* one of the top ten most influential management books ever written. A survey taken by staff writers of *Chief Executive* magazine named *The 7 Habits of Highly Effective People* one of the two most influential books of the twentieth century.[5] Stephen's other bestselling books included *First Things First*, *Principle-Centered Leadership*, *The 7 Habits of Highly Effective Families*, and *The 8th Habit: From Effectiveness to Greatness*. Millions of people worldwide have read his works and experimented with the power of Stephen's thoughts on universal principles of leadership. In February 2010, Stephen returned to academics, joining the faculty of the Utah State University Jon M. Huntsman School of Business as a tenured professor and the "first incumbent of the Jon M. Huntsman Presidential Chair in Leadership."[6]

Throughout his life, Stephen was a faithful Latter-day Saint. At the age of twenty-nine he was called to serve as the first president of the Ireland Dublin Mission; he later served as a bishop, high councilor, and regional representative. He authored several devotional works for Latter-day Saint readers, including *Spiritual Roots of Human Relations* (1970), *The Divine Center* (1982), and *6 Events: The Restoration Model for Solving Life's Problems* (2004). When asked why he believed in the teachings of The Church of Jesus Christ of Latter-day Saints, Stephen answered, "I believe because of my heritage, my disciplined obedience and repentance, and my need for explanation and for power outside myself, because it works and is so life-changing, and because I choose to. . . . God's spirit has filled my whole heart and soul with belief."[7]

Stephen passed away on July 16, 2012, with his beloved wife, children, their spouses, grandchildren, and great-grandchildren present. His legacy to the world is principle-centered leadership woven into seven powerful habits of effectiveness. From the Oval Office in the nation's Capitol to the boardroom, community hall, schoolhouse, and family room, Stephen spoke of achieving a mindset and a skillset to enjoy a successful life. He continues to be admired today for his simple, universal, and timeless teachings.[8]

1   "About Stephen R. Covey," Stephen R. Covey homepage, https://www.stephen-covey.com/about/about.php.

2   Lena M. Harper, "The Highly Effective Person," *Marriott Alumni Magazine*, Summer 2012, 5–7, http://marriottschool.uberflip.com/i/148963/8.

3   Ibid., 6.

4   Ibid.

5   "About Stephen R. Covey."

6   Ibid.; see also Donald Q. Cannon, Richard O. Cowan, and Arnold K. Garr, *Encyclopedia of Latter-day Saint History* (Salt Lake City: Deseret Book, 2001), 259.

7   *Why I Believe* (Salt Lake City: Deseret Book, 2001), 122.

8   "About Stephen R. Covey."

OLIVER COWDERY
Truth

Courtesy of Religious Education
Image Project, Brigham Young
University.

THE NAME OF OLIVER COWDERY was intertwined with that of Joseph Smith during the early days of the Church. Oliver scribed most of the Book of Mormon. Along with the Prophet Joseph, he received the Aaronic Priesthood from John the Baptist and the Melchizedek Priesthood from the ancient Apostles Peter, James, and John. Several of the early revelations in the Doctrine and Covenants are instructions to Oliver Cowdery. On December 5, 1834, Oliver was ordained an Assistant to the President of the Church and on April 3, 1836, he received priesthood keys from Elijah, Elias, and Moses in the Kirtland Temple. Of Oliver, Wilford Woodruff wrote, "I have seen Oliver Cowdery when it seemed as though the earth trembled under his feet. I never heard a man bear a stronger testimony than he did when under the influence of the Spirit."[1]

Oliver Cowdery, son of William Cowdery Jr. and Rebecca Fuller, was born on October 3, 1806, in Wells, Vermont. After receiving a rudimentary education in Vermont and New York, Oliver became a schoolteacher. While teaching school in Manchester, New York, he learned of the prophetic calling of Joseph Smith. In April 1829 he accompanied Samuel Smith to Harmony, Pennsylvania, to meet Joseph. "Near the time of the setting of the Sun, Sabbath evening, April 5th, 1829, my natural eyes, for the first time beheld this brother," wrote Oliver. "On Tuesday the 7th, [I] commenced to write the book of Mormon."[2]

Although Oliver had many glorious manifestations and held positions of trust in the Church, nine formal charges were drawn against him on April 7, 1838, including the charge that he persecuted the brethren "by urging on vexatious law suits against them" and that he sought "to destroy the character of Joseph Smith Jr."3 Oliver refused to attend the high council meeting where the charges were presented. "*Give me my freedom or take my life!*" he wrote. "I shall no longer be bound by the chains of hell. I shall speak out when I see a move to deceive the ignorant."4 Oliver was excommunicated on April 12, 1838, at Far West, Missouri.

In spite of Oliver's separation from the Church, Joseph continued to reach out to him and invited members of the Quorum of the Twelve to do the same: "Write to Oliver Cowdery and ask him if he has not eaten husks long enough? If he is not almost ready to return, be clothed with robes of righteousness, and go up to Jerusalem?"5 For years, Oliver rejected their entreaties and even became a charter member of the Methodist Protestant Church in Tiffin, Ohio. However, by 1847, Oliver, who was then living in Elkhorn, Wisconsin, expressed interest in reuniting with the Church. News of his interest was conveyed to the Twelve. On November 22, 1847, Brigham Young wrote to Oliver, "Return to our father's house, from whence thou hast wandered, and partake of the fatted calf and sup and be filled . . . and renew thy testimony to the truth of the Book of Mormon. . . . His sons and daughters will with open arms hail thee as their long lost brother found in the New and Everlasting Covenant."6

Oliver journeyed from Elkhorn to Kanesville, Iowa, to join the Saints. At a conference held in Kanesville on October 21, 1848, he addressed the assembled congregation: "Friends and Brethren,—My name is Cowdery, Oliver Cowdery. In the early history of this Church I stood identified with her, and one in her councils. . . . I wrote, with my own pen, the entire Book of Mormon (save a few pages) as it fell from the lips of the Prophet Joseph Smith. . . . That book is true." The next month Oliver appeared before the high council at Kanesville and formally requested fellowship in the Church, saying, "Brethren, for a number of years, I have been separated from you. I now desire to come back. . . . I seek no station. I only wish to be identified with you."7 On the motion of Orson Hyde, Oliver was received back into the fellowship of the Saints.

After his rebaptism, Oliver was assigned to help Orson Hyde with the *Frontier Guardian* publication. He did so until April 1849, when he and his wife traveled to Richmond, Missouri, to visit her family. From

Richmond, Oliver wrote of his struggles with his "old difficulty of the lungs."[8] His chronic lung condition advanced to consumption, and on March 3, 1850, at the home of David Whitmer, Oliver died. Just before his death, he admonished his loved ones "to live according to the teachings set forth in the Book of Mormon and he promised them that if they were faithful to this they would be assembled with him in Heaven."[9]

1   "Testimony of Wilford Woodruff," *Deseret News Weekly* 35:391, as cited in Stanley R. Gunn, *Oliver Cowdery: Second Elder and Scribe* (Salt Lake City: Bookcraft, 1962), 73.

2   Oliver Cowdery, *Messenger and Advocate* 1, no. 1 (Oct. 1834): 14.

3   Gunn, 151, 152.

4   Huntington Library Letters, microfilm no. 87, as cited in Gunn, 230.

5   *History of the Church*, 5:368.

6   Brigham Young to Oliver Cowdery, Nov. 22, 1847, as cited in Gunn, 191, 193.

7   Andrew Jenson, *Latter-day Saint Biographical Encyclopedia* (Salt Lake City: Deseret Book, 1936), 1:249, 250.

8   Oliver Cowdery, letter written from Richmond, 1849, as cited in Gunn, 207.

9   Gunn, 209.

MATTHEW COWLEY

Kia Ngawari—Childlike

Courtesy of the Church History
Library, The Church of Jesus
Christ of Latter-day Saints.

MATTHEW COWLEY HAD A GREAT love for the Maori people—he spent thirteen of his fifty-six years as a missionary among them. Matthew wanted the Maori to be *kia ngawari*, meaning "changeable . . . willing to follow the leadership of the Church, and make all the necessary changes to do so." He enjoyed saying that *kia ngawari* was "the thirteenth article of faith in two words."[1] Matthew was the epitome of *kia ngawari* to the Maori people.

Matthew Cowley, son of Matthias F. Cowley and Abbie Hyde, was born on August 2, 1897, in Preston, Idaho. In 1897, the year of Matthew's birth, his father accepted a call to the Quorum of the Twelve Apostles. Due to his father's calling, the family moved from Idaho to "Apostle Row" in Salt Lake City, where Matthew enjoyed a rambunctious childhood. He was often in trouble with neighbors, but just as often seen confessing his guilt and making amends.[2] His shenanigans made such an impression on the neighborhood that when Matthew received his mission call to Hawaii, close neighbor Anthon H. Lund of the First Presidency of the Church told him, "You know, Matt, the Hawaiian Mission isn't far enough away. The farther we can get you away from this neighborhood the better it is going to be for all of us." President Lund added, "The Spirit told me you should go to New Zealand instead of Hawaii. . . . If it is all right with you, I will tell President Smith in the morning and you will be sent to New Zealand."[3]

On November 23, 1914, sixteen-year-old Matthew arrived in Auckland, New Zealand. Soon after his arrival, he became severely ill and was unable to proselyte. Matthew spent much time convalescing and learning the Maori language. With temporal and linguistic help from a woman he fondly referred to as his "Maori mother,"[4] Matthew became proficient in the Maori language. In fact, he was so well-versed in the language that the First Presidency asked him to translate the Book of Mormon into Maori. He completed the translation in 1917 and was then asked to translate the Doctrine and Covenants and the Pearl of Great Price into Maori, a task he completed over the next two years.[5]

In 1919, after finishing his mission to New Zealand, Matthew returned to Salt Lake City and enrolled in the University of Utah. After graduating from the university, he enrolled in George Washington University Law School in Washington, DC. He interrupted his studies to marry Elva Taylor on July 13, 1922. To their union were added one daughter, Jewell, and an adopted Maori boy, Toni. To support his growing family, Matthew worked for Senator Reed Smoot of Utah.

After graduating from law school, Matthew and his family returned to Salt Lake City, where he practiced law for thirteen years. He was a good attorney, but "it was generally conceded, however, that he was too honest and too much a humanitarian at heart to amass any wealth." Though he genuinely cared about those he represented—guilty or innocent, repentant or otherwise—his conviction to truth disallowed him from cheating the law or clients out of money. He built a good reputation in his legal practice with *kia ngawari* as his standard. When asked if he would return to New Zealand and leave his legal practice, Matthew responded, "I am not thinking anything about it. If I am called, I will go, if I am not called, I won't."[6]

In 1938, Matthew's law career ended when he became president of the Pacific Mission. His philosophy as president was that "the most important factor of missionary work is not so much the making of converts as the making of friends. Once we make friends the remainder of the work will be comparatively easy."[7] He exemplified this philosophy and welcomed the Maori as part of his own family.

Matthew selected Glen L. Rudd as his assistant in the mission. Elder Rudd quickly learned that his president's travels were unplanned—"he just went where the Lord wanted him to go."[8] Often they visited Maori and missionaries who had been praying for the president to come and help them. Elder Rudd recalled that "people prayed President Cowley all over the mission."[9] One Maori who prayed for the president's help was the father of a small child who had been blind since birth. The father requested that Matthew give his child a name and his eyesight. Matthew recalled, "It shocked me, but then I said to myself, why not? . . . I had faith in that father's faith."[10] Matthew later reported that the child grew to be a troublemaker, but a troublemaker who could see.

In 1945, Matthew was released as president of the Pacific Mission and sustained as an Apostle of the Lord Jesus Christ. In November 1953, after serving faithfully for eight years in the Quorum of the Twelve Apostles, he told Elder Rudd, "I'm not going to live very long." He then said that he would die in his sleep at the same time that he would have awakened in the morning. Elder Rudd protested that if anyone knew about his impending death, that person would be unable to sleep. Matthew responded, "Oh yes, you would; you know as well as I do that life is eternal." True to his word, on December 13, 1953, at age fifty-six, Matthew took his last breath at the very time that he would have awakened in the morning.[11]

To the Maori Latter-day Saints, Matthew was like the *kauri*, "a species of huge tree . . . a veritable monarch of the forest." At his death, it was said of Matthew by the Maori that "a great and noble *kauri* has fallen . . . by the tender hand of him who is Master of the forest and who sees and knows the eternal potential of his trees."[12]

1   Glen L. Rudd, "Memories of Matthew Cowley: Man of Faith, Apostle to the Pacific," in *Pioneers in the Pacific*, ed. Grant Underwood (Provo: BYU Religious Studies Center, 2005), 18.

2   Henry A. Smith, *Matthew Cowley: Man of Faith* (Salt Lake City: Bookcraft, 1954), 34.

3   Ibid., 42.

4   Rudd, 21.

5   Smith, 53.

6   Ibid., 72, 76–77.

7   Ibid., 60.

8   Rudd, 20.

9   Ibid., 21.

10 Matthew Cowley, "Miracles," *Ensign*, Oct. 2004, 46.

11 Rudd, 30–31.

12 Smith, 2.

LaVell Edwards

Teamwork

Photo by Mark Philbrick, BYU
Photography.

LaVell Edwards is a celebrity in collegiate football and a member of the College Football Hall of Fame. Under his skillful coaching, the Brigham Young University Cougar football team appeared in twenty-one bowl games and won nineteen conference championships, a Heisman Trophy, two Outland Trophies, four Davey O'Brien Awards, a Doak Walker Award, a Maxwell Award, seven Sammy Baugh Awards, and thirty-one all-American citations. In 1984, LaVell was named the National Coach of the Year for the second time in his career after the BYU Cougars finished their season 13–0 and won the national championship.

LaVell Edwards, son of Philo and Addie May Edwards, was born October 11, 1930, in Orem, Utah, the eighth of fourteen children. LaVell played football for Utah State University, where he was team captain and earned all-conference honors in 1950 and 1951.

After receiving his bachelor's degree from Utah State in 1951, he served a two-year commitment in the army. Following his military service, he began coaching football at Granite High School in 1954. After eight years of coaching his high school team to victories and receiving a master's degree from the University of Utah, LaVell accepted the position of assistant football coach at Brigham Young University in 1962.

During his years as assistant coach and later head coach of the BYU Cougars, LaVell assembled a strong coaching team, inspired countless young men, and trained some amazing quarterbacks. Under his guidance, Cougar quarterbacks threw more than eleven thousand passes for more than a hundred thousand yards and completed six hundred and thirty-five touchdowns, leading the BYU Cougars to national recognition as the "Quarterback Factory." LaVell led the BYU Cougars from 1972 to 2000, chalking up two hundred and fifty-seven career victories.

LaVell has received countless accolades and honors from state and national organizations for his accomplishments on the field and for the integrity, distinction, and innovation he has brought to the game of football. LaVell is respected for his calm and unassuming demeanor on and off the football field, his ability to lead by example, and his willingness to bring out the best traits in his players. Former BYU football player Timothy R. Clark wrote of LaVell,

> As a hall-of-famer, he is accorded legend status, a distinction reserved for a small, elite fraternity of coaches who break from the ranks and set themselves apart. . . .
>
> . . . In disposition, Coach Edwards was disarming, pleasant, friendly and self-effacing. He was genuinely interested in his players, not just the X's and O's. . . .
>
> . . .Coach Edwards made it abundantly clear that it's impossible to build an organization and summon its institutional will if you don't really like people. You may get lucky and win a championship, but you'll end up leaving a landfill, not a legacy.
>
> During his career, Coach Edwards earned a room full of trophies and a bag full of garish championship rings—the customary emblems of the win column. More than that, he earned the admiration, respect and loyalty of a generation of broken-down football players who stand when a man called LaVell enters the room. . . .
>
> To my old coach, that stone-faced visage, that genuine article, that iconic builder of men who mentored so many, I salute you.[1]

While rubbing shoulders with the top echelon of football greats, LaVell has willingly accepted Church callings, including that of bishop of a BYU student ward. From 1962 to 1968, LaVell and his beloved wife, Patti, served a mission in New York City. Of his testimony, LaVell said, "I know that The Church of Jesus Christ of Latter-day Saints is the Lord's church. I know that Jesus Christ is my Savior and that He lived, died, and lives again for me. I know that He loves me. This knowledge has brought balance and perspective to my life. In the coaching profession, priorities tend to get skewed, and my testimony helps keep me focused on what is truly important in life."[2]

LaVell retired after the 2000 football season with a 257–101–3 record for a .717 winning percentage, making him the seventh all-time victorious coach in college football history. Following LaVell's retirement, the football stadium at Brigham Young University was renamed the LaVell Edwards Stadium in his honor.[3]

1   Timothy R. Clark, "Timothy R. Clark: What I Learned from Lavell Edwards," *Deseret News*, Jan. 10, 2011, http://www.deseretnews.com/article/705364041/What-I-learned-from-LaVell-Edwards.html?pg=1.

2   *Why I Believe* (Salt Lake City: Deseret Book, 2002), 137.

3   "Lavell Edwards Staff Bio: Head Football Coach," Official Home of the BYU Cougars, http://byucougars.com/staff/m-football/lavell-edwards.

RICHARD L. EVANS
Tireless

WHEN RICHARD L. EVANS WAS sixteen years old, an inspired patriarch blessed him that he would have a "bright career" and "stand in holy places and mingle with many of the best men and women upon the earth." The patriarch told Richard that his "tongue [would] be loosened and become as the pen of a ready writer in dispensing the word of God and in preaching the gospel to [his] fellow men."[1] In fulfillment of that blessing, Richard was for forty-one years the announcer, writer, and producer of *Music and the Spoken Word*, a weekly radio program that was broadcast to millions of people throughout the world. In each broadcast, the Mormon Tabernacle Choir sang hymns of praise to God, and Richard shared messages of hope and goodwill.

Richard Louis Evans, son of John and Florence Evans, was born on March 23, 1906, in Salt Lake City, Utah. Ten weeks after Richard's birth, his father missed his footing while trying to exit a streetcar and fell to the ground. Within a few weeks, his father was dead and his mother was left a widow with nine children to support.[2]

At age eleven, Richard was wounded in a mock battle when a neighborhood playmate shot a loaded BB gun at him. A pellet from the gun struck Richard in the left eye. With blood streaming down his face, Richard ran home, pleading with his sister, "Don't cry; pray for me." Richard lost his eye and had it replaced with an artificial one. His artificial eye did not hamper Richard when it came to finding employment in his youth. He delivered newspapers, sold flowers, washed dishes, drove trucks, and was a traveling salesman. He excelled at school and was the editor of his high school newspaper and yearbook, a champion debater, and the recipient of the Heber J. Grant scholarship award.

Richard interrupted his schooling at the University of Utah to accept a mission call to England. On that mission, he served as secretary of the European Mission, the associate editor of the *Millennial Star*, and the writer of the centennial history of the British mission.[3] After his mission, Richard completed his bachelor's and master's degrees at the University of Utah, graduating with honors. He married Alice Thornley of Kaysville, Utah, on August 9, 1933.

At age twenty-four, Richard was employed by KSL Radio as an announcer, and in 1930 was given the assignment to announce the weekly nationwide Mormon Tabernacle Choir radio program that had begun ten months earlier. In addition to the weekly broadcasts, for five years Richard wrote a syndicated newspaper column for William Randolph Hearst's King Features Syndicate, which circulated to millions of homes across the United States. He also wrote articles for *Reader's Digest* and *Encyclopedia Britannica*. "What is a Mormon?" was an article Richard wrote for the October 1954 issue of *Look* magazine and "was one of the best statements about the Mormons and their beliefs to appear in the national press up to that time, and it further established Richard as an authoritative writer for the Church as well as its best-known voice through his Tabernacle Choir broadcasts."[4] "What is a Mormon?" was later reprinted as a missionary tract.

At age thirty-two, Richard was called to serve in the First Council of Seventy. He was the youngest man to be called as a General Authority in more than thirty years. After Richard had served in that council for fifteen years, President David O. McKay announced at the October 1953 general conference that the newest member of the Quorum of the Twelve Apostles was Richard L. Evans. After the sustaining vote, President McKay introduced Richard by saying, "Elder Evans, whom you know and have known because of his work on the radio and his service in the stakes, and whom the entire nation knows,—Richard L. Evans,—will now speak to us."[5]

As a special witness of Jesus Christ, Richard took on new and more demanding assignments. Yet he remained the voice of *Music and the*

Spoken Word, rarely missing a broadcast and still producing, writing, and announcing the weekly message. In addition, Richard wrote sixteen books, most of which were compilations of his messages given on *Music and the Spoken Word*. His books were read by millions of people throughout the world and reviewed by the most prestigious media outlets of the day, including the *New York Times*.

Richard was also involved in civic affairs, the most notable being the Rotary Club. In 1966 Richard became president of Rotary International. That same year, he and his wife addressed audiences in sixty countries and twenty-five states in the United States. It is estimated that he traveled to ninety countries in his years of service to Rotary International.[6]

Richard's unexpected death was caused by a viral infection. He was only sixty-five years old when he died just after midnight on November 1, 1971, in Salt Lake City. "It is with subdued hearts that we remember our beloved Richard L. Evans," said President Harold B. Lee. "We know that there are heavenly choirs, and maybe they needed an announcer, and one to give the Spoken Word. If so, maybe the need was so great that he is called to a higher service in that place where time is no more."[7]

1   Richard L. Evans, Jr., *Richard L. Evans—The Man and the Message* (Salt Lake City: Bookcraft, 1973), 23.

2   Richard L. Evans, Jr., 18; see also David W. Evans, *My Brother Richard L. Evans* (Beatrice Cannon Evans, 1984), 2.

3   The history was subsequently updated and published in 1937 under the title *A Century of Mormonism in Great Britain*.

4   David W. Evans, 51; the article appeared originally in *Look*, Oct. 5, 1954, 67–68. A condensed version was printed in *Reader's Digest*, 66 (June 1955): 143–46.

5   David O. McKay, *Conference Report*, Oct. 1953, 128.

6   Richard L. Evans, Jr., 75.

7   Harold B. Lee, *Conference Report*, April 1972, 3.

HENRY EYRING
Truth Seeker

Courtesy of the Church History
Library, The Church of Jesus
Christ of Latter-day Saints.

PROFESSOR HENRY EYRING OF PRINCETON University asked a fellow scientist if he would like to collaborate on a chemical kinetics research project. The scientist refused, believing "they would never live long enough to finish the problem." Henry countered, "That's true if we don't learn anything while we are working on the problem."[1] When asked how the world began, Henry answered, "I believe whichever way it turns out actually to have been."[2] His open attitude in the pursuit of truth led him to discoveries that caused the scientific community to sit up and take notice. But to Henry, no truth was more satisfying than his discovery of a pleasing harmony between religion and science.

Henry Eyring, son of Edward Christian Eyring and Caroline Romney, was born February 20, 1901, on a ranch in Colonia Juárez, a Mormon colony in Chihuahua, Mexico. His parents encouraged him to do well in his studies and to pursue eternal truths. His mother often said, "Henry, I hope you'll not just be good but that you'll be good for something."[3] During the Mexican Revolution of 1912, Henry's family moved from the Mormon colonies to Pima, Arizona. In Pima, Henry attended and graduated from high school with a $500 scholarship awarded for excellence in academic performance.[4] In 1923 Henry received his bachelor's degree in mining engineering from the University of Arizona. In 1924 he earned a master's degree in metallurgical engineering and in 1927 a PhD in chemistry from the University of California at Berkeley.

While employed as a researcher and lab instructor at the University of Wisconsin, Henry met Mildred Bennion, a University of Utah professor. They were married on August 24, 1928, in the Chicago Mission home and later sealed in the Salt Lake Temple.[5] Mildred encouraged Henry in his pursuit of scientific truths. Together they traveled to Berlin, Germany, so Henry could research at the Haber Institute. When they returned to the United States, Henry accepted a professorship at Princeton University. As a professor, he encouraged struggling students by simplifying complex concepts. "The world knocks them down," said Henry. "I try to build them up."[6]

Although Henry was admired and respected by his students, it was his scientific discoveries that propelled him to the forefront of academia. He received a prestigious prize from the American Association for the Advancement of Science. In 1933 the *New York Times* reported that Henry had applied truths of quantum mechanics to chemistry, finding that the principles of mechanics also held true in other branches of science.[7] In 1946 Henry left Princeton to become dean of the Chemistry Department at the University of Utah.

Anticipating Henry's move, Church authorities invited him to serve on the General Sunday School Board and to chair the Gospel Doctrine Committee.[8] In these capacities, Henry associated with Church leaders who often remarked about his unusual ability to blend science and religion. "If an idea is wrong, it will fail," Henry told the brethren. "If it is right, nothing can stop it."[9] Henry once told President Joseph Fielding Smith that he recognized that "the church is committed to the truth whatever its source."[10] Henry was a strong proponent of the concept that there was no person too insignificant to learn the truths that he knew; there was no one too small to be dismissed as incapable of contributing to the cause of finding truth.

Henry made a marked difference through his unwavering Church service. Yet when his wife, Mildred, was diagnosed with cancer, he devoted most his time to her, even moving into the hospital to be by her side. Following Mildred's death, Henry found that he had a cancerous tumor. After overcoming his own health problems, Henry married

Winifred Brennan Clark in 1971. With Winifred's encouragement, he returned to his scientific studies and research. In 1976 he was awarded the prestigious Berzelius Medal, an honor that pleased him greatly because the award was given "only once every 50 years."[11] He was nominated for a Nobel Prize and awarded the coveted Wolf Prize in chemistry for his "imaginative applications to chemical and physical processes."[12]

A year after receiving the award, Henry died of recurrent cancer on December 26, 1981. Henry wrote more than six hundred published articles on topics ranging from chemistry to religion, and the scientific papers he was writing before his death were published posthumously.

1   Douglas Henderson, "My Friend, Henry Eyring," *The Journal of Physical Chemistry* 87, no. 15 (1983): 2639.

2   Steven Harvey Heath, "Henry Eyring Mormon Scientist," master's thesis, University of Utah, 1980, 181.

3   Ibid., 27.

4   Henry J. Eyring, *Mormon Scientist: The Life and Faith of Henry Eyring* (Salt Lake City: Deseret Book, 2007), 12.

5   Heath, 153–154.

6   Eyring, 278.

7   Heath, 55–56.

8   Ibid., 160.

9   Edward L. Kimball, "A Dialogue with Henry Eyring," *Dialogue: A Journal of Mormon Thought* 8, no. 3 (Autumn–Winter 1973):106.

10   Walter Kauzmann, "Biographical Memoirs: Henry Eyring," National Academies Press; Dec. 26, 1981, http://www.nap.edu/html/biomems/heyring.html.

11   Henderson, 2640.

12   "Henry Eyring Winner of Wolf Prize in Chemistry—1980," Wolf Foundation, http://www.wolffund.org.il/index.php?dir=site&page=winners&cs=121&language=eng.

AVARD FAIRBANKS
Artist

AVARD FAIRBANKS WAS A PROLIFIC twentieth-century American sculptor and faithful Latter-day Saint whose artistic work is prominently displayed at the United States Capitol Building, in several state capitol buildings, and in other locations throughout the world. Avard sculpted more than a hundred public monuments and hundreds of artistic masterpieces during his nearly eighty-year career in the field of art.

Avard Tennyson Fairbanks, son of John B. Fairbanks and Lilly Annetta Huish, was born on March 2, 1897, in Provo, Utah. Avard's father was a pioneer artist and an art instructor at Brigham Young Academy. At age twelve, Avard sculpted a model of his pet rabbit for the 1909 Utah State Fair and won first prize. Unfortunately, the judge, a university professor, refused to give him the prize, explaining that the contest was for professionals, not for boys. Deeply disappointed, Avard "resolved to become an accomplished artist so that the professor would in time recognize him as a sculptor. 'I'll show him some day!' he said."[1]

As a teenager, Avard studied at the Art Student League in New York and at the Ecole Nationale des Beaux Artes in Paris, France. At age seventeen, he was the youngest artist ever to be admitted to the French Salon. Avard earned academic degrees from the University of Utah, Yale, and the University of Michigan. After completing his degrees, Avard served on the faculties of five American universities and was the founding dean of the College of Fine Arts at the University of Utah.[2] In and out of the university setting, it was Avard's belief that "art should be simple and understandable, not only to the educated and technically trained, but also to children and the untutored. He believed art should be uplifting and represent the finer qualities of life to all men and women."[3]

In 1918 Avard and his brother, J. Leo Fairbanks, were commissioned by the LDS Church to sculpt four friezes for the Laie Hawaii Temple. While working on the friezes in Hawaii, Avard convinced his sweetheart—Maude Fox, of Taylorsville, Utah—to join him in Hawaii and marry him on the island. They became the parents of eight sons and two adopted daughters, all successful in their own way. Of Avard's artistic talent, his son Jonathan said, "I think he was a person who saw the world in larger terms than his art." His son David added, "He was a man who kept the faith with his artwork, he kept the faith with his testimony and he kept the faith with his wife and family."[4]

Avard's nonreligious monuments include the ancient lawgiver of Sparta, *Lycurgus*, for which Avard was awarded a medal by King Paul of Greece. Avard's many other works include his depiction of the *Pioneer Family*, now housed at the state capitol in Bismarck, North Dakota; *Daniel Jackling*, now housed at the Utah State Capitol; *Prime Minister of Canada McKenzie King*, which is at the parliament buildings in Ottawa, Canada; *George Washington*, now housed at the Washington State Capitol Building; *Abraham Lincoln*, which is at the Ford Theater and the United States Supreme Court; and *John Burke, Esther Morris*, and *Marcus Whitman*, which are on display at the U.S. Capitol Building in Washington, DC. During his professional career, Avard had many honors bestowed upon him, including the Herbert Adams Memorial Medal for distinguished service to sculpture.[5]

Among his many religious sculptures are *Jesus Christ, Joseph Smith the Prophet, Three Witnesses, Restoration of the Melchizedek Priesthood,* and *Restoration of the Aaronic Priesthood*. Nine sculptors submitted designs for the angel Moroni statue to be placed atop the Washington DC Temple, where thousands of people traveling the Capital Beltway would view the sculpture each day. Avard's design of a graceful angel holding a trumpet to his lips and a replica of the gold plates in his left arm was selected. Of his design, Avard said, "I wanted the [angel Moroni] statue to conform to the spirit and architecture of the temple, that of aspiring upward. I wanted the feeling of that upward reach, accomplished by the stress of vertical lines."[6] Avard's depiction of the angel Moroni now graces the Washington DC Temple and has been replicated for other temples throughout the world.

In addition to creating religious and nonreligious sculptures, small and large bronzes, marble carvings, medals, and relief panels, Avard was commissioned by the Chrysler Motor Company to create a hood ornament for the 1932 Dodge automobile. When he designed a ram symbol, leaders of Chrysler inquired of him what a ram had to do with the Dodge. Avard explained to them that when people see a ram coming down the road, they would say, "Dodge!"[7]

Just before Christmas 1986, Avard had a heart attack. As he began to improve, he optimistically formulated plans for sculpting the biblical John the Revelator. From his hospital bed, Avard arranged for a ton of clay to be delivered to his studio. Although the clay arrived, a second heart attack took his life on January 1, 1987, just two months short of his ninetieth birthday.[8] On his desk was found the following admonition:

> When one proclaims a disbelief in God and his powers, then one becomes an atheist or agnostic and divorces himself from celestial support and the influence of the Holy Spirit. He gives up his heritage and relationships with the holy family bonds and ties.
>
> Thus one becomes spiritually alone in a physical world of greed, suspicion, and intrigue, and is subject to physical survival.[9]

Generations now have the privilege of viewing Avard's legacy of talent and faith in bronze and stone monuments atop temples, in government buildings, and in museums spread across the land.

1   Eugene F. Fairbanks, *A Sculptor's Testimony in Bronze and Stone* (Salt Lake City: Publisher's Press, 1972), 1.

2   Donald Q. Cannon, Richard O. Cowan, and Arnold K. Garr, *Encyclopedia of Latter-day Saint History* (Salt Lake City: Deseret Book, 2001), 355.

3   "Avard T. Fairbanks," J. Willard Marriott Library, University of Utah, http://www.lib.utah.edu/collections/utah-artists/UAP-Avard-Fairbanks.php.

4   "Avard Fairbanks' Art Exhibited in Visitors' Center," *LDS Church News*, June 24, 1995, http://gospelink.com/library/document/84845?highlight=1.

5   Fairbanks, 8.
6   J. Michael Hunter, "I Saw Another Angel Fly," *Ensign*, Jan. 2000, 12.
7   "Avard T. Fairbanks."
8   Fairbanks, 9.
9   Ibid., 147.

JAMES E. FAUST

Listening

Courtesy of the Church History
Library, The Church of Jesus
Christ of Latter-day Saints.

JAMES E. FAUST SERVED AS an Apostle and special witness of the Savior Jesus Christ for twenty-nine years and as a General Authority for thirty-five years. He was the Second Counselor in the First Presidency of the Church from 1995 until his death in 2007. Of James it has been said, "[He] always strove to reach out in a spirit of kindness and brotherhood. His conference addresses often reflected the Savior's two great injunctions: to love and serve God and to love and serve His children. With warmth, wit, and wisdom, President Faust brought a grandfatherly grace to the pulpit, blessing the lives of all who heard his witness and heeded his counsel."[1]

James Esdras Faust, son of George A. Faust and Amy Finlinson, was born on July 31, 1920, in Delta, Utah. James's family moved to Salt Lake City when he was a small boy so that his father could attend law school at the University of Utah. Although James liked growing up in Salt Lake City, he spent holidays and many summers with his grandparents, who lived in Oak City, near Delta. James attended Granite High School, where he lettered in football and track and excelled in debate and on the student court.

After graduating from high school in 1937, James attended the University of Utah and ran the 440-yard and mile relay for the university. James interrupted college life in 1939 to accept a mission call to Brazil. Before completing that mission in 1942, he was appointed a district president.

Upon returning to the United States, James was drafted into the Army Air Corps. On April 21, 1943, in the Salt Lake Temple, while on military leave, James married Ruth Wright, a beautiful young woman he had known in high school. Of their marriage, Elder Neal A. Maxwell wrote, "Chief among the 'great souls' who have influenced [James] is his wife, Ruth. They met as students at Granite High School and were sealed in the Salt Lake Temple while President Faust was on a brief military leave and before the long journey into the Pacific. His deep devotion to Ruth may be gauged by the fact that, while they were separated during World War II, he wrote a letter every day to her. The letters arrived irregularly, and one day Ruth Faust received ninety letters; her employer thoughtfully let her have the afternoon off to go home and read them!"[2] James and Ruth became the parents of five children.

At the end of World War II, James, ranked a first lieutenant in the Army Air Corps, was discharged. He returned to Ruth and to his studies at the University of Utah. After going to school year-round, he graduated from law school in the spring of 1948, at the same time earning his bachelor's degree, the last two years of which he completed during that same three-year period in 1948. A year later he was called to be bishop of the Cottonwood Second Ward and elected on the Democratic ticket to the Utah House of Representatives. He then practiced law in Salt Lake City for many years.[3]

James believed that it was important for him to give service to his community and Church as well as to the legal field. He accepted an opportunity to serve on the Utah Legislative Study Committee and the Utah Constitutional Revision Commission. He also served as president of the Utah Bar Association from 1962 to 1963 and as an adviser to the *American Bar Association Journal*. United States President John F. Kennedy appointed James to the Civil Rights Commission. In 1996 James received the Distinguished Lawyer Emeritus Award from the Utah Bar Association. In 1998 he was given a Brazilian national citizenship award and made an honorary citizen of the city of São Paulo—honors bestowed upon only a few world leaders.

As a General Authority, first as an Assistant to the Quorum of the Twelve in 1972 and then as a Seventy in 1976, James served as president of the International Mission, adviser on Church-related affairs in South America, executive director of the Church Curriculum Department, director of Welfare Services, and editor of three monthly magazines—the

Friend, the *Ensign*, and the *New Era*. He also served as managing director of the Melchizedek Priesthood Mutual Improvement Association.[4] In each of these important assignments, James served with honor and efficiency.

On September 30, 1978, James was sustained as a member of the Quorum of the Twelve Apostles. Of his calling to the Apostleship, James said, "I understand that a chief requirement for the holy Apostleship is to be a personal witness of Jesus as the Christ and the Divine Redeemer. Perhaps on that basis alone, I can qualify. This truth has been made known to me by the unspeakable peace and power of the Spirit of God."[5] James served faithfully in the Quorum of the Twelve until March 12, 1995, when he was set apart as second counselor to President Gordon B. Hinckley in the First Presidency of the Church. The presidency of Gordon B. Hinckley, Thomas S. Monson, and James E. Faust constitutes the longest continuously serving First Presidency in Church history.

On August 10, 2007, at age eighty-seven, James died at his home in Salt Lake City of causes incident to age. Of him, Elder Maxwell said, "Early on, the gospel seed found fertile soil in James Esdras Faust. When only seventeen, he was called to serve as a counselor in his ward Sunday School superintendency. At twenty-eight he was ordained as a bishop. Since then he has done it all in terms of Church service: stake high councilor, stake president, regional representative of the Twelve, Assistant to the Twelve, Seventy, and Apostle. In each of these callings he demonstrated that a good leader is always a good listener. . . . When he assert[ed] himself, it [was] after listening. Again and again, colleagues have seen him listen patiently to discussions which swirl about the edges of a matter and then create a focus on the key issues. He does this thoughtfully but, if necessary, boldly."[6]

1   "President James E. Faust, Beloved Shepherd," *Ensign*, Oct. 2007.

2   Neal A. Maxwell, "President James E. Faust: Pure Gold," *Ensign*, Aug. 1995, 12.

3   James Bell, *In the Strength of the Lord: The Life and Teachings of James E. Faust* (Salt Lake City: Deseret Book, 1999), 66–68.

4   "President James E. Faust Dies at Age 87," *Deseret News*, Aug.10, 2007, http://www.deseretnews.com/article/695199591/President-James-E-Faust-dies-at-age-87.html?pg=all.

5   Bell, 131.

6   Maxwell, 12–17.

HARVEY FLETCHER

Innovating

Courtesy of the Church History
Library, The Church of Jesus
Christ of Latter-day Saints.

HARVEY FLETCHER SPENT A LIFETIME pursuing scientific excellence as a professor, researcher, and engineer. He invested his energy in discovering ways to better the lives of those who were hard of hearing, and saw his efforts rewarded when he witnessed them using his hearing aids and "with tears running down their cheeks crying, 'I can hear! I can hear!'"[1] His discoveries in stereophonic sound have benefited every generation since. In the scientific community, Harvey is known as the "father of stereophonic sound."

Harvey Fletcher, son of Charles Eugene Fletcher and Elizabeth Miller, was born September 11, 1884, in Provo, Utah. Harvey received an eighth-grade education, the highest level of coursework available in Provo at that time. He repeated the second half of the eighth grade, claiming there was "nothing else to do."[2] Though academically minded, Harvey was contented to remain in his hometown after graduation and to help his father build houses and his uncles deliver groceries. Eventually, however, he became bored and was easily persuaded to attend Brigham Young Academy. In the fall of 1900, Harvey began a lifelong relationship with science at the academy.

Unfortunately, Harvey's love for science started off on the wrong foot when he failed his first physics class. He retook the class and passed with an A-plus. Harvey's early achievements were not limited to the classroom, however; Harvey and a classmate submitted a bid for a Provo City construction job and won. They completed the job, made a profit, and "found themselves 'way ahead in experience' as a result of the project."[3]

Later, under the guidance of Professor Ernest Partridge, Harvey and two classmates undertook the challenge of placing three large letters—B, Y, and U—on the side of the mountain overlooking the campus. After much planning, Harvey and his classmates directed other students to whitewash the letters. After the students worked for six hours on the letter "Y," they had doubts about the size and proportion of the letter. Because of their doubts, the students refused to whitewash any more letters after filling in the "Y," which remains the sole letter on the mountain. To Harvey's credit, the "Y" was perfectly proportioned when viewed from the ground level.[4]

Harvey graduated from Brigham Young Academy in 1907. His first employment was an opportunity to teach physics and mathematics at the same academy. During this time, he courted Lorena Chipman. When Harvey decided to pursue a PhD degree at the University of Chicago, he asked Lorena to marry him. Harvey and Lorena were married on September 9, 1908, and soon moved to Chicago, even though Harvey had not been accepted into the PhD program at the university.

Harvey was rejected from pursuing a graduate program at the University of Chicago because he had only three years of university experience. Discouraged, he sought the help of Professor Robert Millikan, who advised him to register as a special student taking graduate-level classes in order to prove his ability to succeed. Harvey followed his advice and reflected, "I was as well, if not better, prepared in physics and mathematics than any of my classmates . . . but I was below them in my knowledge of subjects in the general educational field."[5] He was admitted as a graduate student after completing one year of general education courses.

When Harvey asked Professor Millikan for suggestions on a dissertation topic, Millikan asked him to find the charge of an electron using a medium other than water. Harvey made great headway in using oil and eventually published several papers with Millikan, documenting revolutionary findings on the charge of the electron and proving its existence. Though there is some controversy on the authorship of the papers, Harvey said, "People have frequently asked me if I had bad feelings toward Millikan for not letting me be a joint author with him on the first paper, which really led to his getting the Nobel Prize. My answer has always been no."[6] Harvey expressed gratitude to Professor Millikan for the opportunity he had to work with him.

In 1911, after graduating with a PhD degree from the University of Chicago, Harvey was offered a job at the American Telephone and Telegraph Company and the Western Electric Company. Harvey refused both positions in order to return to Provo and teach at his alma mater, Brigham Young University.

For several years, the Western Electric Company of New York sent Harvey letters asking if he was now ready to leave academia and work for their company. By 1916 Harvey was ready to accept their offer, but George H. Brimhall, president of Brigham Young University, did not want to lose such an excellent professor. President Brimhall took the matter before Joseph F. Smith, President of The Church of Jesus Christ of Latter-day Saints. President Smith advised Harvey to accept the employment offer with the Western Electric Company of New York, but cautioned him to keep his testimony and maintain his Church activity, saying, "If you can do so you can do more good for the Church in New York City than you could do here at the BYU at the present time."[7]

In compliance with President Smith's prophetic counsel, Harvey moved his family to New York in 1916 and began working for Western Electric. He stayed with that company for thirty-three years, working on acoustics. Harvey developed two ways of relating sound that are still used today: binaural and stereophonic.[8] His research and inventions took on worldwide acclaim as they influenced individuals who were hard of hearing and future researchers who have built and continue to build upon his work. Following the counsel to remain active, Harvey served as president of the New York Branch for a decade and as president of the New York Stake for another decade.[9]

In 1952 Harvey returned to Brigham Young University to serve as the director of research. In his remaining years in academia, he formed an engineering course and became chair of the Department of Engineering. He was known for working closely with students until 1960. At that time, he left the university to devote himself to researching musical tones. Harvey died in Provo on July 23, 1981.

Harvey made a career out of listening to others. He lived to see his scientific pursuits flourish while never failing to fortify his testimony. He proclaimed after receiving his PhD, "I know better than I have ever known before that the Church of Jesus Christ of Latter-day Saints is the true church and is the power of God unto salvation."[10]

1 Harvey Fletcher, "Autobiography of Harvey Fletcher" (unpublished manuscript), 57, quoted in Stephen H. Fletcher, "Harvey Fletcher 1884–1981," in *Biographical Memoirs, National Academy of Sciences* 61 (Washington, DC: National Academy Press, 1992), 180–181.

2 Michael Fletcher Perry, "'Good and Great': A Biography of Harvey Fletcher," honors thesis, Brigham Young University, 2006, 15.

3 Perry, 18–19.

4 Ibid., 20–21.

5 Harvey Fletcher, "My Work with Millikan on the Oil-drop Experiment," *Physics Today* 35 (June 1982): 43.

6 Fletcher, "My Work with Millikan," 47.

7 Perry, 62.

8 *Encyclopedia Britannica*, "Harvey Fletcher," http://www.britannica.com/EBchecked/topic/210055/Harvey-Fletcher.

9 Edward L. Kimball, "Harvey Fletcher and Henry Eyring: Men of Faith and Science," *Dialogue: A Journal of Mormon Thought* 15 (Autumn 1982): 79.

10 Gordon B. Hinckley, "'Seek First the Kingdom of God . . .': The Story of Harvey Fletcher, the Great Scientist—A Humble Man Who Believed Implicitly," *Improvement Era*, July 1950, 582.

BRANDON FLOWERS
Testimony

Courtesy of Lucy Hamblin and
CC-BY-SA-3.0.

As a little boy, Brandon Flowers was driven by his mother in the family car up and down the Las Vegas Strip in hopes of finding his father, who had a gambling and drinking addiction. The nightly searches ended when Brandon was six years old and his father quit his vices after receiving a testimony of the truthfulness of The Church of Jesus Christ of Latter-day Saints. Through the years Brandon also gained a testimony of Jesus Christ. That testimony has been an anchor to him as he has honed his talents as a rock musician.[1]

Brandon Flowers, son of Terry Flowers and Jean Barlow, was born June 21, 1981. When Brandon was eight years old, his family moved to Payson and then to Nephi, Utah, trying to get out of the "rat race" of Las Vegas. Though Brandon "liked the freedom of being a kid in a small town," he "never really got over the culture shock" of moving from the lights of Las Vegas to quiet, rural Utah.[2] When he was sixteen years old, his parents let him move back to Las Vegas to finish high school.[3]

After high school graduation, Brandon worked in casinos and shops in Vegas. An advertisement in a Las Vegas newspaper announcing that Dave Keuning was starting a band and looking for like-minded musicians captured his attention and changed his life. Dave Keuning, Ronnie Vannucci, Mark Stoermer, and Brandon formed the rock band

The Killers and had their first gig in August 2002. Of Brandon's talent, band member Ronnie Vannucci said, "Brandon wasn't afraid to just get up there and just do it. You need that when you're trying to get something off the ground."[4]

As success and stardom followed the band, Brandon made a conscious decision to never succumb to the vices of a typical rock star. He wanted to be different and to stand for righteous principles. "There are a lot of connotations that come along with popular music or rock music, and it's usually very sex driven or money driven," he said. "I realized early on that it wasn't the road for me and that maybe because of the foundations that were laid in my life by my mom taking me to church that I wanted to take a different road."[5]

Since then The Killers have sold more than 16 million albums worldwide. Brandon has also released a solo album titled *Flamingo* that charted at number one in the United Kingdom in September 2010. The Killers have performed with Coldplay and Bruce Springsteen. Sir Elton John named Brandon one of his top five heroes.[6]

Most people would not see "rock stardom" as compatible with living a Latter-day Saint lifestyle. But in Brandon's case, his testimony of the gospel of Jesus Christ takes precedence over fame: In "numerous interviews and articles . . . he's affirmed his Mormonism over the years."[7] Columnist Craig McLean observed, "When asked about his Mormon faith . . . [Brandon is] aware of how uncool it is to talk about your religion. But he talks nonetheless. He can't help himself. He's polite and funny, but honesty and directness shoot out of him."[8] Brandon finds "a lot of people love to come up to me and tell me they were raised in the church. And they expect there to be this camaraderie about 'Oh, we've outgrown it now, and we're smart enough now not to be in it.' And it started happening so often that it really made me take a look at myself and I realized I was raised in it, and . . . there's still a fire burning in there!"[9]

In 2012 Brandon had a conversation with famed atheist Richard Dawkins on a Swedish talk show. Brandon told Dawkins that some of the things he loved about his Mormon faith were "my mother teaching me to pray, and that I have that communication with my heavenly Father. . . . There are answers to questions that my church has . . . it's a beautiful thing to me, and I'm happy."[10]

Family is also an important part of Brandon's life. "It's definitely not normal in this business at my age for me to have a wife and children," said Brandon, "but I guess for me it ties back to my roots and the example set from my parents. They were married for 44 years, and there was always a happiness in my home, and that's what I want."[11] Brandon married Tana Mundkowsky on August 2, 2005, on the island of Oahu. Brandon and Tana are the parents of three sons, one of whom is named Ammon after the Book of Mormon missionary. Brandon said of being a father, "There's nothing better than being a parent and there's not a song you could write that would beat having those kids. I prefer being with them than on the road, although I love my job."[12]

Brandon continues to enjoy success in the music industry, yet his goals for the future are much more than having another hit song. "I feel like I want to be a positive force in the world," he said. "I want to uplift people."[13]

1   Tim Teeman, "Indie Rocker Brandon Flowers Builds on His Faith," *The Australian News*, Sept. 4, 2012, http://www.theaustralian.com.au/news/world/indie-rocker-builds-on-his-faith/story-fnb64oi6-1226464223898#.

2   Craig McLean, "Songs of Praise," *The Observer*, Sept. 23, 2006, http://www.theguardian.com/music/2006/sep/24/popandrock.killers.

3   Teeman.

4   McLean.

5   Brandon Flowers, "I'm a Mormon," Mormon.org video, mormon.org/me/5233.

6   Flowers.

7   Christopher Jones, "Conveying Joseph Smith: Brandon Flowers, Arthur King, and the Mormon Rock Star Image," *Juvenile Instructor*, Oct. 19, 2011, http://www.juvenileinstructor.org/conveying-joseph-smith-brandon-flowers-arthur-kane-and-the-mormon-rock-star-image/.

8   McLean.

9   Flowers.

10   Katherine Weber, "Dawkins Lays into Brandon Flowers over Mormon Faith," *The Christian Post*, Sept. 21, 2012, http://www.christiantoday.com/article/dawkins.lays.into.brandon.flowers.over.mormon.faith/30681.htm.

11   Flowers.

12   Teeman.

13   Flowers.

JIMMER FREDETTE
Goodness

Courtesy of *Deseret News.*

AFTER JIMMER FREDETTE'S SUCCESSFUL BASKETBALL career at Brigham Young University and his honor as Player of the Year, President Barack Obama said, "Unbelievable. Best scorer obviously in the country. Great talent."[1] Of Jimmer, now a professional basketball player with the New Orleans Pelicans, *Sports Illustrated* writer Kelli Anderson wrote, "Facing the opposition's best defender (or, more often, defenders), [Jimmer] pulls up going right or going left. He shoots off the dribble, off the wrong foot, off balance, off the glass. He finishes in traffic with a dozen deft moves, including a funky scoop shot, originating from his waist, that he can make with either hand."[2]

James Taft Fredette, son of Al and Kay Fredette, was born on February 25, 1989, in the blue-collar town of Glen Falls, New York. Jimmer's father, a Latter-day Saint, was employed at the Finch Paper Mill near the Hudson River and his mother, a Catholic, was employed as an occasional substitute teacher. Although Jimmer grew up in a "tiny house, with just two bedrooms for the five family members to share, and sloped ceilings upstairs that make standing up straight a challenge for full-grown adults," he said, "My childhood was just so magical. My dad . . . would always come outside and play with us when he got home from work." Concerning his mother, Jimmer said, "She didn't really care if we wrecked things because we didn't really have nice things anyway. . . . And she made a rule when we were younger that we could dribble a ball in the house."[3]

Jimmer's backyard was the gathering place for neighborhood friends; Jimmer recalled, "We would play every kind of game you could think of. It would get very competitive." He became so good at basketball as a kid that "it didn't take long before Jimmer's jumpers became an unofficial halftime show" at the basketball games held at Glen Falls High School. "Fans were tickled by the curly-haired little kid—still chubby—who was swishing three-pointers from all over."[4]

Hoping to keep his young son grounded in spiritual matters, Jimmer's father told him, "The most important thing you're ever going to do in this life is be a good person. . . . If your role model is Christ, you're going to follow his example. You can be the best athlete there ever was, but if you're not a good person, nobody will like you."

Jimmer worked hard to become a strong and likable player on the basketball court. He practiced hard and concluded, "It's not about being the most athletic, quickest, or fastest but knowing how to use your body to your advantage, so you can be successful. I can stop on a dime, and that's how I'm able to create the space I need when I shoot the ball." And create space he did. Whether playing ball at high school games or challenging inmates at the nearby penitentiary, Jimmer was at his best: "He scored more than 2,400 points at Glen Falls High, sixth-most in New York state history."[5]

Yet Jimmer was a second-tier prospect when it came to being recruited at the college level. The exception was Brigham Young University. Head coach Dave Rose watched Jimmer play ball at a summer basketball camp at BYU. "Rose saw a guy with big feet and an occasionally awkward way of shooting the ball. But he also saw a player with a limitless repertoire of unorthodox moves and ways to score."[6]

At BYU, Jimmer was recognized as "one of the most accurate foul shooters in the nation, making at least 85 percent of his free throws each season." By the end of his junior year, Jimmer "was a third-team All-American; the Cougars [had] won an NCAA tourney game for the first time since 1993; and Jimmer [had] averaged 22.1 points and 4.7 assists." At this point, his thoughts turned to the NBA until former BYU player and Boston Celtics general manager Danny Ainge told Jimmer that "his own senior year was one of the best years of his life—not just playing basketball but being in college and enjoying that lifestyle as long as possible."[7]

During his senior year, Jimmer's success in BYU basketball was unprecedented—fans coined the term "Jimmermania" to show their enthusiasm for his performance. In 2011 Jimmer passed Danny Ainge as the top scorer at BYU with a career-high fifty-two-point game against New Mexico. "He won Player of the Year awards named for Dr. James Naismith (inventor of the game of basketball), John Wooden (winner of a record 10 national championships), and Oscar Robertson (arguably the most versatile player in college basketball history)."[8] With Jimmer as the leading scorer, BYU advanced to the NCAA Sweet Sixteen for the first time since 1981.

On June 23, 2011, Jimmer was drafted as the number ten overall pick by the Sacramento Kings. Jimmermania moved to Sacramento and recharged Sacramento Kings merchandise sales by a 540 percent increase. On March 2, 2014, he negotiated a buyout with Sacramento and signed with the Chicago Bulls, where he played until signing with the New Orleans Pelicans on July 24, 2014.

Occasionally, Jimmer bumps into college coaches like Mike Berg of Notre Dame and Jay Wright of Villanova who shake their heads and say, "How did we miss you?" Of his professional success, his mother, Kay, said, "Thank heavens for Jimmer's success in basketball because it pulled us all through some really rough times. . . . Jimmer still doesn't realize to this day how much he helped us all. His success was the shining light that got us through the darkness."[9]

1 "Obama Heaps Praise on BYU's Jimmer Fredette," KSL.com., March 17, 2011, http://www.ksl.com/?sid=14751208.

2 Kelli Anderson, "A Real Jimmer Dandy," *Sports Illustrated*, Jan. 31, 2011, http://si.com/vault/article/magazine/MAG1181209/index.htm.

3 Pat Forde, *The Contract: The Journey of Jimmer Fredette from the Playground to the Pros* (Salt Lake City: Shadow Mountain, 2012), 18, 20, 23.

4 Ibid., 21, 26.

5 Ibid., 38, 57, 93.

6 Ibid., 99.

7 Ibid., 94, 122, 127.

8 Ibid., 165.

9 Ibid., 103, 13.

ARNOLD FRIBERG

Magnifying Talents

Courtesy of the Church History
Library, The Church of Jesus
Christ of Latter-day Saints.

WHEN ARNOLD FRIBERG WENT TO see his bishop about serving a mission, his bishop advised him to "forego the mission." The bishop seemed to know that Arnold had another full-time mission to fulfill, for he told Arnold, "You will do more good through developing your talent than you could do in two years of door-to-door tracting."[1] Although barely a young adult at that time, Arnold had already been formally trained in cartoon and commercial artistry, worked as an illustrator and painter, and won three national art awards.[2] He credited his unusual artistic talent to a desire to serve others and to worship God. Today his artistic renderings are some of the most widely recognized works of religious art. They appear in scriptures, manuals, and LDS meetinghouses worldwide.

Arnold Friberg, son of Sven Peter Friberg and Ingeborg Solberg, was born on December 21, 1913, in Winnetka, Illinois. When Arnold was three years old, he and his Swedish father and Norwegian mother moved from Illinois to Arizona with the hope that the warmer climate would help improve his father's health. In Arizona, the Friberg family was introduced to and baptized members of The Church of Jesus Christ of Latter-day Saints.

By age seven, to the delight of family and friends, Arnold's budding talent for art was recognized. After graduating from high school, Arnold attended the Chicago Academy of Fine Arts before working as a freelance artist in New York City. Due to a misunderstanding about his apartment lease in the Big Apple, Arnold moved to Chicago, where he met and courted Hedve Baxter until he was drafted into the United States Armed Forces to serve in World War II. After his military service, Arnold settled in San Francisco, where Hedve would move. Their friendship blossomed into romance and they were married on December 26, 1946.[3] They had two children—a son and a daughter—during their marriage.

Always conscious of his artistic gifts, Arnold dedicated his life to his work. To him, "art . . . [was] a service, to bring enrichment to people's lives."[4] In 1947, to celebrate the centennial of the first Mormon pioneers entering the Salt Lake Valley, Arnold created a float with "working fountains and live landscaping" for the Days of '47 Parade.[5] The float was a favorite of parade goers.

Arnold and Hedve moved to Salt Lake City three years later on New Year's Eve in 1949. In Salt Lake, Arnold accepted a teaching position in the art department at the University of Utah. His close proximity to the LDS Church Office Building put him in a position to be commissioned by Church leaders to create an artistic rendering of the first Sunday School meeting of the Church. His painting, *Pioneer Sunday School*, garnered worldwide recognition.

After seeing *Pioneer Sunday School*, Adele Cannon Howells, president of the General Primary Association, commissioned Arnold to depict twelve scenes from the Book of Mormon for the Primary Association. Howells sold some of her possessions to raise the needed $12,000 to pay for his artwork. Relying on the influence of "a master's hand," Arnold painted the requisite Book of Mormon scenes that Howells desired in the way they both imagined—communicating spiritual events that a child could understand. "What I do I am driven to do," Arnold said. "I follow the dictates of a looming and unseen force. . . . I try to become like a musical instrument, intruding no sound of its own but bringing forth such tones as are played upon it by a master's hand."[6] He added, "I want my art to be perfectly understood. I hope no one ever has to explain my pictures."[7] Arnold confessed, "I don't belong in the art world at all. I'm a storyteller."[8]

While painting the Book of Mormon scenes, Arnold was visited by Herman Stolpe, a Swedish art publisher asked by Hollywood producer Cecil B. DeMille to find an artist who could paint scenes for his film production of *The Ten Commandments*. Stolpe had told DeMille, "The man you're looking for is in Salt Lake City."[9] During his visit with Arnold, Stolpe was given prints of eight completed artworks for the Book of Mormon project. These prints were shared with DeMille, who immediately recognized Arnold's talents and offered him a contract to do the artwork for *The Ten Commandments*. Arnold designed fifteen large paintings, countless sketches, and many letter designs for the film production. His talents received worldwide recognition, including an Academy Award nomination for best costume design.

In 1975, with feelings of patriotism running high, Arnold felt compelled to paint a commemorative rendering of George Washington praying at Valley Forge for the United States Bicentennial that was to be held the following year. In this painting he wanted "to pay tribute to the tall and heavy-burdened man who held our struggling nation together"[10] and "to help rekindle a reverence for the deep spiritual roots of our country." His artistic rendering, *The Prayer at Valley Forge*, received nationwide acclaim.

Amid the applause that seemed to always surround him, Arnold never pushed to the background nor forgot his dependence on his wife, Hedve. She patiently kept meals warm while he finished his work and filtered phone calls so that unnecessary distractions did not "'derail' his creative concentration."[11] When Hedve died in 1986, Arnold noted that "a darkness came into the pictures," and he felt discouraged.[12] Heidi Wales, who handled "the business side of his studio," brought happiness back into his life.[13] In 1989 Arnold and Heidi were married, adding Heidi's two sons from a previous marriage to Arnold's family.[14]

In June 2010, Arnold fell and broke his hip. He underwent hip surgery but never fully recovered. Arnold died at age ninety-six on July 1, 2010. Arnold believed that "art has always been at its best when it has served a cause greater than the artist."[15] Such was the case in his life. Through art, Arnold depicted the "power and majesty of the word of God."[16]

1   Robert T. Barrett and Susan Easton Black, "Setting a Standard in LDS Art: Four Illustrators of the Mid-Twentieth Century," *BYU Studies* 44, no. 2 (2005): 30.
2   Barrett and Black, 30.
3   Ted Schwartz, *Arnold Friberg: The Passion of a Modern Master* (Flagstaff, AZ: Northland Press, 1985), 44.

4 "Arnold Friberg," Friberg Fine Art, 2010, http://www.fribergfineart.com/arnold-Friberg.html.
5 Schwartz, 3.
6 Barrett and Black, 32.
7 T. Rees Shapiro, "Arnold Friberg, Painter of 'Prayer at Valley Forge,' Dies at 96," *The Washington Post*, July 7, 2010, B7.
8 Shapiro, B7.
9 Barrett and Black, 34.
10 "Arnold Friberg," Friberg Fine Art, 2010.
11 Schwartz, 126.
12 Barrett and Black, 37.
13 Schwartz, 125.
14 "Obituary: Friberg, Arnold," *Deseret News*, July 4, 2010, B10.
15 Schwartz, 3.
16 Barrett and Black, 33.

HEBER J. GRANT

Perseverance

Courtesy of the Church
Archives, The Church of Jesus
Christ of Latter-day Saints.

WHEN HEBER J. GRANT WAS ten years old, he wanted to participate in a singing class. The voice teacher told Heber that he would never be able to sing due to his being tone-deaf. Another voice teacher told him that he could sing, but not to do so until the teacher was at least forty miles away. Though friends begged him to not sing and one suggested his singing could be mistaken for a patient having a tooth pulled, Heber was not deterred. After five months of practicing the hymn "O My Father" as many as 115 times a day, he sang the hymn in a Church setting. Although all agreed that his singing was a failure, Heber persisted and practiced other hymns.[1] Such was the determination of Heber J. Grant, who taught the entire LDS Church the importance of perseverance.

Heber Jedediah Grant, the only son of Jedediah Grant and Rachel Ivins, was born November 22, 1856, in Salt Lake City, Utah. Nine days after Heber's birth, his father died. His mother believed that Heber was destined for greatness. Eliza R. Snow held the same opinion and told Rachel that Heber would become a great man in the Church. Rachel often said to Heber, "Behave [yourself] and that honor [of Apostleship will] come to [you]."[2]

Rachel worked as a seamstress to support herself and her son. Heber recalled sitting on the floor and pumping the pedals of his mother's treadle sewing machine with the intent of relieving the pain in Rachel's "tired limbs."[3] In his youth, Heber adopted a motto from Ralph Waldo Emerson: "That which we persist in doing becomes easier for us to do; not that the nature of the thing itself is changed, but that our power to do is increased."[4] With this motto as his guide, Heber succeeded in becoming an acclaimed penman, baseball pitcher, banker, and businessman.

In the Salt Lake 13th Ward, Heber met and courted Lucy Stringham. Heber and Lucy were married and sealed for eternity on November 1, 1877, in the St. George Temple. Living the principle of plural marriage, Heber also married Augusta Winters and Emily Wells.

In 1882 President John Taylor called Heber to the Quorum of the Twelve Apostles. Heber felt inadequate to fulfill the calling of an Apostle even though his mother knew years before that he would someday be an Apostle. Heber viewed the Apostleship as a calling "beyond anything I was worthy of, and . . . the thought came to me, 'You know . . . that John Taylor is a prophet of God, and to decline this office . . . is equivalent to repudiating the prophet.'" Heber said to President Taylor, "I will accept the office and do my best."[5]

Yet for months Heber struggled with feelings of personal failure and turned to the Lord in prayer. One day while praying, he saw in vision a council in heaven. "In this council the Savior was present, my father was there, and the Prophet Joseph Smith was there," recalled Heber. "The Prophet Joseph Smith and my father mentioned me and requested that I be called to that position [Apostleship]. . . . It was given to me that I had done nothing to entitle me to that exalted position, except that I had lived a clean, sweet life. . . . It was because of their faithful labors that I was called. . . . From that day it depended upon me and upon me alone as to whether I made a success of my life or a failure."[6] From that day forward, Heber never again worried about his worthiness to serve in the Quorum of the Twelve.

From 1918 to 1945 Heber served as President of The Church of Jesus Christ of Latter-day Saints. More than any prophet before or since, Heber took an adamant and persistent stance on the need to observe the Word of Wisdom. So often did he speak on this doctrine that some Latter-day Saints wondered if he could speak about anything else. "There is seldom a conference when someone does not take it upon himself to tell us: 'Please do not speak on the Word of Wisdom,'" said Heber at a general conference. "'We hear it so much, we are sick and tired of it.'. . . No . . . Latter-day Saint [who] is keeping the Word of Wisdom is ever sick and tired of hearing it."[7]

As President, Heber strenuously opposed the repeal of prohibition and the Eighteenth Amendment to the United States Constitution. Despite his plea for Latter-day Saints to not repeal prohibition, Utah became the thirty-sixth state—the deciding state—to vote for the repeal of prohibition. When Heber heard of the vote, he lamented, "I have never felt so humiliated in my life over anything as that the state of Utah voted for the repeal of prohibition."[8] From that point on Heber became even more adamant about the need for Latter-day Saints to live the Word of Wisdom.

Another important topic to Heber was counseling members to live within their means and avoid debt. He believed that debt and speculation were the major causes of the Great Depression. Under his guidance and direction the Church implemented the welfare program. When the United States became embroiled in World War II, his was the voice of comfort that buoyed up Latter-day Saints.

Heber died on May 14, 1945. At his funeral, his counselor David O. McKay characterized him as "loyal to friends, to truth, [and] to God."[9]

1   Heber J. Grant, *Conference Report*, April 1900, 61; Joan Oviatt, "I Have Learned to Sing," *Ensign*, Sept. 1984, 43.

2   Heber J. Grant, *Conference Report*, Oct. 1919, 32.

3   Heber J. Grant, "Faith-Promoting Experiences," *Millennial Star* 93, no. 47, Nov. 19, 1931.

4   Heber J. Grant, *Gospel Standards*, comp. G. Homer Durham, 5th ed. (Salt Lake City, UT: Deseret News Press, 1942), 355.

5   Grant, *Gospel Standards*, 194.

6   Ibid., 195–196.

7   Heber J. Grant, *Conference Report*, April 1937, 13.

8   James H. Wallis, "President Grant—Defender of the Word of Wisdom," *Improvement Era* 39, no. 11, Nov. 1936, 698.

9   "President Heber J. Grant," *Improvement Era* 48, no. 6, June 1945, 361.

John Hafen
Imaginative

Courtesy of L. Tom Perry
Special Collections, Harold B.
Lee Library, Brigham Young
University.

ALTHOUGH JOHN HAFEN'S ARTWORK WAS slow to be embraced by the public, he is now considered "the most appealing of any of the early Utah stylists" and has been called "Utah's greatest artist."[1] John believed that his artistic abilities were a gift from God.

John Hafen was born March 22, 1856, in Scherzingen, Switzerland. When John was six years old, he and his family migrated to the United States. On the way to the Salt Lake Valley, his family spent twelve days in Winter Quarters, Nebraska, where John's two-year-old brother died. After his burial, the family trekked on to the Salt Lake Valley and settled in Payson, Utah, before making Salt Lake City their permanent home in 1868.

As a youth, John showed a propensity for art and enrolled in the Twentieth Ward Academy in Salt Lake City to receive lessons and instruction in drawing. Over the next decade, Utah artists George Ottinger and Dan Weggeland encouraged John to seek traditional art training outside Utah.[2] Before he followed their encouragement, John married Thora Twede in 1879. Thora "believed in her husband's dreams of success and in his ability to paint, and always supported his quest for fulfillment no matter how great the sacrifice. She loved John Hafen, bore him ten children, kept his home, and urged him on to success for the thirty-one years they spent as man and wife."[3]

In 1890 John and artists Edwin Evans, Lorus Pratt, and John B. Fairbanks were set apart as missionaries and sent to Paris, France, to study art.[4] The Church paid for their art education in Paris with the agreement that upon completion of their studies, these artists would return to Utah and paint murals for the Salt Lake Temple and would complete other paintings for the Church.[5] On July 26, 1890, John wrote to his wife from Paris, "What I have seen is of inestimable benefit to me. It has humbled me as a child. I feel that I will have to commence at the bottom and submit myself to my Heavenly Father." He then expressed to Thora that his ability to become the painter the Lord wanted him to be depended "wholly upon my faithfulness to the Gospel and the assistance of Almighty God." A few weeks later, John wrote to Thora, "God's servants have blessed me with power to accomplish my mission and get all the knowledge of art required and I know that God is able to help me to live so that I will realize these blessings."[6]

John and the other artists returned to Salt Lake City with a new impressionistic style that not only adorned the Salt Lake Temple, but also influenced a generation of Latter-day Saint artists. John achieved acclaim as a landscape artist and portrait painter, painting several portraits of the General Authorities. President Heber J. Grant commissioned John to paint more than two hundred artistic renderings for the Church.

John was known as an eccentric when it came to his commitment to art. He refused to accept employment in a trade other than art at a time when most men—especially men with a large family like John's to feed and clothe—were farmers or worked in several trades to make a living. As a result, John and his family lived most of their days in poverty. John attempted to fight poverty "as best he could with the weapons of a romantic," which included teaching art at Brigham Young Academy and making frequent trips across the country to sell his paintings.[7]

Hoping to find a better lifestyle, John moved his family to Indiana. In that state, he was recognized as one of Indiana's finest impressionist artists. After painting the governor's portrait, John and his family resided in an attractive cottage overlooking a beautiful valley where many friends surrounded them. Unfortunately, just as John was beginning to realize his lifelong dream of providing for his family through his art, he contracted pneumonia and died on June 3, 1910, in Indianapolis at age fifty-four.[8]

Of the early artists in Utah, John is acclaimed for best communicating the beauty of God's creations. As artist B. F. Larson said of him, "John Hafen loved and understood nature. To him it was created by a personal God. He approached nature with a reverent attitude. In many of his comments about the out-of-doors his speech is characterized by words of praise and thanksgiving to God. . . . Hafen lived close to God. He had a prophetic, sensitive spirit. He knew that his ideas seemed childish to those who did not understand."[9]

1 "Hafen, John (1856–1910)," Springville Museum of Art, http://www.springvilleartmuseum.org/collections/browse.html?x=artist&artist_id=2; Robert S. Olpin, William C. Seifrit, and Vern G. Swanson, *Artists of Utah* (Salt Lake City: Peregrine Smith Books, Gibbs-Smith Publisher, 1999), 45.

2 Ibid.

3 William Lee Roy Conant Jr., "A Study of the Life of John Hafen," master's thesis, Brigham Young University, Aug. 1969.

4 Jay M. Todd, "John Hafen," *Ensign*, Aug. 1976, 60.

5 See Giles H. Florence Jr., "Harvesting the Light: The 1890 Paris Art Mission," *Ensign*, Oct. 1988.

6 Todd, 60.

7 Olpin, Seifrit, and Swanson, 115.

8 "Hafen, John (1856–1910)," Springville Museum of Art.

9 Todd, 60.

GAIL HALVORSEN

Compassion

Courtesy of PD-USGOV-
MILITARY-AIR-FORCE.

COLONEL GAIL HALVORSEN IS A retired Air Force career officer and command pilot. During the 1948–1949 Berlin airlift, Gail delivered food, coal, and necessary supplies in his C-54 airplane to the people of Berlin who had been blockaded by the Soviets. He also began Operation Little Vittles, in which he dropped parachutes containing candy to the children of East and West Berlin. To the children, Gail was known as the "Candy Bomber"—or, in German, the *Rosinenbomber*.

Gail Halvorsen was born October 10, 1920, in Salt Lake City, Utah. He grew up in Utah and Idaho on small farms where he learned the value of hard work, integrity, and honor. Growing up with his "face down in the dirt all the time," Gail liked to look up and watch planes fly overhead and wished that he were "up there with them."[1]

When asked how he went from being a farm boy to a pilot, he said,

> The government was trying to build the pilot base for the looming war and offered a non-college pilot training program at a ground school in Ogden. I competed with about 150 other people, and they gave 10 flight-training scholarships. . . .
>
> My first cross country, learning to fly in '41, I came up over the farm. Dad was down in the sugar beets with

two horses, pulling the cultivator, and Mother was in the garden. I thought, *Boy, I'll show 'em I can fly this airplane!* So I circled a few times, gunning the engine. They didn't even stop. So I climbed up another 1,000 feet or two, then cut off the power and did a two-turn spin over the farm. I came back that night, and my dad met me at the door. "You're through. You're grounded." I asked, "Why?" He said, "Well, your mom just about had a heart attack. She knew it must be you after circling a few times, and she started watching. She's not feeling well yet." I said, "Oh no, hey, I won't do that again!" And so the next time over the farm, I just circled and wiggled the wings.[2]

Fortunately, Gail continued to fly and to wiggle the wings of aircrafts. In 1942 he joined the Army Air Corps and received flight training with the Royal Air Force. During World War II, Gail served in the Air Force as a C-47 and C-54 transport pilot. After the war, he flew in the Berlin airlift, where he became known as "Uncle Wiggly Wings" and the "Berlin Candy Bomber." As to Gail's acquiring the name "Berlin Candy Bomber," this is how it happened: One day on a flight to the Tempelhof air base in West Berlin, Gail

noticed a group of children watching through barbed wire as the airplanes landed. . . . Touched [by the scene], Gail dug in his pocket for a couple sticks of gum and distributed them, promising to return the next day with more candy. The children wondered how they would recognize his plane. Don't worry; as I approach, I'll wiggle my wings, [he] replied. Back at his base, Halvorsen made parachutes by tying strings to the corners of handkerchiefs and then attaching the strings to candy bars. The next day he released the handkerchiefs on approach to Tempelhof and saw the kids joyously clutching their candy. Soon large crowds had gathered and Halvorsen was receiving mail addressed to "Uncle Wiggly Wings" and the "Chocolate Flier." . . .

Halvorsen knew what he had been doing violated Air Force regulations, and when his colonel found out, the young pilot got an earful. But Berlin newspapers had already gotten wind of Halvorsen's candy drops and airlift

commander General William Tunner approved the con-
tinuation of "Operation Little Vittles." What began with a
pilot's spare handkerchiefs and candy his crew bought at the
local commissary soon spread throughout the airlift, with
25 participants in his squadron alone. . . .

The American Confectioners Association donated tons of
candy for the cause . . . and [American] school children assembled the candy parachutes and sent them on to Germany.
By January 1949 some 250,000 parachutes had been dropped
over Berlin, and the operation helped reassure citizens that
the West would not abandon them. As one young Berliner
later told Halvorsen, "It wasn't [just] chocolate. It was hope."[3]

Gail has been an outstanding ambassador for The Church of Jesus
Christ of Latter-day Saints wherever he has traveled in the world. He
wrote a memoir of his military experiences called *The Berlin Candy Bomber*
and has served as a stake president, a bishop, and a high councilman.[4]
Whatever his calling has been, Gail has always demonstrated a special
love for the youth of the Church, taking advantage of opportunities to tell
them to live the gospel with enthusiasm and to reach their goals.

Gail married Alta Jolley of Zion National Park on April 16, 1949.
They became the parents of five children. (Approaching fifty years of
marriage, Alta died in January 1999. Gail is now married to Lorraine
Pace, a high school friend from more than six decades ago.) Three of
their grandchildren were privileged to attend a school named for Gail
in Frankfurt, Germany, and in 2013 a secondary school in the Berlin
suburb of Zehlendorf was named in his honor. Gail has received many
honors and awards, including the Cheney Award for his humanitarian
work, and since 2004 the United States Air Force has annually given the
Colonel Gail Halvorsen Award to a pilot in air transportation.

Gail maintains his ties to Germany, attending anniversary celebrations
of the airlift and conducting commemorative candy drops. At the 2002
Winter Olympic Games, he led the German Olympic team into Rice-
Eccles Stadium for the opening and closing ceremonies. During the
Mormon Tabernacle Choir's annual Christmas concerts in December
2012, renowned broadcaster Tom Brokaw narrated the story of the Candy
Bomber during four concerts to more than eighty thousand people in the
Conference Center in Salt Lake City.[5]

Since Gail's act of compassion to the children of a blockaded city, thousands of Air Force humanitarian airlifts have tried to replicate his kindness. "Those two sticks of gum changed my life forever," said Gail. "I received many honors and gifts on behalf of the pilots who volunteered for the candy drops. However, all the gifts and other worldly things that resulted did not bring near the happiness and fulfillment that I received from serving others—even serving the former enemy, the Germans, who had become friends."[6]

1   "The Berlin Airlift: Gail Halvorsen," PBS, Jan. 19, 2007, http://www.pbs.org/wgbh/amex/airlift/peopleevents/p_halvorsen.html.
2   http://www.historynet.com/interview-with-gail-halvorsen-the-berlin-candy-bomber.htm.
3   "The Berlin Airlift: Gail Halvorsen."
4   See Gail S. Halvorsen, *The Berlin Candy Bomber* (Bountiful, Utah: Horizon Publishers, 1990).
5   R. Scott Lloyd, "Bitter, Sweet Night for Mormon Tabernacle Choir at Christmas Concert," *Deseret News*, Dec. 15, 2012, http://www.deseret-news.com/article/765617897/Bitter-sweet-night-for-Mormon-Tabernacle-Choir-at-Christmas-concert.html?pg=all; Blair Howell, "Concert Review: Mormon Tabernacle Choir's Christmas Concert Relates Gifts of Love, Tells Story of Candy Bomber," Dec. 17, 2007, http://www.deseretnews.com/article/865568925/Concert-review-Mormon-Tabernacle-Choirs-Christmas-concert-relates-gifts-of-love-tells-story-of.html?pg=all.
6   Michael O. Tunnell, *Candy Bomber: The Story of the Berlin Airlift's "Chocolate Pilot"* (Watertown, MA: Charlesbridge, 2010), ix.

HAROLD I. HANSEN
Charisma

Courtesy of Betty Hansen
Gibbons.

IN 1937, WHILE SERVING A MISSION in the Eastern states, Harold Hansen was asked to direct an outdoor play at the Hill Cumorah in Palmyra, New York. Using his charisma and unique theatrical talents, Harold directed the first Hill Cumorah Pageant. The outdoor pageant attracted large crowds that first summer and has continued to do so every summer since for the next seven decades.[1] As a result, Harold is the longest-standing director of a single production in the history of theater.

Harold Ivan Hansen, son of Hans Dederick Hansen and Nielsine Caroline Hartman, was born March 14, 1914, in Logan, Utah. When Harold received a mission call to the Eastern states, he was disappointed. Being of Danish descent and speaking fluent Danish, he anticipated a mission call to Denmark, not the eastern United States. If it had not been for the counsel of parents, local priesthood leaders, and Elder David O. McKay of the Quorum of the Twelve Apostles, he might have refused the call. Due to their wise counsel, Harold left Utah confident that he was needed in the East.[2]

Upon Harold's arrival in the mission field, his mission president, Don Colton, asked him to go to Cumorah and work on an outdoor pageant. "You've been in theater," said President Colton. "There might be something you could do to help out." Fifty missionaries had been assigned to produce a pageant at the Hill Cumorah, and "everything was in rehearsal and [the pageant] was pretty well ready."[3] Once at Cumorah, Harold was disappointed to find that the pageant was anything *but* ready. As he came upon the scene and saw the missionaries still trying to pull things together, he felt that his "first day at the hill was a total waste," and he asked himself, "Is this what I came on the mission for?" He was so distraught with the rehearsal that he refused to pray that night.[4] The next day, however, as he directed the first scene, within five minutes he had set up the scene perfectly. Recognizing Harold's charisma, the senior elders put him in charge of the pageant.

The day before the formal production of the pageant, Harold was still considering asking to be released from the mission. He told President Colton, "If this thing ever comes off, I'll have a testimony."[5] Harold recounted his experience at the opening night to President Colton: "I saw things happen on that hill that were never touched by any of us there . . . and we knew it beyond a shadow of a doubt."[6] At the close of the evening, President Colton asked Harold, "How's your testimony?"[7] Harold expressed confidence that he was in the right place and had a peaceful assurance of his calling.

After returning from his mission in 1940, and while working on a master's degree at Iowa State University, Harold received a request to return to New York and once again direct the pageant. Knowing that he was being divinely commissioned, he agreed. He also had another reason for returning—a certain sister missionary. Sister Betty Kotter, then serving her mission, participated in the 1938 and 1939 productions of the pageant. When she completed her mission, romance blossomed and Harold and Betty were married on the Hill Cumorah. They were sealed for time and all eternity in the temple when they returned to Utah.[8]

During the next six years, Harold finished a PhD and started a professorial career at the University of Iowa. But Harold and Betty felt the pageant was their calling and dedicated themselves to the production each summer.

In 1951 Harold met with Ernest L. Wilkinson, president of Brigham Young University, to ask him for a job.[9] During the interview, Harold "charmed the socks off of Wilkinson and walked out of the office with the position of department chair."[10] Harold devised a plan for the pageant that he explained to Wilkinson: "My plan was to invite principally women volunteers from the west to do as the missionaries do and pay their own way to participate in the pageant."[11] By the time he directed his last pageant, there were almost two hundred and fifty participants in the pageant and many more applying for the opportunity. Most participants claimed that it was Harold's personality that elicited their tremendous support and loyalty for the pageant. "Remarkably, from 1953 to 1977, [Harold] never had to send a volunteer home or pull a cast member from a performance."[12] How did he cultivate such loyalty? Lael Woodbury, a participant in the pageant (1950–1962) and later dean of the College of Fine Arts at BYU, said that Harold was "one of the most charismatic men he had ever met."[13]

Harold's charisma was also instrumental in establishing relationships between Latter-day Saints and residents in the eastern United States. "As the Pageant was produced year after year, changes were occurring which made it evident that there was a softening of the attitude toward [Latter-day Saints], and that there was a feeling of . . . welcome."[14] In 1977, the First Presidency presented Harold with a formal written release and retirement as director of the Hill Cumorah Pageant. During his last pageant performance, Harold said, "I tried to run away from this assignment. . . . When you've been willing to give everything that you have of yourself, when you have been up against something that just seems insurmountable, and everything you have you've poured out to the Lord, asking: that's when you'll find your faith. . . . I thank my Heavenly Father that He didn't let me go [forty years ago]."[15]

When Harold passed away in 1992, he left not only a devoted wife and four daughters but generations of Hill Cumorah Pageant participants and audiences who had been blessed by his charismatic direction.

1   For more information on the Church's acquisition and development of the Hill Cumorah, see Rex C. Reeve Jr., "The Hill Called Cumorah," *Regional Studies in Latter-day Saint Church History*, ed. Larry C. Porter, Milton V. Backman, and Susan Easton Black (Provo, UT: Department of Church History and Doctrine, Brigham Young University, 1992): 71–91.

2   Harold I. Hansen, "Cumorah's Lonely Hill," typescript, 1986, typescript in possession of Charles A. Henson, Provo, Utah, 29–30.

3   Hansen, 13–14.

4   Walter Boyden Jr., "The Road to Hill Cumorah," PhD dissertation, Brigham Young University, 1982, 33–34.

5   Hansen, 293–330.

6 Boyden, 291.

7 Hansen, 30.

8 Ibid., 46–48.

9 Lael Woodbury, oral history interview by Mary Jane Woodger, Sept. 19, 1999, Provo, Utah.

10 Lael Woodbury interview.

11 Hansen, 75.

12 Derek Spriggs, oral history interview by Mary Jane Woodger, Sept. 9, 1999, Provo, Utah; Betty Ann Hansen Gibbons and Patty Hansen Phillips, oral history interview by Mary Jane Woodger, June 3, 1999, Provo, Utah.

13 Lael Woodbury interview.

14 Harold I. Hansen to Elder Mark E. Petersen and Elder Richard L. Evans, June 5, 1962, Harold I. Hansen Collection, Mss1701, Box 27, Fd. 1, L. Tom Perry Special Collections, Brigham Young University, Provo, Utah.

15 Baker et al., "Inventory of the Harold I. Hansen Collection," typescript, June 1993 (revised July 1998): xi, Harold I. Hansen Collection.

FRANKLIN S. HARRIS

Vision

Courtesy of the Church History
Library, The Church of Jesus
Christ of Latter-day Saints.

THOUSANDS OF PEOPLE ENTER THE Harris Fine Arts Center on the Brigham Young University campus each year, yet few know of the remarkable life and contributions made by Franklin Harris to Brigham Young University. Franklin was president of BYU for twenty-four years from 1921 to 1945, the longest tenure of any BYU president. He was also the first president of BYU to hold a PhD. During his administration, BYU moved from an intermountain denominational college toward being a full university as Franklin organized new colleges and added graduate and research divisions to upgrade the scholarship and academic standing of the university.[1]

Franklin Stewart Harris, son of Dennison Harris and Eunice Stewart, was born August 24, 1884, in the small farming community of Benjamin, Utah, a few miles southwest of Provo. Both of his parents were teachers before and after their marriage. In the 1890s Franklin and his family moved to the Mormon colonies in the Mexican state of Chihuahua so that his father could teach at the Juarez Academy. Franklin's own career as a teacher began in 1904, when at the age of twenty and after only one year of college at BYU he taught science at the Juarez Academy in Chihuahua.[2]

Franklin returned to the United States and finished his bachelor's degree at BYU in 1907 before enrolling in Cornell University in New York, where he earned a PhD in agronomy. Upon completing his doctorate, Franklin was employed as a professor of agronomy and an agronomist on the staff of the Experiment Station at Utah State Agricultural College. On June 18, 1908, he married Estella Spilsbury in the Salt Lake Temple and they became the parents of six children.[3]

In 1921, at age thirty-six, Franklin was named president of Brigham Young University. By this point in his life, Franklin had a national reputation in agronomy, a love for the arts, and a vision of crafting a great university. In his inaugural address, Franklin outlined his ambitious plan to lead BYU to higher academic levels: "The first task of the future is to preserve at the institution this spirit that comes to us from the past—the true spirit of the Brigham Young University. This spirit places character above learning, and indelibly burns into the consciousness of the student the fact that the most enduring joy is dependent on spiritual growth which looks toward eternal progression."[4]

While president of BYU, Franklin traveled the world, visiting scores of universities and educational institutions around the world in an effort to bring BYU out of obscurity. For example, in Russia, Iran, and Mexico, he gave extended service to the broader world community.[5] In Japan and Syria, he not only promoted the values of a BYU education but served short-term missions. Standing on the BYU campus—where as a country boy from Benjamin, Utah, he had dreamed of the future—Franklin said at the BYU Founder's Day celebration of 1923, "Behold the greatest university campus in all the world—in embryo. More students will come, the faculty will be enlarged, new colleges will be added, and there is no end to the improvements which can be made. Truly the campus is the setting of what will undoubtedly be the greatest university in the world, a place to train for leaders."[6]

Franklin's vision of BYU was shared by Heber J. Grant, seventh President of the Church and president of the BYU Board of Trustees, who wrote a letter of appreciation to Franklin as he concluded his service as president of BYU:

> We are deeply grateful to you for your long and distinguished incumbency of the Presidency. . . . You have advanced the University to a place among the leading institutions of the nation. . . . You have done all this with a minimum of expense that is a marvel to school administrators generally, that has given to the tithe payers of the

Church a feeling of gratitude for your careful expenditure of their hard earned funds . . . and that has always afforded the First Presidency and the Board of Trustees a complete confidence in your integrity and honesty in the performance of your duties.[7]

Following his tenure at BYU, Franklin served as president of Utah State University from 1945 to 1950. In the early 1950s Franklin had an extended stay in Iran, where he was president of the LDS branch in Tehran. Franklin served for many years on the YMMIA General Board and became the author of several books, including *The Young Man and His Vocation*, as well as nearly two hundred scientific papers.[8]

After a life of administration, teaching, integrity, and academic contributions, Franklin died on April 18, 1960, at age seventy-five. Oxford University scholar Karl Young summarized Franklin's achievements: "A life could be written of F. S. Harris the Humanist, or of Harris the World Citizen, or of Harris the Educator, or of Harris the Man of Religion, or of Harris the Big Brother to All His Fellows. But Franklin Harris' greatest work in life was in education."[9]

1   Charlene Winters, "Frank S. Harris," *BYU Magazine*, Fall 1998, http://magazine.byu.edu/?act=view&a=312.
2   Ernest L. Wilkinson, ed., *Brigham Young University, The First One Hundred Years*, 4 vols. (Provo, UT: BYU Press, 1975), 2:26.
3   Andrew Jenson, *LDS Biographical Encyclopedia*, 4:240.
4   "Inaugural Address: Franklin S. Harris," BYU Archives, http://aims.byu.edu/sites/default/files/foundationdocuments/Inaugural_Address—Franklin_S_Harris.pdf.
5   Wilkinson, 411.
6   "Franklin S. Harris," Office of the President, Brigham Yong University, http://president.byu.edu/p/harris.
7   Wilkinson, 415.
8   Jenson, 4:240.
9   Wilkinson, 26.

MARTIN HARRIS
Taking Risks

Courtesy of Religious Education
Image Project, Brigham Young
University.

JOSEPH SMITH HESITATED TO ASK Martin Harris to finance the publication of the Book of Mormon. However, neither young Joseph nor his father—a wheat farmer, cooper, and day laborer—were in a position to secure a publisher's agreement. Oliver Cowdery, a schoolteacher and scribe of the Book of Mormon translation, likewise lacked the necessary means for collateral. The same could be said of Joseph Knight Sr., Peter Whitmer Sr., and other believers. Joseph Smith knew that there was only one man who had the means to secure the publisher's note and relieve the awkward financial situation—Martin Harris. But would Martin provide security when past associations with the translation had made him a target of public ridicule and marital strife? Knowing full well that accepting the printer's debt would place his reputation, finances, and marriage in jeopardy, Martin agreed to finance the publication of the Book of Mormon.

Martin Harris, son of Nathan Harris and Rhoda Lapham, was born May 18, 1783, in Easton, New York, and was reared to manhood in Palmyra, New York. At age twenty-five, he married his sixteen-year-old cousin, Lucy Harris. For more than twenty years, they resided in Palmyra on property given to them by Martin's father. During those years, Martin became a "gentleman and a farmer of respectability" as well as a patriot, serving in the 39th New York Militia during the War of 1812.[1]

It was not until 1824 that Martin's reputation in the community became tarnished, beginning when he hired Joseph Smith Sr. and his son Hyrum. During their employ, Martin learned of the prophetic calling of young Joseph. Historian Willard Bean wrote that "Martin was thrilled beyond expression. He requested that he be kept posted on any new developments."[2] Martin was not only curious about but was supportive of Joseph. He gave Joseph fifty dollars to help defray expenses when Joseph journeyed to Harmony, Pennsylvania. Martin also carried by hand transcribed characters from the Book of Mormon to linguists Charles Anthon and Dr. Mitchell in New York City, afterward testifying, "The translation that I carried to Professor Anthon was copied from the same plates; also, that the professor did certify to it being a correct translation, I do firmly believe and do know that Joseph Smith was a Prophet of God; for without I know he could not have had that gift, neither could he have translated the same."[3]

Martin was the scribe to the book of Lehi translation. Unfortunately, the manuscript pages of the translation were lost. Historical recounting of the lost manuscript differs in detail, but scholars agree that Martin's wife played a central role. Martin's repentance was sincere, and in June 1829 he became one of the Three Witnesses of the Book of Mormon. He then mortgaged his farm acreage to ensure the publication of the Book of Mormon.

Martin was baptized April 6, 1830, in the Seneca River by Oliver Cowdery. In August 1831, Martin was told to "be an example unto the Church, in laying his moneys before the bishop of the church." He faithfully complied. In 1832 Martin served a mission with his brother, Emer Harris, baptizing a hundred "persons at Chenago Point, . . . New York," and another eighty-two persons in Pennsylvania.[4] After driving a wagon in the Zion's Camp march to Missouri, Martin became one of three men to select the original members of the Quorum of the Twelve Apostles. On February 17, 1835, Martin was named to the first high council in Kirtland, Ohio.

During his service on that council, Martin failed to heed a warning in his patriarchal blessing that admonished him to "be humble and meek in heart or Satan will seek to raise thee up to pride and boasting."[5] In September 1837, Martin was ejected from the high council. Angered by the ejection, Martin estranged himself from the LDS Church for the next thirty-two years. During these years, he vacillated from one dissenting sect to another, including the Strangites, the Whitmerites, and even a group led by William Smith.

At age eighty-six Martin requested that Brigham Young be told of his impoverished circumstances in Kirtland and of his desire to visit Utah. "Tell him I should like to visit Utah, my family, my children—I would be glad to accept help from the Church, but I want no personal favor," said Martin. "Wait! Tell him that if he sends money, he must send enough for the round trip. I should not want to remain in Utah." Upon hearing of his request, Brigham Young replied, "I was never more gratified over any message in my life. Send for him! Yes, even if it were to take the last dollar of my own."[6] In his eighty-eighth year, Martin journeyed to the Salt Lake Valley. After his arrival, as he gazed on the temple, tabernacle, and the developing city, he exclaimed, "Who would have thought that this Book of Mormon would have done all this?"[7]

Martin's final testimony was recorded by William Pilkington: "On the 9th day of July 1875, while [Martin] was dying, I knelt by his cot. . . . I wanted to get what I thought would be his last words, but he could not talk audibly." Pilkington prayed that Martin's last words could be understood and later reported. "Strength was given to [Martin] and he bore his testimony as he had done many times before and I understood every word. He then bore the same testimony to the whole world and then laid back exhausted."[8] Martin died on July 10, 1875, in Clarkston, Utah. He was buried with the Book of Mormon in his right hand and the Doctrine and Covenants in his left, both scriptures he had generously financed.[9]

1   Madge Harris Tuckett and Belle Harris Wilson, *The Martin Harris Story: Special Witness to the Book of Mormon* (Provo, UT: Maasai Inc., 1983), 10.

2   Willard Bean, *History of Palmyra* (Palmyra, New York: P. Courier Co., Inc., 1938), 35, as cited in Tuckett and Wilson, 15–16.

3   Letter of Martin Harris, November 23, 1870, as cited in Tuckett and Wilson, 23.

4   Tuckett and Wilson, 54–55.

5   Ibid., 59.

6   William Harrison Homer, "The Passing of Martin Harris," *Improvement Era* 29 (March 1926): 470–471.

7   *Journal History of the Church of Jesus Christ of Latter-day Saints*, June 1, 1877.

8   William Pilkington, testimony sworn before Joseph W. Peterson, April 3, 1934.

9   Andrew Jenson, *LDS Biographical Encyclopedia* 1:276.

ORRIN HATCH

Patriotic

UTAH SENATOR ORRIN HATCH IS now serving his seventh term in the United States Senate—which makes him the most senior Republican in the Senate and the longest-serving senator in Utah's history. Utah Governor Gary Herbert said of Orrin, "Probably nobody in Utah's history has made more impact on national policy than Orrin Hatch. Early in his career he set the tone for conservative thought [and] . . . helped pave the way for Ronald Reagan [to win the presidency]."[1]

Orrin Hatch, son of Jesse and Helen Hatch, was born on March 22, 1934, in Pittsburgh, Pennsylvania, and was reared in a blue-collar, devout Latter-day Saint family who lived in humble circumstances. As a youth, Orrin was recognized for his excellence in academics and athletics. He was also recognized for standing up for the underdog and for making a positive difference among his classmates in Pittsburgh.

In the early 1950s, Orrin accepted a mission call to serve in the Great Lakes Mission, which essentially covered large parts of Indiana, Michigan, and Ohio. When he arrived in the region, Orrin told his mission president that "he was going to fulfill two missions during the two years, one for himself and one for his brother who was killed in World War II." On his mission, Orrin averaged sixty-six hours a week proselytizing and was credited with distributing more than three thousand copies of the Book of Mormon. At the end of Orrin's mission, his mission president said that Orrin had fulfilled the equivalent of two missions during two years, calling him "the most wonderful missionary the Church ever had." Decades later, while serving as a United States senator, Orrin named his mission experience as "the most important two years of my life."[2]

Orrin was the first in his family to attend college, receiving a degree in history from Brigham Young University in 1959. While at the university, he met and married Elaine Hansen of Newton, Utah, on August 28, 1957, in the Salt Lake Temple. Orrin and Elaine became the parents of six children. Soon after their marriage, they moved to Pittsburgh so that Orrin could attend the University of Pittsburgh Law School on an honors scholarship and receive his law degree. While a law student, Orrin worked as a janitor, construction worker, and an all-night dormitory desk attendant to support his growing family before earning a law degree in 1962.

Following graduation from law school, Orrin practiced law first in Pennsylvania and then in Utah until his election to the United States Senate (his first elective office) in 1976. Orrin was elected by an unexpected nine-point margin, defeating a three-term Democratic incumbent. Over his decades of service in the Senate, Orrin has served as chairman of the Health, Education, Labor, and Pensions Committee and as chairman of the Senate Judiciary Committee. He has championed numerous legislative issues, including the Welfare Reform Bill and the Religious Freedom Restoration Act. Among his many initiatives have been the Balanced Budget Amendment to the Constitution, Strengthening Our Commitment to Legal Immigration and America's Security Act, and the Utah School Trust Lands Exchange Act. Orrin is currently the chairman of the Senate Finance Committee and a member of the Judiciary Committee; the Health, Education, Labor, and Pensions Committee; and the Joint Committee on Taxation. He also serves on the board of directors for the United States Holocaust Memorial Museum in Washington, DC. In 1999 Orrin was a Republican presidential candidate.[3] As the current President *pro tempore* of the Senate, he is third in line of succession to the U.S. presidency (behind the Vice-President and the Speaker of the House of Representatives).

Orrin is a respected statesman, family man, and something of a Washington "renaissance man." In addition to his passion for public policy, his interests include religion, music, poetry, sports, and art. He has published several nonfiction books as well as scores of poems and songs.[4] He has received many awards for his political and artistic contributions, including six honorary doctorates.

Through his years in the political whirlwind at the nation's capital, Orrin has been steadfast and immovable in his devotion to The Church of Jesus Christ of Latter-day Saints. He has been a bishop, high councilman, and gospel doctrine teacher. Of the importance of his testimony, Orrin said, "Knowing that God exists is one of the greatest blessings of our lives. A belief in God helps us endure the vicissitudes and challenges, pains and sufferings, and everyday difficulties of this life. Assurances of a loving God warm our souls and help to make life worthwhile."[5]

1   Lee Roderick, *Courage—Orrin Hatch, Leading the Fight for Constitutional Rights* (Alexandria, VA: Probitas Press, 2011), xviii.

2   Roderick, 4–5.

3   "Orin Hatch: United States Senator for Utah," www.hatch.senate.gov.

4   Roderick, 510–511.

5   *Why I Believe* (Salt Lake City: Deseret Book, 2001), 168.

GORDON B. HINCKLEY
Tenacity

Courtesy of the Church
Archives, The Church of Jesus
Christ of Latter-day Saints.

ALTHOUGH GORDON B. HINCKLEY DESCRIBED himself "as a shy and bashful boy—freckle-faced and awkward," he was destined for greatness.[1] Gordon's parents knew something of his greatness before his birth, for his father's patriarchal blessing had promised, "Your posterity will become great, from your loins shall come forth statesmen, prophets, priests and Kings to the most High God. The Priesthood will never depart from your family, no never. To your posterity there shall be no end . . . and the name of Hinckley shall be honored in every nation under heaven."[2] His mother's patriarchal blessing spoke of her responsibility to prepare a noble posterity: "The eye of the Lord has been upon thee from thy birth and a decree of the Father has gone forth that thou shalt have a mission to fill, a work to do. . . . Thy name shall be perpetuated and live in the memory of the Saints."[3] The life of Gordon B. Hinckley was a credit both to his parents and to his God.

Gordon Bitner Hinckley, son of Bryant Stringham Hinckley and Ada Bitner, was born June 23, 1910, in Salt Lake City, Utah. Gordon was descended from a long line of faithful progenitors, including his grandfather, Ira Nathaniel Hinckley, who was called by Brigham Young in 1867 to oversee the construction of Cove Fort, and his father, Bryant Hinckley, who presided over a stake in Salt Lake City, served on the YMMIA General Board, and served as president of the Northern States Mission.

As a child, Gordon was sickly. He suffered from allergies, asthma, hay fever, and whooping cough that was aggravated by the smoke of coal-burning stoves in Salt Lake City. As a youth, Gordon attended public schools and worked as a newspaper carrier for the *Deseret News*, a Salt Lake City daily paper. Later he attended and graduated from the University of Utah. He accepted a call to serve a mission in Great Britain. On that mission, Gordon wrote to his father about discouraging events in the mission field. Instead of sympathizing with him, his father penned, "Forget yourself and go to work." His wise counsel set the stage for the rest of Gordon's life.[4]

After his mission, Gordon married his childhood, across-the-street neighbor, Marjorie Pay, on April 29, 1937, in the Salt Lake Temple. Theirs was an exemplary sixty-seven-year marriage of love, loyalty, and good humor. Gordon and Marjorie became the parents of five children—three daughters and two sons.

To support his family, Gordon accepted employment as the executive secretary of the Church Radio, Publicity, and Literature Committee. This employment gave him daily contact with the leading Brethren of the Church, and he was quickly recognized by the Brethren as a hard worker and a leader among men. Gordon served as president of the Salt Lake East Millcreek Stake until April 6, 1958, when President David O. McKay called him to be an Assistant to the Quorum of the Twelve Apostles. At the October 1961 general conference, Gordon was sustained as a member of the Quorum of the Twelve Apostles. From 1981 to 1995, he served in the First Presidency of the Church as a counselor to presidents Spencer W. Kimball, Ezra Taft Benson, and Howard W. Hunter.

On Sunday, March 12, 1995, Gordon became the fifteenth President of The Church of Jesus Christ of Latter-day Saints. As President, he exhibited an inexhaustible desire for work, a quick wit, a keen mind, and an uncompromising testimony of restored truths.[5] He encouraged members to reach out in love to neighbors and to those who had strayed from the faith. He traveled the world to speak with Church members in more than sixty countries. Through television interviews and national press publications, including appearances on *60 Minutes* and *Larry King Live*, and hundreds of newspaper and magazine articles, Gordon increased media attention and improved the public image of the Church. He addressed the National Press Club in Washington DC, the Religion

News Writers Association, the U.S. Conference of Mayors, and twice addressed the Los Angeles World Affairs Council.

Gordon was honored by the National Conference for Community and Justice (formerly the National Conference of Christians and Jews) for his contributions to tolerance and understanding in the world, and was the recipient of the Distinguished Service Award presented to him by the National Association for the Advancement of Colored People. He also received the Silver Buffalo Award from the Boy Scouts of America. In 2004 Gordon was awarded the Presidential Medal of Freedom by President George W. Bush in the White House in Washington, DC. In addition, he received seven honorary doctoral degrees.[6]

Some notable hallmarks of Gordon's administration include the construction of the twenty-one-thousand-seat Conference Center in Salt Lake City, the presentation of *The Family: A Proclamation to the World* in a general Relief Society meeting, the establishment of the Perpetual Education Fund, and the expansion of the Quorums of the Seventy. In addition, Gordon wrote and edited several manuals, pamphlets, scripts, and books, including the best-selling *Standing for Something*, written for a general audience. Wanting to extend temple blessings to more members worldwide, Gordon began the most intensive temple-building program in Church history.

On January 27, 2008, Gordon died at age ninety-seven, surrounded by loved ones in Salt Lake City. At the time of his death, no one in the history of the Church had worked for more years in more assignments at the headquarters of the Church than he had. It was obvious to Latter-day Saints worldwide that the Lord had prepared and placed Gordon in a pivotal position to lead the Church into the twenty-first century. After all, he understood and appreciated the past but had the tenacity to step boldly into the future.

1   "Strong Testimony Came Early to President Hinckley," June 6, 1994, *LDS Church News*, http://www.deseretnews.com/article/357553/STRONG-TESTIMONY-CAME-EARLY-TO-PRES-HINCKLEY.html.

2   Sheri Dew, *Go Forward with Faith: The Biography of Gordon B. Hinckley* (Salt Lake City: Deseret Book, 1996), 22.

3   Ibid., 21.

4   Ibid., 64.

5   Craig Manscill, Robert Freeman, Dennis Wright, eds., "Gordon B. Hinckley," in *Presidents of the Church: The Lives and Teachings of the Modern Prophets* (Springville, Utah: Cedar Fort, 2008), 407–442.

6   "Beloved Church President, Gordon B. Hinckley, Dies at 97," Jan. 27, 2008, http://www.mormonnewsroom.org/article/beloved-church-president-gordon-b-hinckley-dies-at-97.

HOWARD W. HUNTER

Christlike Living

Courtesy of the Church
Archives, The Church of Jesus
Christ of Latter-day Saints.

HOWARD W. HUNTER SERVED AS President of The Church of Jesus Christ of Latter-day Saints for only nine months, yet his influence will be felt for generations to come. Through his patriarchal blessing, Howard learned that "the Lord foreknew [him]," for he had shown "strong leadership among the hosts of heaven" and had been ordained "to perform an important work in mortality in bringing to pass [the Lord's] purposes."[1] That important work included admonishing Latter-day Saints to see the temple as a symbol of their Church membership and to teach their children the importance of temple covenants.

Howard W. Hunter, son of John William Hunter and Nellie Marie Rasmussen, was born November 14, 1907, in Boise, Idaho. During Howard's childhood, his father was not a member of the Church but was supportive of Howard's participation in Church activities. Howard gained a testimony of the gospel of Jesus Christ in his early years, but his father asked him to wait to be baptized. Five months after his twelfth birthday, with his father's consent, Howard was baptized in an indoor swimming pool complex in Boise.[2]

In his youth, Howard was known for being hardworking and ambitious. He excelled in school and earned his Eagle Scout award, becoming only the second teenage boy to reach the rank of Eagle Scout in Idaho. Howard loved music and played several instruments with proficiency. After graduating from high school, he organized Hunter's Croonaders, a band that performed on weekends in Idaho and for two months on a cruise ship en route to Asia.

In his early twenties, Howard moved to Southern California with the hope of furthering his musical career. In California, he met his eternal companion, Clara May Jeffs. Howard and Clara were married June 10, 1931, in the Salt Lake Temple. They became the parents of three sons. Soon after their marriage, Howard decided to forgo his music career for a stable family life.

Howard supported his growing family by working in the title department of the Los Angeles County Flood Control District. At night, he attended evening courses offered by the Southwestern University Law School. After five years of taking a full load of evening courses, Howard graduated *cum laude* from the Southwestern University Law School and passed the California Bar exam. Howard opened a successful law practice in Los Angeles. He believed that his success in the field of law was due to his honesty. As his law practice grew, Howard refused to charge clients who were unable to pay for his legal advice.[3]

Although Howard was busy with his family and career responsibilities, he never turned down a chance to serve in the Church. He was a Scoutmaster, bishop of the El Soreno Ward, high priest group leader, and president of the Pasadena Stake. On October 9, 1959, Howard was called to be an Apostle of the Lord Jesus Christ by President David O. McKay. He served as an Apostle for thirty-four years, including ten years as President of the Quorum of the Twelve, until becoming the fourteenth President of The Church of Jesus Christ of Latter-day Saints on June 5, 1994.

Howard's presidency was the shortest tenure of any President in the history of the Church, lasting only nine months. Among the hallmarks of his ministry was his focus on Christlike living and temple worthiness. He encouraged Latter-day Saints to study the life of the Savior and to follow the Savior's example of love, compassion, and forgiveness. Howard asked that all adult members of the Church possess a temple recommend.

Howard was admired for the loving care he extended to his dear wife as her health deteriorated. Elder James E. Faust said of Howard, "In 1983 his beloved wife, Clara Jeffs Hunter, passed away. . . . President Hunter [had] tended to her needs, providing loving care with respect and an uncommon devotion for many years, with a complete disregard for his own health. . . . We have never seen such an example of devotion of a husband to his wife. Theirs was a many-splendored love affair."[4] Seven years after the death of his wife, Howard married Inis Stanton, a woman he had known years earlier in California.

Like many prophets, Howard was no stranger to adversity and pain. It was his steadfast faith that strengthened him through trials. "I acknowledge God's miraculous hand in my life," he said. "He has repeatedly spared my life and restored my strength, has repeatedly brought me back from the edge of eternity, and has allowed me to continue in my mortal ministry for another season."[5] After enduring the pain of cancer, Howard died on March 3, 1995. His last words were "'thank you' to those [attending] him."[6]

Those who knew Howard best remember him for his counsel to be "a temple-attending and a temple-loving people. Let us hasten to the temple as frequently as time and means and personal circumstances allow. Let us go not only for our kindred dead, but let us also go for the personal blessing of temple worship. . . . The temple is a place of beauty, it is a place of revelation, it is a place of peace. It is the house of the Lord. It is holy unto the Lord. It should be holy unto us."[7]

1 Eleanor Knowles, *Howard W. Hunter* (Salt Lake City: Deseret Book, 1994), 71.

2 Craig Manscill, Robert Freeman, and Dennis Wright, eds., "Howard W. Hunter," in *Presidents of the Church: The Lives and Teachings of the Modern Prophets* (Springville, UT: Cedar Fort, 2008), 375–404.

3 Knowles, 86, 93, 117–119.

4 James E. Faust, "The Way of an Eagle," *Ensign*, Aug. 1994, 2.

5 "Exceeding Great and Precious Promises," *Ensign*, Nov. 1994, 7.

6 Gordon B. Hinckley, "A Prophet Polished and Refined," *Ensign*, April 1995, 33.

7 Howard W. Hunter, "A Temple-Motivated People," *Ensign*, Oct. 2010.

Jon M. Huntsman Sr.
Generosity

Courtesy of *Deseret News.*

Jon M. Huntsman, a prominent LDS businessman and humanitarian, is the executive chairman of the board of the Huntsman Corporation, which operates in dozens of countries around the world. Over the past decades, Jon is perhaps better known as one of the world's most generous benefactors. Broadcaster Larry King wrote, "Jon Meade Huntsman may well be the most remarkable billionaire most of America has never heard of. . . . Jon Huntsman is living proof you can do well by doing right."[1] Jon's story is a Horatio Alger tale of what happens to a man who helps other people.

Jon Meade Huntsman, son of Alonzo Blaine Huntsman and Kathleen Robison, was born June 21, 1937, in a two-room house with no plumbing in the small town of Blackfoot, Idaho. His father moved their family to small towns in southern Idaho and later to Fillmore, Utah, seeking work as a schoolteacher, and to Palo Alto, California, in pursuit of a doctorate degree in education. Jon learned the value of hard work from his father and spent his youthful summers working full-time while many of his friends played baseball or went fishing. Jon was elected student body president of Palo Alto High School and was recruited by Harold Zellerbach, chairman of Crown-Zellerbach Paper Company, to attend the Wharton School of the University of Pennsylvania on a scholarship. Jon graduated at the top of his class from the Wharton School in the spring of 1959.

Jon married Karen Haight, daughter of David B. Haight (who would later become a member of the Quorum of the Twelve Apostles), in June 1959. Karen described Jon as "one of the poorest boys I knew."[2] In July 1959 Jon began his two-year service in the U.S. Navy. After completing his military obligations, he worked full-time while completing his MBA degree at night from the University of Southern California's Marshall School of Business. To date, Jon has been awarded thirteen honorary doctorate degrees.

One of Utah's most successful entrepreneurs, Jon founded Huntsman Corporation, which became the largest privately held chemical company in North America by the time it became a public company in 2005. Under his guidance, his initial start-up, Huntsman Container Corporation, developed a plastic clamshell container which he sold to McDonalds to package hamburgers. Huntsman's company went on to develop about seventy other packaging products, including the first plates, bowls, dishes, and carry-out containers made of plastic. He then purchased businesses that manufactured the basic raw materials that went into his products. Today, Huntsman Corporation produces more than 12,000 products in their seventy-five global locations, where they employ more than 13,000 people with annual revenues of $13.5 billion. Jon is known for his business acumen and integrity. A noted attorney wrote of him, "Jon Huntsman is not your average CEO. Jon is a true rarity in the corporate world: a hugely successful entrepreneur whose conscience is as sharp as his business sense, whose word is known as an unbreakable bond. From his very first job, picking potatoes in rural Idaho at age eight, to his current position of running the world's largest private chemical company, he has always put ethical concerns on equal, if not greater, footing than his business concerns."[3]

Despite Jon's hardscrabble upbringing, Jon's family has always emphasized giving. In 1960, when Jon was a lieutenant in the Navy, he took $50 out of his $320 monthly paycheck to give to veterans' families in the Navy Relief Program in addition to the $32 he tithed to the LDS Church. "The time to give away money is when you make it," he said. According to *Forbes* magazine, of more than twelve hundred billionaires worldwide, Jon is one of nineteen who has donated at least a billion dollars to charity. In 2010, Jon donated so much to the Huntsman Cancer Foundation that he dropped off the *Forbes* 400 list of the richest men in the world. Before he dies, Jon plans to give all of his money away. In 2013, *Forbes* once again declared him one of the country's ten most generous Americans for his lifetime giving. He believes that other wealthy individuals need to step up and give more. "It becomes a game to see how much you can accumulate," Jon said. "Why should someone who has $5 billion only give away $2.5 billion? They can't take it with them."[4]

Neil Cavuto, host of a Fox business program, wrote of Jon, "In Jon Huntsman's world, giving is a sacred duty. He doesn't think much of billionaires who wait until they are dead to give away their money. I sometimes think Jon would be happiest if he could coincide his final breath with giving away his last dollar to someone in need, thus allowing him to leave this world the way he entered it."[5] Jon has received many humanitarian awards, including the Distinguished American Award from the Horatio Alger Association and awards from the National Conference of Christians and Jews and from Pope John Paul II.

After being diagnosed with cancer and treated twice, Jon recognized a void in cancer care in the state of Utah. On his road to recovery, Jon and his wife committed themselves to advancing cancer research and caring for others. In 1995, the Huntsman family pledged $100 million to construct a state-of-the-art cancer center in Salt Lake City. Five years later, the Huntsmans pledged another $125 million. Today the Huntsman Cancer Institute and Hospital at the University of Utah is world-renowned, and Jon assumed the mantle of principal benefactor. He and Karen have contributed more than $400 million and raised or generated hundreds of millions in gifts from generous organizations and agencies. Other beneficiaries of Huntsman generosity include institutions of higher education, hundreds of recipients of college scholarships, religious organizations, community centers, shelters for the homeless and the abused, and countless other worthy causes.

Jon has served in many capacities in the LDS Church, including president of the Washington DC Mission, stake president, regional representative, and Area Seventy. He said of his membership in the Church, "I thank God every day for the anchor of the Church."[6] He and his beloved wife are the parents of nine children, including son Jon Huntsman Jr., who was twice elected governor of the state of Utah and then appointed as United States ambassador to China.

When asked to reflect on his life, Jon said,

I think I could sum it up best by saying that if I had to write a book about my life, I would simply title it, "Lucky, Lucky Me!" Because I understand so well that, if everything were stripped away from us that had to do with affluence or material possessions, Karen and I would be just as happy today as the day we were married. If we had to return to Idaho where I started, that would be a great blessing. I don't think we would miss one iota the trappings of our life. I must say that when the Lord has blessed one with affluence and with material goods, there is not only an obligation but there is a duty, a very critical duty, that one has to impart a substantial part of that material gain to others, particularly those who are suffering.[7]

1   Jon M. Huntsman, *Winners Never Cheat: Everyday Values We Learned As Children (But May Have Forgotten)* (Philadelphia, PA: Pearson Prentice Hall, 2005), xxi, xxvii.

2   Gerry Avant, "A True-to-Life Horatio Alger Saga," *LDS Church News*, Oct. 25, 1997.

3   Huntsman, xviii.

4   David Whelan, "Jon Huntsman on Giving Away $1.2 Billion," *Forbes* magazine, May 18, 2011, http://www.forbes.com/forbes/2011/0606/focus-jon-huntsman-buffett-gates-charity-in-one-pocket-out-other.html.

5   Huntsman, 185.

6   Avant.

7   Ibid.

ORSON HYDE

Prophesying

Courtesy of L. Tom Perry
Special Collections, Harold B.
Lee Library, Brigham Young
University.

ON JUNE 27, 1844, ORSON HYDE "felt very heavy and sorrowful in spirit, and knew not the cause. . . . He never felt so before, and knew no reason why he should feel so then." Days later, he learned the cause of his great sorrow was the martyrdom of the Prophet Joseph Smith and Joseph's brother Hyrum. Of their deaths and the future of the Church, Orson declared before a crowd in Boston, Massachusetts, "I will prophesy that instead of the work dying, it will be like the mustard stock that was ripe, that a man undertook to throw out of his garden, and scattered seed all over it, and next year it was nothing but mustard. It will be so by shedding the blood of the Prophets—it will make ten saints where there is one now."[1]

Orson Hyde, son of Nathan Hyde and Sally Thorpe, was born January 8, 1805, in Oxford, Connecticut. Of his younger years and those of his siblings, Orson wrote, "In our early childhood, we were left an orphan. We grew up to manhood, a stranger to a father's protection and to a mother's care . . . few seemed to care for us, or take any interest in our welfare."[2] In 1819, fourteen-year-old Orson journeyed to Ohio, where he supported himself by working in a small iron foundry, in a woolen mill, and in the Gilbert and Whitney store in Kirtland.

In 1827 Orson joined the Methodist church and became a class leader. He was convinced by Sidney Rigdon's logical arguments to abandon the teachings of the Methodists and to affiliate himself with the Campbellite movement. Orson became a Campbellite pastor to congregations in Elyria and Florence, Ohio.

It was the Book of Mormon that changed Orson's religious course, although his first impression of the book was unfavorable. While preaching against that book, he later recorded, "For the first time, [I] thought that the 'Mormon' bible might be the truth of heaven; and fully resolved before leaving the house, that I would never preach against it any more until I knew more about it, being pretty strongly convicted in my own mind that I was doing wrong."[3] On October 30, 1831, Orson was baptized in the Chagrin River by Sidney Rigdon.

On November 1, 1831, two days after his baptism, Orson and other faithful elders were commanded by the Lord to "go ye into all the world, preach the gospel to every creature" (Mark 16:15). Of his mission with Samuel Smith to the Eastern states, Orson wrote, "Wherever we were received and entertained, we left our blessing; and wherever we were rejected, we washed our feet in private against those who rejected us."[4]

Upon returning to Kirtland, Orson taught in the School of the Prophets. Of his scholarship, he said, "I have once memorized the Bible, and when any one quoted one verse, I could quote the next. I have memorized it in English, German, and Hebrew."[5] On June 6, 1833, Orson was called to be a clerk to the First Presidency of the Church. He is credited with recording the Kirtland revelations from 1831 to 1834, the Book of Commandments, the Kirtland council minutes, Joseph Smith's letter book, and patriarchal blessings.

In 1834 Orson served on the first high council in Kirtland until enlisting in Zion's Camp to help redeem exiled Saints in Missouri. At the conclusion of Zion's Camp, he returned to Kirtland, where he was called to the Council of the Twelve Apostles and blessed by Oliver Cowdery that "he shall go forth according to the commandment, both to Jew and Gentile, and to all nations, kingdoms and tongues."[6] In fulfillment of this promise, Orson was one of the first Apostles to serve in the British Isles. "When we came in sight of Liverpool, the Spirit of God rested down upon us to a very great degree," wrote Orson. "Let me assure you . . . that the Lord God Omnipotent is with us."[7] Of Orson's preaching with Heber C. Kimball and John Goodson in England, the Reverend James Fielding penned, "Kimball bored the holes, Goodson drove the nails, and Hyde clinched them."[8]

When Orson returned to the United States, his testimony of the Restoration of the gospel faltered and he was numbered among the apostates. On October 24, 1838, he affixed his signature to the slanderous affidavit of Thomas B. Marsh that vilified Joseph Smith. As a result, Church fellowship was withdrawn from him. By spring of 1839, Orson felt sorrowful for his actions and lamented, "Few men pass through life without leaving some traces which they would gladly obliterate. Happy is he whose life is free from stain and blemish. . . . I sinned against God and my brethren; I acted foolishly. . . . I seek pardon of all whom I have offended, and also of my God."[9] His confession was accepted and his Apostleship was restored to him.

Orson was blessed by Joseph Smith and told, "In due time thou shalt go to Jerusalem, the land of thy fathers, and be a watchman unto the house of Israel; and by thy hand shall the Most High do a great work, which shall prepare the way and greatly facilitate the gathering together of that people." The opportunity for fulfilling this blessing came in the 1840s when Orson journeyed from Nauvoo to England and from there through Europe to Palestine. On October 24, 1841, he climbed the Mount of Olives and dedicated Jerusalem for the return of the Jews and the building of the holy temple. In his dedicatory prayer, Orson petitioned the Lord to "remove the barrenness and sterility of this land, and let springs of living water break forth to water its thirsty soil. Let the vine and olive produce in their strength, and the fig-tree bloom and flourish. Let the land become abundantly fruitful when possessed by its rightful heirs."[10]

Upon Orson's return to Nauvoo, it was publicly announced that he was called to serve a mission to St. Petersburg, Russia. This mission was never fulfilled, as Orson was sent instead to Washington, DC, to present a memorial that reviewed the persecution of the Saints in Missouri to government officials. As the leadership of the Church fell to the Quorum of the Twelve after the martyrdom of Joseph Smith, Orson was given the responsibility of supervising the completion of the Nauvoo Temple before joining the Saints in small encampments in Iowa Territory.

It was not until 1852 that Orson migrated to the Salt Lake Valley, where he served as an associate judge of the Utah Supreme Court, a member of the Utah Territorial Legislature, president of the Utah Senate in 1870, and a regent of the University of Deseret. He was the senior member of the Quorum of the Twelve Apostles from 1847 to 1875.

In June 1875 Brigham Young adjusted the seniority of the Twelve, partially because of Orson's prior estrangement from the Church. As a result, Orson was removed as president of that quorum, and John Taylor assumed the position. If Orson felt any disappointment or resentment at the change, it is not recorded.

Orson died on November 28, 1878, in Utah. The inscription on his tombstone reads, "Orson Hyde, Apostle of the Lord Jesus Christ, Defender of truth, preacher of righteousness." Orson lived long enough to see that his prophecy that "shedding the blood of the Prophets . . . will make ten saints where there is one now" was beginning to be fulfilled.[11] At the time of Joseph's death, there were 26,146 known members of the Church. At the time of Orson's death, the number of members had increased more than sixfold to 180,294.

1   *History of the Church*, 7:132, 198.

2   *Frontier Guardian*, Dec. 26, 1851, 2, as cited in Howard H. Barron, *Orson Hyde: Missionary, Apostle, Colonizer* (Bountiful, Utah: Horizon Publishers, 1977), 16.

3   Orson Hyde, "History of Orson Hyde," *Millennial Star* 26, no. 48 (Nov. 26, 1864): 760.

4   Orson Hyde, "History of Orson Hyde," *Millennial Star* 26, no. 49 (Dec. 3, 1864): 774–775.

5   *Journal of Discourses*, 2:81.

6   *History of the Church*, 2:189.

7   Letter of Orson Hyde, *Messenger and Advocate* 3, no. 11 (Aug. 1837): 551.

8   As cited in Heber C. Kimball, "Synopsis of the History of Heber Chase Kimball," *Millennial Star* 26, no. 39 (Sept. 24, 1864): 614.

9   Hyde, "History of Orson Hyde," *Millennial Star* 26, no. 50 (Dec. 10, 1864): 792.

10 *History of the Church*, 4:xxxi, 457.

11 Ibid., 7:198.

ANDREW JENSON

Record Keeping

Courtesy of the Church History
Library, The Church of Jesus
Christ of Latter-day Saints.

OF ANDREW JENSON'S LIFETIME OF gathering documents and writing histories, Senator William H. King of Utah said, "Your historical and other writings stand out as a most remarkable achievement and are of incalculable value to the entire membership of the Church."[1] *The New York Times* reported that Andrew "since 1898 compiled and edited 850 manuscript volumes of the church's history, covering period 1830 to 1900, and histories of stakes, wards, and conferences of the church . . . [and has] traveled almost 1,000,000 miles on church business, twice circling the globe, collecting on the way much material for his comprehensive personal library on Mormon Church history."[2]

Andrew Jenson, son of Christian and Kirsten Jenson, was born on December 11, 1850, in the Torsleu parish of Hjorring, Denmark. Four years after his birth, his parents became members of The Church of Jesus Christ of Latter-day Saints. Andrew recalled growing up on the "literary diet" of the Bible, the Book of Mormon, and other Church publications. At age thirteen, Andrew was invited to keep a personal journal by Latter-day Saint missionaries. Their invitation led Andrew to a lifetime of record keeping.

In May 1866 Andrew and his family set sail for America. "During the voyage, fifteen-year-old Andrew recorded the dates of marriages, births, and deaths of the passengers."[3] In October 1866 he and his family arrived in the Salt Lake Valley. Upon seeing the valley, Andrew shouted for joy, for "as long as I can remember I had prayed and hoped for the opportunity to gather to Zion." Andrew and his family settled in Pleasant Grove, where Andrew herded cows, sold lithographs, and labored on railroads. For him, such employment opportunities were less than satisfactory, for "I aspired to do something worth while."[4]

On April 9, 1873, Andrew was called to serve a mission in Denmark. Of the call, he wrote, "I must acknowledge that the thought of filling a mission, inexperienced as I was, caused me many sleepless nights." But when he was set apart for the mission by George Q. Cannon, he felt peace because of the promise that "I on this mission should be blessed with the power of utterance, so that I should bear powerful testimonies to my countrymen and bring many of them to a knowledge of the truth."[5]

After fulfilling a successful mission, Andrew married Kirsten Marie Pederson, a young woman he had met in Denmark. Andrew and Kirsten made their home in Pleasant Grove, Utah. Although Andrew found employment building a tramway up Little Cottonwood Canyon, he was "depressed" and "wondered if the Lord had nothing else for me to do except working with pick and shovel. I thought that the common manual labor to which I had been subject could be done by anyone possessing physical strength and ordinary intelligence. Should I not see the day when some of my dreams would come true?"[6]

In May 1879 Andrew accepted a second mission call to Denmark, where he served as president of the Copenhagen branch, translated scriptures into Danish, and acted as mission president. Years later, a third mission call came to serve as president of the Scandinavian mission.

In April 1888, Andrew was sustained as Assistant Church Historian. He was assured of his worth through a divine manifestation in which he was told, "Thou has not lost thy position in the Church as an historian, thy zeal and integrity in that capacity are known to God and are pleasing in his sight, and it is God who hath inspired thee to do the work which thou has already done." In his capacity as Assistant Church Historian, Andrew was assigned to visit all the stakes of the Church in the United States and review their records. On his visits, Andrew was disappointed to find "most of the Church records in a 'deplorable condition.'" He reported to the First Presidency, "In many instances no regular records are being kept at all, and those few which are kept . . . have long ago been lost, misplaced or destroyed and consequently about half the members of the Church are in perfect ignorance today as regards the dates of their blessings, baptisms, confirmations, ordinations, etc."[7]

Realizing the need to improve record keeping in the stakes of Zion, General Authorities encouraged Andrew to teach Latter-day Saints about the importance of recordkeeping. Andrew was assigned in May 1895 "to travel to all the countries of the world where Latter-day Saint missionaries had been assigned" and gather documents for Church history purposes. Wilford Woodruff told Andrew that he "would be greatly blessed on this mission and accomplish much good. He also told him 'it was the Lord's will that I should go on this mission and accomplish much good for the Church.'" The notes and records that Andrew gathered on his worldwide tour now "constitute the foundation and outline for histories of nearly every stake, ward, branch, quorum, association, etc., of the Church, in its gathered state, and of every mission, conference, branch, etc., abroad," from the time of the organization of the Church."[8]

In spite of his travels, Andrew is best known for his historical writings, which include *The Historical Record, Church Chronology, Latter-day Saint Biographical Encyclopedia*, and *Encyclopedia History of the Church of Jesus Christ of Latter-day Saints*. Of his writings, Andrew said, "[I] do not expect any one of you to ever read all of these lengthy manuscript histories, but they are all very important as works of reference. These volumes and the many that hereafter will be added, may consistently be termed the 'fathers' of the new dispensation."[9]

By the time of his death on November 18, 1941, Andrew had written a "Journal History" from the organization of the Church on April 6, 1830, to December 31, 1930.[10] James H. Anderson wrote of the many other accomplishments of Andrew, stating, "No man has done more—if any has done so much—in the cause of abundant and correct data for the Church records."[11] The First Presidency of the Church eulogized him by writing, "[Andrew's] devotion to historical research was of the Highest character. He never wearied in finding facts and making a record of them. His testimony was perfect. The gospel was his whole concern. The Church will miss him."[12]

1   Keith W. Perkins, "A Study of the Contributions of Andrew Jenson to the Writing and Preservation of LDS Church History," master's thesis, Brigham Young University, May 1971, 121.

2   *The New York Times*, Nov. 20, 1941.
3   Perkins, 6.
4   Andrew Jenson, *Autobiography of Andrew Jenson* (Salt Lake City: Deseret News Press, 1938), 25–26, 36.
5   Perkins, 10, 11.
6   Ibid., 14.
7   Ibid., 59, 81, 86.
8   Ibid., 91, 92, 98.
9   Ibid., 113.
10 Ibid., 118.
11 James H. Anderson, "One Andrew Jenson," *Improvement Era* 24, no. 9 (July 1921): 787.
12 *Deseret News*, Nov. 19, 1941.

HEBER C. KIMBALL
Trusting God

Courtesy of Religious Education
Image Project, Brigham Young
University.

FINANCIAL REVERSES WITHIN THE KIMBALL family forced nineteen-year-old Heber Kimball to venture from his home and seek his fortune. "I found myself cast abroad upon the world, without a friend to console my grief," recalled Heber. After several weeks of suffering "for the want of food and the comforts of life," he accepted an offer from his brother to board with him and learn the potter's trade.[1]

An unusual evening was spent by the apprentice potter on September 22, 1827, in Mendon, New York, where he beheld an army marching in the sky and engaging in combat with opposing military forces. Heber later learned that on that very evening Joseph Smith had received the plates from the angel Moroni. Heber joined Joseph in Kirtland, Ohio. "The Gospel and plan of salvation that I have embraced, is music to me," said Heber. "It is sweet to my body, and congenial to my spirit; and it is more lovely than anything else I have ever seen since I have been in the world. I love it."[2]

Heber C. Kimball, son of Solomon Farnham Kimball and Anna Spaulding, was born June 14, 1801, in Sheldon, Vermont. On June 4, 1837, Joseph Smith said, "Brother Heber, the Spirit of the Lord has whispered to me: 'Let my servant Heber go to England and proclaim my Gospel, and open the door of salvation to that nation.'" In obedience to the prophetic prompting, Heber "felt a determination to go at all hazards."

He journeyed from Ohio to New York and then sailed on the *Garrick* to Liverpool. When the ship anchored, a small boat took him to shore. "When we were within six or seven feet of the pier, I leaped on shore," wrote Heber. "For the first time in my life I stood on British ground, among strangers. . . . I put my trust in God, believing that He would assist me in publishing the truth, give me utterance, and be a present help in time of need."[3]

The success Heber enjoyed on English shores was remarkable. For example, after preaching to a gathering in Chatburn, he wrote, "I felt someone pulling at my coat, exclaiming, 'Maister, Maister.' I turned round and asked what was wanted. Mrs. Elizabeth Partington said, 'Please sir, will you baptize me?' 'And me?' 'And me?' exclaimed more than a dozen voices. Accordingly I went down into the water and baptized twenty-five."

Upon returning to the States, he met with friends, "some of whom were so glad to see us," wrote Heber, "that tears started in their eyes when we took them by the hand."[4] Heber's testimony of the gospel of Jesus Christ did not lessen at the martyrdom of Joseph Smith, for he knew the Twelve held "the keys to open up the authority of [the Lord's] kingdom upon the four corners of the earth."[5] He pressed forward through trials of threatened mobocracy, rigors of the Iowa wilderness, and the trek to the Salt Lake Valley.

In December 1847 Heber was chosen as a counselor in the Presidency of the Church. This call had been prophesied five years before by Hyrum Smith, who said to Heber, "You shall be blest with a fullness, and shall be not one whit behind the Chiefest as an Apostle[;] you shall stand in the presence of God to judge the People, & as a prophet you shall attain to the Honour of the three."[6]

The remaining two decades of Heber's life were inseparably interwoven with the pioneer development of the intermountain region. He was chief justice and lieutenant governor of the provisional government of Deseret. He traveled throughout the pioneer settlements strengthening the Saints and was everywhere honored and beloved.

Heber died on June 22, 1868, in Salt Lake City. His death was linked to a severe fall from a wagon. His funeral was held on June 24, 1868, in the Salt Lake Tabernacle. The eulogy was offered by Brigham Young, who said, "We can say truly that the day of this man's death was far better to him than the day of his birth. . . . I have been personally acquainted with him forty-three years and I can testify that he has been a man of truth, a man of benevolence, a man that was to be trusted."[7]

1   Heber C. Kimball, "Synopsis of the History of Heber Chase Kimball," *Millennial Star* 26, no. 30 (July 23, 1864): 471.

2   Orson F. Whitney, *Life of Heber C. Kimball*, 3rd ed. (Salt Lake City: Bookcraft, 1967), 15–17, 457.

3   Ibid., 104, 119.

4   Ibid., 171, 203.

5   D&C 124:128.

6   *Early Patriarchal Blessings of The Church of Jesus Christ of Latter-day Saints*, comp. H. Michael Marquardt (Salt Lake City: The Smith-Pettit Foundation, 2007), 214.

7   Whitney, 495.

J. GOLDEN KIMBALL
Simplicity

Courtesy of the Church History
Library, The Church of Jesus
Christ of Latter-day Saints.

IN LATTER-DAY SAINT MYTHOLOGY, J. Golden Kimball is remembered for his rough-around-the-edges honesty, humor, and the occasional swear words that popped up in his sermons. However, his honesty, humor, and colorful language were merely a product of a deeper quality—simplicity. Golden was a simple man who lived without pretense. Motivated by love for the gospel of Jesus Christ and love for all people, Golden lived the creed that, in life, "the bigger things are to love your God, your neighbor, to be generous . . . to be honest, truthful, moral, etc. . . . Sell [all you have] and follow the Master." With this creed as his guide, Golden encouraged all who listened to him to act better and to walk a little closer to God.[1]

Jonathan Golden Kimball, son of Heber C. Kimball and Christeen Golden, was born June 9, 1853, in Salt Lake City, Utah. At age fifteen, Golden recognized the financial predicament his family faced with the passing of his father in 1868. As the oldest son in the family, Golden accepted the responsibility to gain employment to support his family. At that time, he had "enough ambition to have made [him] President of the United States of America." Yet the employment he secured was that of a cowboy driving mules, "a profession of some immediate value" to his financial circumstances.

During this period of his life, Golden gained a reputation as a rugged "contractor-for-hire" of considerable moral repute. "It is reported that he always saw to it that the work was done right and that . . . he never took advantage of people, but was honest in his dealings with every one under all circumstances."[2] Despite his reputation, success, and financial contribution to his family, Golden could not keep his mother or siblings from the effects of poverty.

As for his personal life, Golden reported, "There was no restraint or responsibility placed upon me." He felt free to choose the ways of the cowboy and began to swear, and he confessed that "I was not actively engaged in church work." It was his response to an advertisement for loggers to harvest wood in Logan Canyon for building a temple that brought him back to Church activity. As part of his employment, Golden was assigned to preside over the logging crew at Latter-day Saint Church meetings, organize prayers, and persuade other loggers not to swear. Though this presented a challenge to Golden, he took the responsibility seriously and went to work. At that time, he understood the importance of a leader practicing what he preached, so Golden curbed his swearing and persuaded other loggers to do likewise, "excepting 'hell' and 'damn it.'" In Logan Canyon, none of the loggers, including Golden, considered *hell* or *damn* swear words.[3]

After working as a logger for a season, Golden attended Brigham Young Academy at the invitation of Professor Karl G. Maeser. Upon completing his second year at the academy, he accepted a call to serve in the Southern States Mission. On this mission, he contracted malaria and a doctor warned him that he would die if he didn't "do something for [himself]." Golden responded, "Well, I won't die, as I'm a Mormon— you can't kill them." Such wit was typical of Golden. Elder John Henry Evans said of Golden's simplistic style, "The essence of this normal vision and this normal expression is the sense of humor." To Bryant S. Hinckley, Golden's humor contained "the deepest wisdom."[4]

After serving an honorable mission, Golden returned to Salt Lake City in 1885. One year later, he was called to the Quorum of the Seventy. The following year, Golden married the beautiful Jennie Knowlton. They became the parents of six.

In 1891 Golden was called to preside over the Southern States Mission. While serving as mission president, he was called to be one of the seven presidents of the Quorum of the Seventy. As a president of the Seventy, Golden was given the "responsibility of bearing apostolic witness of the name of Christ."[5] The First Presidency sent him to bear witness of the Savior to Latter-day Saints throughout the United States. The extensive travel did not bother Golden because "[he] was happiest when he was . . . on the road on assignment . . . back to the people he knew and loved; the ranchers, the farmers, the cowboys."[6]

Golden's humorous style of speaking endeared him to Latter-day Saints across the nation. They spoke of Golden as "the favorite man of the folk"—a folk hero beloved by the Saints wherever he spoke.[7] Golden did not view himself as a hero, however. At the October 1926 general conference, he acknowledged his imperfections by stating, "I am a man of weakness; I am a man full of faults; but God knows I have given him the best effort there was in me."[8]

Golden's testimony and love for the gospel of Jesus Christ were his most prized possessions. He divulged, "I would rather be tied to a whipping post and have my flesh stripped from my bones than to lose my faith in this Church and have my spirit killed." Golden was very hurt when disharmony between himself and other General Authorities surfaced. The source of the friction was Golden's use of "those two little [swear] words"—*hell* and *damn*. He "regret[ed] that [his] ways [didn't] always please [the authorities]" but did not change his style of speaking.[9]

After visiting his daughter in Northern California, Golden was in an automobile accident while en route to Salt Lake City. On September 2, 1938, the car in which he and his wife were traveling skidded into a bank. Golden was ejected from his seat and killed upon impact. His wife survived the accident with a few lacerations.

Golden is remembered for his love of people, his humor, and his salty language. His was a simple faith epitomized by the saying, "[God] created us and he never created a failure."[10]

1   Claude Richards, *J. Golden Kimball: The Story of a Unique Personality* (Salt Lake City: Deseret News Press, 1934), 67, 70.

2   Richards, 23–24.

3   Richards, 29, 31, 32–33.

4   Richards, 46, 121–123.

5   Gordon B. Hinckley, "Special Witnesses for Christ," *Ensign*, April 1984.

6   Jim Kimball, *On the Road with J. Golden Kimball*, DVD, aired Nov. 7, 1998 (Camarillo, CA: Goldhill Home Media, 2000).

7   Thomas E. Cheney, *The Golden Legacy: A Folk History of J. Golden Kimball* (USA: KSG Publishing, 1974), xi–xii.

8   J. Golden Kimball, *Conference Report*, Oct. 1926, 131.

9   Richards, 58, 67–69.

10 J. Golden Kimball, 130.

SPENCER W. KIMBALL
Divinely Driven

Courtesy of the Church Archives,
The Church of Jesus Christ of
Latter-day Saints.

SPENCER W. KIMBALL'S OLDER BROTHERS never let him forget that he was short. At Spencer's baptism, his brothers called him "The Chubby Little Bishop." Spencer joked that his height was stunted because his brothers made him carry five-gallon cans of slop to the pigs.[1] Although Spencer was short in stature, there was nothing short or small about his character and drive to get things done. Because of his determination to move the work of God forward, Spencer was able to "lengthen the stride" of the Church membership.

Spencer Woolley Kimball, son of Andrew Kimball and Olive Woolley, was born March 28, 1895, in Salt Lake City, Utah. When Spencer was three years old, his family moved to Thatcher, Arizona, so that Spencer's father could provide assistance to Native Americans residing in the Indian Territory. Spencer worked hard as a child to tame the desert on the family farm in Thatcher. His hardest experience, however, was the death of his mother in 1906 when Spencer was just eleven years old. At the time of Olive's death, Spencer resolved to live up to her memory and make her proud that he had been her son.[2]

With the enthusiasm of youth, Spencer excelled in sports and music and was president of his class each year he attended Gila Academy. After graduating from the academy, Spencer accepted a mission call to the Swiss-German Mission. Due to the outbreak of World War

I, his mission call was changed to the Central States Mission.³ After completing an honorable mission, Spencer returned to Thatcher, where he met Camilla Eyring, a home economics teacher at Gila Academy. Thirty-one days after meeting Camilla, Spencer asked her father if he would approve their marriage. Spencer and Camilla were married November 16, 1917, in Thatcher. At that time, Spencer had only ten dollars to his name and Camilla owed fifty dollars for her schooling. In June 1918, Spencer and Camilla were sealed for eternity in the Salt Lake Temple.

Spencer supported Camilla and their growing family as a bank clerk until 1927. In that year, he invested $150 in the Kimball-Greenhalgh Insurance Agency and went to work for the agency as an insurance salesman. Within the first month of his employment, Spencer had doubled his investment by arriving at work early in the morning and leaving late at night. Due to the hours Spencer kept in the office, coworkers joked that he would die with his shoes on.

In 1943, while serving as a stake president in Thatcher, Spencer was called to the Quorum of the Twelve Apostles. He felt very inadequate to accept such a high calling and wrestled with the Lord for a witness that he was worthy to serve. "There was one great desire, to get a testimony of my calling," he said. "How I prayed! How I suffered! How I wept! How I struggled!" After eighty-five days of praying for an answer, Spencer received a spiritual confirmation that it was the will of the Lord for him to serve as an Apostle.⁴

During his apostolic service, Spencer suffered from debilitating illnesses and afflictions, such as heart attacks, throat cancer, boils, deafness, Bell's palsy, and brain tumors. Any of these maladies would stunt the work of most men, but Spencer refused to let physical limitations prevent him from fulfilling his responsibilities. He encouraged others to follow his example, believing that all would be strengthened by the Lord. As an Apostle Spencer wrote several books, the most quoted of which is *The Miracle of Forgiveness*, a must-read for those seeking peace through the repentance process. Spencer is also remembered for working tirelessly in behalf of Father Lehi's descendants. Whether the descendants were residing in North or South America or living on an isle of the sea, Spencer sought them out and shared with them the gospel of Jesus Christ.

In 1973 Spencer was sustained as the twelfth President of The Church of Jesus Christ of Latter-day Saints. During his administration, he encouraged every member to "lengthen your stride" and "do it." Under his direction, a new LDS edition of the scriptures was published, worthy nineteen-year-old men were called to serve missions, genealogical research expanded, and temple building progressed at a rate never seen before. No other event in his administration, however, was more groundbreaking than his remarkable revelation received in June 1978 that extended the priesthood to all worthy males.

Spencer died on November 5, 1985, in Salt Lake City. There was nothing small or short about Spencer W. Kimball's ministry. Elder Neal A. Maxwell of the Quorum of the Twelve Apostles said of Spencer, "Church members will be nourished and encouraged by the eloquence of the example of this seer in overcoming (or coexisting with) adversity after adversity. His resilience was exemplary. His deft humor occupied the place which might have so easily been commandeered by self-pity. His selfless dedication, time and again, caused him to be up and about his Father's business (sometimes even before he was well). The examples are legendary and will be recounted for many years."[5]

1   Edward L. Kimball and Andrew E. Kimball Jr., *Spencer W. Kimball: Twelfth President of The Church of Jesus Christ of Latter-day Saints* (Salt Lake City: Bookcraft, 1977), 33, 37.

2   Kimball and Kimball, 48–49.

3   Matthew O. Richardson and Timothy Merrill, "Spencer W. Kimball," *Presidents of the Church: The Lives and Teachings of the Modern Prophets*, ed. Craig Manscill, Robert C. Freeman, and Dennis A. Wright (Springville, UT: Cedar Fort, 2008), 321–322.

4   Kimball and Kimball, 195.

5   Neal A. Maxwell, "Spencer the Beloved: Leader Servant," *Ensign*, Dec. 1985, 8.

ARTHUR HENRY KING
Intellectual

Courtesy of L. Tom Perry
Special Collections, Harold B.
Lee Library, Brigham Young
University.

FOR ALMOST THREE DECADES, ARTHUR HENRY KING lectured and taught English in his capacity as assistant director general of the British Council.[1] For teaching English as a second language in Pakistan, Iran, India, Denmark, Sweden, Finland, Belgium, and Germany, he was decorated twice by Queen Elizabeth. He was also acclaimed for writing anti-Nazi propaganda during World War II and for being a widely respected Shakespeare scholar.[2]

Arthur Henry King, son of devout Quaker parents, was born February 20, 1910, in Hampshire, England. From his father he learned that "in landscape you can find evidence of a creative power for good."[3] On an April morning in 1916, his father took Arthur to a shaded area in the woods, where he showed him the bluebells that blanketed the ground. "I could scarcely breathe because the impression was so great," Arthur recalled. The experience was heightened as he realized years later the depth of his father's love when he chose "to do that that morning— to give me that experience."[4]

After graduating with high honors from the University of Cambridge, Arthur enrolled in the University of Sweden, where he earned a doctorate degree.[5] In 1935, while Arthur was teaching at Lund, Sweden, his wife, Maud, gave birth to a son. Their son died seven days later. This untimely death led Arthur to search for "a kind of recompense" for his deceased son.[6] He had grown dissatisfied with the Quakerism of his parents, not liking the class distinctions in Quakerism or the lack of "dogma, something firm [he] could depend on to help answer [his] and others' questionings." Searching for answers to life's questions, Arthur attended an Anglican church for several years, appreciating their hymns and rituals but seeing in this church "no true social group, no force." He then turned to Islam, where he found a sense of community, but viewed Allah as "remote [and] arbitrary." Arthur discovered a family-centered approach to life in Hinduism, but also social prejudice. He thought Buddhism had intense spiritual discipline, but "no place for a personal God." Although Arthur saw "fatal flaws" in the world's religions, he believed that "each [religion] has in it something that points us toward and prepares us for acceptance of [Mormonism]."[7] In March 1966, a year after his wife Maud died, Arthur visited his Uncle Archie. On that visit, he met his second cousin Patricia, a Latter-day Saint who agreed to teach him about the gospel of Jesus Christ. Arthur accepted Mormonism and was baptized, believing that he had at last found the truth. He received a patriarchal blessing that promised him that he would "raise up children in the house of faith."[8] At age fifty-seven, this portion of his blessing confused him, for his wife was deceased and he had no children. The blessing was fulfilled when Arthur married Patricia and enjoyed the blessings of family life.

When President Harold B. Lee learned of the conversion of the "distinguished" Arthur King, he invited Arthur to teach at Brigham Young University.[9] Arthur accepted his invitation and became one of the most sought-after teachers on campus. "There were young people who sought me out," he recalled. "I didn't choose them. They chose me."[10] One student explained why students wanted to enroll in Arthur's classes: "His influence was immediate and arresting . . . his strong British voice thundering in my head." Whatever Arthur taught—art, literature, music, or history—students were confident that classroom instruction would be given "through the gospel lens." Arthur held that "the most important thing we could read ourselves or to our children [was] the scriptures."[11] One student said, "His incisive mind invited awe, not so much for what he knew . . . as for how he opened any subject to a more expansive view."[12]

Arthur died on January 15, 2000, from Parkinson's disease.[13] In his final hours, he was still writing poetry.[14] To future poets, he said, "I think the answer is to practice your technique, endeavor to be a good man, not a great poet, live a good life, and leave the rest to the Lord."[15]

1   Giles H. Florence, "A King's Life: An Arthurian Legend," *Deseret News*, February 17, 2010, http://www.deseretnews.com/article/705376897/A-kings-life-an-Arthurian-legend.html?pg=all.

2   "Obituary: Arthur Henry King, CBE., B.A; M.A. (Cantab); D. Litt; FCP; FIL," *Deseret News*, Jan. 17, 2000, http://www.deseretnews.com/article/738972/Obituary-Arthur-Henry-King-CBE-BA-MA-Cantab-D-Litt-FCP-FIL.html.

3   "Speak That I May See Thee: Arthur Henry King," BYUtv, *LDS Lives*, originally aired 5 Feb. 2008, http://www.byutv.org/watch/a1c4894a-fd76-4729-93b2-8ff896c427cc/lds-lives-speak-that-i-may-see-thee-arthur-henry-king.

4   Arthur Henry King, *The Abundance of the Heart* (Salt Lake City, UT: Bookcraft, 1986), 88.

5   Florence.

6   "Speak That I May See Thee."

7   Arthur Henry King, "A Testimony of My Conversion," *New Era*, Feb. 1971, 34–36.

8   "Speak That I May See Thee."

9   Florence.

10 "Speak That I May See Thee."

11 Joe Cannon, "Reflections on Arthur Henry King," *Deseret News*, Feb. 17, 2010, http://www.deseretnews.com/article/705376893/Joe-Cannon-Reflections-on-Arthur-Henry-King.html?pg=all.

12 Florence.

13 "Speak That I May See Thee."

14 Florence.

15 Douglas E. Airmet, "Mormon Poets Talk about Their Craft," *New Era*, Aug. 1975, 49.

MICHAEL O. LEAVITT

Cooperation

IN 1998 REPUBLICAN GOVERNOR MICHAEL LEAVITT and Democratic Governor John Kitzhaber presented the "Enlibra" plan to elected officials in Washington, DC. Their plan called for a nationwide collaborative "move toward balance" in environmental protection and restoration efforts. Because of their disregard for political party affiliation and their embrace of collaborative efforts, the governors' plan was so unexpected by elected politicians at the capital that political journalist David Broder wrote, "Mr. Kitzhaber [of Oregon] and Mr. Leavitt [of Utah] seemed like creatures . . . from another planet. One where most Americans would like to live."[1] Michael's ability to offer a collaborative approach to even the most difficult issues has earned him the respect of family, friends, colleagues, and peers throughout the nation.

Michael Okerlund Leavitt, son of Dixie Lorraine Leavitt and Phyllis Anne Okerlund, was born on February 11, 1951, in Cedar City, Utah. As a youth, he was employed at his family's insurance brokerage and attended Southern Utah University in Cedar City. At the university, he met Jacalyn "Jackie" Smith, who had come to Cedar City to perform in the Utah Shakespearean Festival. She was beautiful, talented, and mature—he "didn't think he had a chance"[2] with her. But with some encouragement from friends, Michael asked Jackie for a date and by the following summer they were married.

In 1974 Michael graduated with a bachelor's degree in economics and business from Southern Utah University. Two years later, Michael spearheaded his father's campaign for governor of Utah. Although his father lost the election, Michael came away from the campaign with a love for politics. He became an active political operative and before long was "viewed as Utah's premier campaign strategist."[3] He ran the successful campaigns of Senator Jake Garn and Senator Orrin Hatch.

In 1984, after being named chief executive of The Leavitt Group, Michael turned from politics to devote his time and talents to being the leader of the nation's second-largest privately held insurance brokerage.[4] For eight years, he oversaw the expansion of his family brokerage, but in 1992, he was thrust back into the political realm when he accepted an invitation to run for governor of Utah on the Republican ticket. Michael won a majority of votes and served as governor for more than ten years, longer than any other governor in Utah history.

During his tenure, Michael was known for his collaborative and problem-solving skills. It was his practice to "put the best interests of the state above politics."[5] He contended that "the best approach [to solving problems] is when businesses and employees work together."[6] Coworker Jeff Packer said that Michael "consider[ed] opposing positions" before making "an informed call."[7]

On September 11, 2001, when news of the air attack on the Twin Towers and the Pentagon reached Michael, he immediately recognized that "this is not an experience that any generation has had in our country, ever . . . in terms of [attacks on] the mainland." As commander and chief of the Utah National Guard, he foresaw that the attack would bring difficult challenges to the Utah National Guard and their families. Michael and Jackie "concluded to do something for the families to say thank you." So they personally visited and thanked Guard families for their sacrifices and saw "that there was comfort . . . in being together." Michael knew that "it was an important thing for me to see firsthand."[8]

Due to the respect that his fellow governors had for Michael's ability to assess each situation and seek a cooperative solution, they elected him chairman of the Western Governors Association, the Republican Governors Association, and the National Governors Association.[9]

Michael is credited with being a driving force behind the establishment of the Western Governors University, "a multi-state, linked distance learning delivery network" established through the collaboration of eleven governors across the nation.[10] And his reputation as a collaborator and an effective policy-maker led to his appointment as head of the Environmental Protection Agency in 2003. After serving for two years in that position, he was appointed Secretary of Health and Human Services in 2005.

When U.S. President George W. Bush left office in 2008, so did Michael, but he did not leave the political realm. He was an active participant in Mitt Romney's bid for president of the United States. When speaking of his role in the Romney campaign, Michael compared himself to a goat that calms the stallion before a race, but "people who know him [say] he's more like a similar stock of stallion."[11]

Michael's collaborative abilities extend beyond his career in politics and insurance. Once, while Michael was serving as governor of Utah, journalist Susan Whitney caught a glimpse of Michael and Jackie playing a pickup game of basketball with their family. Whitney wrote, "It seems almost effortless the way Mom and Dad make sure everyone is included in the game."[12] Family, friends, and loved ones respect him for his wisdom, caring, and ability to include everyone. Regardless of the situation in which Michael is placed, he has the ability to look at the bigger picture and find ways to cooperate and find amicable solutions.

1   David Broder, "Two Western Governors Show How System Works," *The Blade*: Toledo, OH, Monday, July 20, 1998, http://news.google.com/newspap ers?nid=1350&dat=19980720&id=jwwwAAAAIBAJ&sjid=hgMEAAAAIBA J&pg=3648,1945971.

2   Susan Whitney, "Jackie & Mike Leavitt: Chemistry Brought 'First Couple' Together, but Their Personalities Make It Work," *Deseret News*, Wednesday, Oct. 16, 1996, http://www.deseretnews.com/article/519439/JACKIE--MIKE-LEAVITT--CHEMISTRY-BROUGHT-FIRST-COUPLE-TOGETHER-BUT-THEIR-PERSONALITIES-MAKE-IT.html?pg=all.

3   Jonathan Martin and Alexander Burns, "Mike Leavitt, the Man Planning the Mitt Romney Presidency," *Politico*, June 3, 2012, http://www.politico.com/news/stories/0612/76983.html.

4   "Michael O. Leavitt," Leavitt Partners (blog), http://leavittpartners.com/team/michael-o-leavitt/.

5   "Governor Michael O. Leavitt, Former HHS Secretary and EPA Administrator, Selects WorldWide Speakers Group for Exclusive Representation," PRNewswire, http://www.prnewswire.com/news-releases/governor-michael-o-leavitt-former-hhs-secretary-and-epa-administrator-selects-worldwide-speakers-group-for-exclusive-representation-105253808.html.

6   Michael O. Leavitt, "Better Health; Lower Costs; Shared Responsibility," Leavitt Partners (blog), March 26, 2013, http://leavittpartners.com/2013/03/better-health-lower-costs-shared-responsibility/.

7   Comment by Jeff Packer on Michael Leavitt's LinkedIn page under experience as governor of the state of Utah, http://www.linkedin.com/profile/view?id=69756838&authType=NAME_SEARCH&authToken=n_Su&locale=en_US&srchid=2084557041373490139416&srchindex=3&srchtotal=86&trk=vsrp_people_res_name&trkInfo=VSRPsearchId%3A2084557041373490139416%2CVSRPtargetId%3A69756838%2CVSRPcmpt%3Aprimary.

8   "Project Prologue: The Utah National Guard," Michael O. Leavitt Center for Politics & Public Service, Southern Utah University, http://leavitt.li.suu.edu/leavitt/?p=380.

9   "Michael O. Leavitt," Leavitt Partners.

10 "WGU's First 15 Years: A Timeline," WGU, Western Governors University, http://www.wgu.edu/about_WGU/timeline.

11 Martin and Burns, "Mike Leavitt."

12 Whitney.

HAROLD B. LEE
Steadfast

Courtesy of the Church
Archives, The Church of Jesus
Christ of Latter-day Saints.

A PLAQUE NEAR HAROLD B. LEE's birthplace reads, "Harold B. Lee, eleventh president of The Church of Jesus Christ of Latter-day Saints, touched and changed countless lives."[1] Harold was the epitome of a man who wholly devoted his life to strengthening Latter-day Saints and building the kingdom of God.

Harold Bingham Lee, son of Samuel Lee and Louisa Bingham, was born March 28, 1899, on a farm near Clifton, Idaho. Harold's parents set an example for him of hard work, faithfulness, and compassion. He credited his mother's inspiration and gift of healing to the preservation of his life on many occasions. For example, when Harold was eight years old, he accidently spilled a can of lye all over himself. His mother opened a vat of pickled beets and poured cup after cup of the red vinegar over his head and body, neutralizing the poisonous effects of the lye. When Harold was a teenager and had punctured one of his arteries on a broken bottle, his mother stopped the bleeding and cleaned his wound. In spite of her best efforts, the wound festered and became infected. His mother healed the infection by burning a black sock to ashes and rubbing the ashes into the open wound.[2]

Harold began his educational pursuits at a grammar school near his home in Clifton before enrolling in the Oneida Stake Academy in Preston, Idaho. At age seventeen, he attended Idaho's Albion State Normal School.

After two summers (1916 and 1917) at the Normal School, Harold passed the state's fifteen-subject test and received two teaching certificates. By age eighteen, he was appointed as a school principal in Oxford, Idaho. While in Oxford, Harold founded the Oxford Athletic Club, started a women's choir, and served as elders quorum president in his ward.

At age twenty-one, Harold accepted a mission call to the Western States Mission. On his mission, Harold met Fern Lucinda Tanner, a sister missionary from Utah. Following their missions, Harold and Fern renewed their acquaintance and were married November 14, 1923, in the Salt Lake Temple. They became the parents of two daughters.

To better his employment opportunities and support his growing family, Harold enrolled in the University of Utah. After completing further coursework, he was hired to be a principal in the Granite School District. While working as a principal, Harold also served as president of the Salt Lake Pioneer Stake. Being a stake president during the Great Depression was difficult for Harold, for most Latter-day Saints in his stake had lost their savings, livelihood, and hope. Concerned for his people, Harold initiated a program of self-reliance and relief that proved so successful that it was later adopted worldwide as the welfare system of the Church.

On April 10, 1941, at age forty-two, Harold was ordained an Apostle of the Lord Jesus Christ by President Heber J. Grant. At the time of his call to the Quorum of the Twelve Apostles, Harold was nearly twenty years younger than any other member of the quorum. As an Apostle, Harold was assigned to oversee and implement the welfare program of the Church for more than twenty years. Under his watchful guidance, Church welfare was extended to needy individuals and communities in many countries throughout the world.

During these same years, Harold's wife, Fern, was by his side sustaining his humanitarian outreach efforts. After thirty-nine years of marriage, however, Fern died on September 21, 1962. Harold married Freda Joan Jensen on June 17, 1963. At the time of their marriage, Freda was a member of the general board of the Primary Association and director of elementary education in the Jordan School District.[3]

Soon after Harold's marriage to Freda, President David O. McKay appointed Harold to be chairman of the Church Correlation Committee. In that capacity, Harold pioneered the worldwide coordination of Church materials and activities. He initiated organizational changes within the Church that improved the efficiency and effectiveness of councils, programs, and events so that Church leaders and members alike could better serve the "one" and teach the rising generation principles of the gospel of Jesus Christ.[4]

After thirty-one years of service in the Quorum of the Twelve Apostles, Harold was sustained as President of the Church on July 7, 1972. "Never think of me as the head of the Church," he said. "Jesus Christ is the head of this Church, I am only a man, his servant."[5] In his last talk as Church President, Harold said, "If it were not for the assurance that I have that the Lord is near to us, guiding, directing, the burden would be almost beyond my strength, but because I know that He is there, and that He can be appealed to, and if we have ears to hear attuned to Him, we will never be left alone."[6]

After only eighteen months as President of the Church, Harold B. Lee died of a fatal pulmonary hemorrhage on December 26, 1973, in Salt Lake City. At that time, he was the youngest Church President to die since the martyrdom of Joseph Smith. At Harold's funeral, some felt that his passing was untimely, but the death of a righteous man is never untimely. President Spencer W. Kimball said, "A giant redwood has fallen and left a great space in the forest."[7] Although his death at age seventy-four was unexpected by Latter-day Saints worldwide, it was not unexpected by his wife, Freda, for Harold had said to her, "God is very near."[8]

1   Donald Q. Cannon, Richard O. Cowan, and Arnold K. Garr, *Encyclopedia of Latter-day Saint History* (Salt Lake City: Deseret Book, 2000), 651.

2   *Presidents of the Church Student Manual* (Salt Lake City: The Church of Jesus Christ of Latter-day Saints, 2003), 180.

3   Ibid., 181–188; see also Garr, Cannon, and Cowan, 653.

4   Ibid., 187–188.

5   Garr, Cannon, and Cowan, 653.

6   "Harold B. Lee's Closing Remarks," *Ensign*, Jan. 1974, 129.

7   *Presidents of the Church Student Manual*, 193.

8   Emerson R. West, *Profiles of the Presidents* (Salt Lake City: Deseret Book, 1974), 336.

REX E. LEE

Endurance

Courtesy of L. Tom Perry
Special Collections, Harold B.
Lee Library, Brigham Young
University.

FOR MORE THAN FIFTY YEARS, Rex Lee enjoyed near perfect health. Energetic and active, he ran thirteen marathons, was a father to seven, worked as a lawyer, and became president of Brigham Young University. After he was diagnosed with cancer, his active lifestyle ended. Despite physical limitations, Rex endured his recurring cancer with courage and optimism. Even as assistance was needed for him to carry out ordinary tasks, Rex insisted on preparing a case to be argued before the United States Supreme Court. Though Rex did not live to argue the case, his positive attitude and endurance remains a legacy for family and friends to admire.

Rex Edwin Lee, son of Rex Lee and Mabel Whiting, was born February 27, 1935, in Arizona. About four months before Rex's birth, his father was killed in a hunting accident. Following her husband's death, Rex's mother married Wilford Shumway, who became a father and mentor to Rex and his siblings. Rex attributed his work ethic to working alongside his stepfather in the sawmills at St. Johns, Arizona.[1]

When Rex was a sophomore in high school, he announced to friends that one day he would be a lawyer. After graduating from high school, Rex enrolled in Brigham Young University. At the beginning of his freshman year, he wondered if "a boy from [such a small town] could make it at a big university." He knelt by his bed and prayed for assurance, later writing of his answer: "I felt that I was not alone, that

I had a partner who was interested in me and willing to help. Though my earthly parents were located hundreds of miles to the south, my Heavenly Father was very much there with me."[2]

Rex interrupted his university studies to serve a mission in Mexico. In Mexico City, he met Janet Griffin. After completing an honorable mission, Rex sought out Janet at Brigham Young University and they were married on July 7, 1959, in the Mesa Arizona Temple.

After graduating from the university in 1960, Rex enrolled in the University of Chicago Law School and graduated at the top of his class. He worked as a law clerk for an associate justice of the United States Supreme Court before becoming a partner in a prestigious Phoenix law firm. Within four years of graduating from law school, Rex had argued his first case before the U.S. Supreme Court. Though he called his initial argument "a disaster," it marked the beginning of fifty-nine oral arguments he presented before that court.[3]

In 1972 Rex was invited to be the founding dean of the J. Reuben Clark Jr. Law School. As dean, he was responsible for recruiting both faculty and students. Following his deanship, Rex was named assistant attorney general of the Civil Division in the United States Department of Justice and later solicitor general of the United States. In these positions, he honorably represented the U.S. government before the Supreme Court.[4] Though his legal ability was heralded as superior, Rex faced opposition for holding firm to what he knew was right even when his job was on the line. He clung to the philosophy "It is not enough to do the right thing. You must do the right thing the right way." Though many disagreed with Rex and his standards, among his legal associates he was known as a man of "principle, not mere politics."[5]

After leaving his position as solicitor general, Rex entered private practice and joined the faculty of the J. Reuben Clark Jr. Law School. However, when he was diagnosed with cancer, Rex and his wife moved from Utah to Maryland so that he could receive treatment at the NIH Medical Center. Cancer took a toll on Rex and his family as they anxiously watched him battle the illness. Yet his son Mike recalled, "We never felt deprived because when Dad was home, he was home. He played with us, supported us, taught us, and loved us. . . . He never excused his absence from the family. He was *with* the family."[6] After months of intensive treatment, the cancer went into remission.[7]

Though Rex was well aware that his cancer could return, he accepted the offer to become president of Brigham Young University in 1989. Within a short time of becoming president, Rex was again diagnosed with cancer. Though this cancer was less aggressive than the previous type, it was incurable. As the effects of cancer worsened, Rex kept working and remained positive despite extreme pain. "Probably the most important thing I have learned," said Rex of his fight with cancer, "is the value of life. I clearly recognize how essential it is to appreciate life and the many blessings it offers—not just as we look back in retrospect, but right now, at the very moment that the good things in life are happening to us."[8] Of Rex's work as president of Brigham Young University, President Gordon B. Hinckley said, "[Rex gave] unstintingly of [his] time, [his] talents, [his] means, and [his] heart."[9]

Rex resigned from the university in 1995 and died on March 11, 1996.[10] Reflecting on the day of his death, his wife, Janet, wrote, "We knew that Rex's earthly life was coming to a close. Our seven children joined me in his hospital room as we spoke of favorite shared experiences, of our love for him, and of our faith in God. . . . Then, as efficiently and purposefully as he had lived his life, surrounded by our eternal family and with his hand in mine, Rex left mortality."[11] In honor of Rex Lee, a race is held each year at Brigham Young University to raise funds for cancer research.

1   Rex Lee, Janet Lee, and Jim Bell, *Marathon of Faith* (Salt Lake City: Deseret Book, 1996), 1–2, 35.
2   Ibid., 1–5.
3   Ibid., 5–9; Richard Wilkins, "In Memoriam: Rex E. Lee," Clark Memorandum, Spring 1996, 4.
4   Wilkins, 4; David Binder, "Rex Lee, Former Solicitor General, Dies at 61," *New York Times*, March, 13, 1996.
5   Wilkins, 4.
6   Ibid., 4; Peter B. Gardner, "Brothers in Law," *BYU Magazine*, Spring 2011.
7   Lee, Lee, and Bell, 46, 49–50, 87, 97.
8   Ibid., 164.
9   Greg Hill, "Funeral Speakers Laud Life of Rex E. Lee," *LDS Church News*, March 23, 1996, 4; Wilkins, 5.
10 "Obituaries: Rex Edwin Lee," *Deseret News*, March 13, 1996, A7.
11 Lee, Lee, and Bell, 184.

DON L. LIND

Determination

Courtesy of Don L. Lind.

NASA ASTRONAUT DON LIND UNDERSTANDS the admonition "never give up." When he first tried to enter the astronaut training program, Don recalled, "I applied, and they turned me down, and I appealed, and they turned me down, and I asked for a waiver, and they turned me down, and I wrote to everybody that I could think of. I had written so many times [that] I was on a first-name basis with Jack [G.] Cairl in the Personnel Office."

It was not until a call was issued for a fifth group of astronauts that Don met all of the requirements. When he called the personnel office, he remembers the secretary humorously saying, "Oh yes, Dr. Lind. . . . We were wondering how soon you'd call."[1] After surviving initial cuts, many interviews, and "absolutely unbelievable" physicals, in April 1966 Don was selected from a pool of 3,200 applicants as one of nineteen men to enter the NASA space program.[2] His determination and hard work paid off as Don fulfilled his lifelong dream of becoming an astronaut.

Don L. Lind, son of Leslie and Elizabeth C. Lind, was born May 18, 1930, in Midvale, Utah.[3] In childhood, he developed a love and fascination for the endless universe and began preparing to one day be part of the space program. His father, an electrician, explained to Don the principles of physics, from inclined planes to phases of the moon. His mother, a schoolteacher, taught Don to read before he entered first grade. His parents "instilled in [him] a feeling that [he was] capable of doing anything [he] set [his mind] to do."[4] By age six, Don was climbing trees in a meadow near his home and shaking tree branches to simulate pretend flights through space. The adventures of comic book explorers Buck Rogers, Flash Gordon, and Brick Bradford captivated his imagination.[5]

After spending two years studying physics at the University of Utah, Don served a mission to the New England Mission. After completing an honorable mission, he finished his bachelor's degree in 1953 at the University of Utah. The next year, he enlisted in the Navy, where he learned to land jet airplanes on aircraft carriers and to record cosmic rays while in flight for scientists at the University of California at Berkeley.[6] Don viewed his four-year tour with the Navy as "a great character builder"—a time of "choice spiritual experiences."[7] After completing his tour with the Navy, he earned a doctorate degree in high-energy nuclear physics at the University of California at Berkeley.[8]

After completing this degree, Don worked at the Goddard Space Flight Center in Maryland before accepting employment as a NASA astronaut. For nineteen years, he worked on many different projects for NASA, such as designing and developing experimental gear for satellites and managing the development of experiments for *Apollo 11* that had to be completed in ten minutes or less.[9] He trained to go to the moon, to go on scientific flights to the space station Skylab, and to be in the two-man rescue crew for Skylab if needed. Disappointingly, NASA had to cancel these flights due to government budget cuts, so none of these experiences directly led to his dream of flying in space. This was "an incredible professional disappointment" to him.[10]

The frustration Don experienced in his chosen career path did not spill over to his family life. Don married Kathleen Maughan—a young woman he had met on his mission—on April 1, 1955, in the Salt Lake Temple. They became the parents of seven.[11] Kathleen said of Don, "He has often said that the titles he values most are brother in the gospel, and daddy and husband."[12]

At age fifty-five, Don's lifelong dream of entering space was about to be realized. He is credited with having the longest wait of any NASA astronaut to enter space.[13] But this time was not wasted; he was very busy with other flights, and in his spare time he gave more than two thousand talks at Church youth conferences. On April 29, 1985, Don launched into space on Space Lab 3 and looked at the earth's horizon, seeing about twenty "different layers of intense blue colors . . . and then the blackest, blackest space you can imagine."[14] He noted that when flying in space, "you can hear no family squabbles. You are unaware that there are divorces going on down there and lawsuits and discrimination and poverty. It's a beautiful scene. You see the world as the Lord created it."[15]

For Don, his years of hard work and determination had been worth the reward of seeing earth from space and doing important experiments in the space lab that could not be done on earth. It was a thrill for Don to be a part of the exploration of our corner of the galaxy.

Soon after his once-in-a-lifetime flight, Don left NASA to teach at Utah State University. After nine years of teaching, he retired to serve missions with his wife, Kathleen.[16]

Looking back on his life and the lessons he learned, Don said, "I learned that important things don't come easily or quickly. I learned that persistence pays off. I also learned that you have to be prepared when the opportunity comes."[17]

1   Don L. Lind, oral history, interview by Rebecca Wright, May 27, 2005, Houston, Texas, part of the NASA Johnson Space Center Oral History Project, 4–5.

2   Lind, 5–6; Kathleen Maughan Lind, *Don Lind: Mormon Astronaut* (Salt Lake City: Deseret Book, 1985), 66.

3   Douglas B. Hawthorne, *Men and Women of Space* (San Diego: Univelt, Inc., 1992), 426.

4   Lind, oral history, 1; Lind, *Don Lind: Mormon Astronaut*, 9.

5   Lind, oral history, 1.

6   Hawthorne, *Men and Women of Space*, 427; Lind, oral history, 3.

7   Lind, *Don Lind: Mormon Astronaut*, 46–47, 50.

8   Kristen Moulton, "Utah Astronaut Recalls His Role in Moon Walk," *Salt Lake Tribune*, July 20, 2009.

9   Hawthorne, 427; Lind, oral history, 13.

10   Lind, oral history, 10.

11   Lind, *Don Lind: Mormon Astronaut*, 34, 51.

12   Melvin Leavitt, "Mission Specialist One: The Story of a Latter-day Saint on the Final Frontier," *New Era*, April 1985, http://www.lds.org/new-era/1985/04/mission-specialist-one?lang=eng.

13   Moulton.

14   Lind, oral history, 44.

15   Don L. Lind, "Mine Eyes Have Seen the Glory," *New Era*, July 1983, 36–41.

16 Lind, oral history, 47; Moulton.
17 Don L. Lind, "The Heavens Declare the Glory of God," *Ensign*, Nov. 1985, 37–39.

TRUMAN G. MADSEN
Scholarship

Courtesy of *Deseret News.*

THOUSANDS KNOW THE HISTORY OF Joseph Smith as a man and as a prophet because of Truman Madsen's articulate and passionate teaching. After hearing Truman teach and testify of Joseph Smith, listeners came away with a deeper knowledge, testimony, and love for the Prophet of the Restoration. Truman spent a lifetime studying, testifying, and teaching of the Prophet Joseph Smith and the everlasting truths of the gospel of Jesus Christ.

Truman Grant Madsen, son of Axel A. Madsen and Emily Grant, was born December 13, 1926, in Salt Lake City, Utah. Truman was a grandson of Heber J. Grant, seventh President of The Church of Jesus Christ of Latter-day Saints. "I grew up in the environment [of] Eighth Avenue and A Street [President Grant's home] in Salt Lake City [which] overlooks Temple Square," Truman recalled. "You could say that was our playground. It was." For Truman, seeing the Salt Lake Temple as a child filled him with "a sense of covenant, a sense of belonging, and a sense of, 'I have to be true to that heritage.'" To him, "That was in my childhood. That came with breathing."[1]

From Truman's years at kindergarten to receiving a master's degree, Salt Lake City was his hometown. After graduating from East High School in 1944, he served an honorable mission to the New England states. He earned a bachelor's and master's degree in philosophy at the University of

Utah before marrying Ann Nicholls on June 16, 1953, in the Salt Lake Temple. Truman and Ann became the parents of three and a foster Navajo youth.

On their honeymoon, Truman and Ann received word that Truman had been accepted into the PhD philosophy program at Harvard University in Cambridge, Massachusetts. Knowing in advance that attending the academic setting of Harvard might threaten his testimony of the gospel of Jesus Christ, Truman determined to keep himself grounded in religious matters. To keep that resolve, he hung a picture of the Salt Lake Temple on a wall in their small apartment in Boston, read literature about the Restoration to balance his academic studies, and "accept[ed] and fulfill[ed] whatever calling in the Church his local leaders might assign."2

After graduating from Harvard, Truman accepted a faculty position in philosophy at Brigham Young University. During his thirty-five years as a faculty member, Truman had many academic accolades. For twenty years, he was the Richard L. Evans Professor of Christian Understanding at BYU. He also served as the director of the BYU Jerusalem Center for Near Eastern Studies. Truman is credited with building bridges between Christians, Jews, and Muslims and traveling the world to strengthen those relationships. As a result of Truman's outreach efforts, his close friends included many renowned scholars and leaders of churches all over the world. In addition, Truman was appointed by the president of the United States to serve on the board of the National Endowment for the Humanities.

Truman was a guest professor at Northeastern University, Haifa, and the Graduate Theological Union in Berkeley, California. He sponsored several symposia on comparative religion published as *Reflections on Mormonism*, *The Temple in Antiquity*, and *Chosenness and Covenant in Judaism and Mormonism*. Among his volumes on Mormon thought are *Eternal Man*, *Christ and the Inner Life*, *Four Essays on Love*, *The Highest in Us*, and *The Radiant Life*. Truman was also an editor and a contributor to the *Encyclopedia of Mormonism*. His books, CDs, DVDs, articles, and tapes are still widely circulated. *Joseph Smith Tapes* (1978), *Joseph Smith CDs*, and *On Sacred Ground* continue to be distributed. Through this media and others, Truman took the truths of the gospel to the academic world and to Latter-day Saints in countless firesides and other Church settings throughout the United States and around the world.

Through his years of academic excellence, Truman not only taught and mentored students but remained true to his pledge to fulfill whatever calling in the Church was assigned to him. Truman served as bishop of the BYU 11th Ward, president of the New England Mission, a member of the Sunday School General Board, president of the BYU 5th Stake, and patriarch of the Provo Sharon East Stake. "'He was just so loving and kind' . . . that many young people in his stake knew nothing of his career and simply knew him as a loving patriarch," said Kevin J. Worthen, president of the Sharon East Stake.[3]

Truman died on May 28, 2009, at his home in Provo at age eighty-two, following a yearlong battle with cancer. "Truman Madsen was one of a kind," said Sheri Dew, CEO of Deseret Book Company and executive vice-president of Deseret Management Corporation. "He not only spoke the language of the scholar, but he had the rare capacity to teach even the most complex concepts in a way that meant something to the rest of us."[4] Truman will long be remembered as a much-quoted philosopher, author, speaker, teacher, and biographer.

1   Truman G. Madsen, Wheatley Interview Transcript, Aug. 18, 2008.
2   "Truman G. Madsen Bio," Trumanmadsen.com, shttp://trumanmadsen.com/bio.php.
3   Lynn Arave, "Former BYU Professor Truman Madsen Dies," *Deseret News*, May 29, 2009, http://www.deseretnews.com/article/705307069/Former-BYU-professor-Truman-Madsen-dies.html.
4   Ibid.

KARL G. MAESER
Teaching

Courtesy of L. Tom Perry
Special Collections, Harold B.
Lee Library, Brigham Young
University.

OF KARL MAESER'S TEACHING, James E. Talmage wrote, "His time to him was too valuable to be reckoned in terms of earthly wage. He labored to discharge a trust, which with the fulness of his great soul he believed to have been given him of Heaven. How well he has succeeded let the multitude who have been honored by enrollment among his pupils answer!"[1]

Karl Gottfried Maeser, son of Johann Gottfried Maeser and Christina Fredrica Zocher, was born January 16, 1828, in Vorbrucke, Germany. Karl's father was a talented artist who painted chinaware to support his family. Karl attended parochial and normal schools in Germany, graduating in 1848 with high honors. After graduation, he accepted a teaching position in Dresden, Germany. Three years later, he entered the First District School as a professor, the beginning of many professorial positions for Karl. In 1854 he was appointed director of the Budich Institute Neustadt in Dresden.

After marrying his sweetheart, Anna Mreth, Karl began a serious study of Mormonism. He wrote to the president of the Swiss Italian Mission asking for literature about The Church of Jesus Christ of Latter-day Saints. After reading the literature sent to him, Karl again wrote to the president asking that a missionary be sent to Germany to baptize him. On October 14, 1855, Karl became the first baptized member of the Church in Saxony, Germany. As he came out of the baptismal water, Karl recalled, "I lifted both my hands to heaven and said Father, if what I have done just now is pleasing unto Thee, give me a testimony, and whatever Thou shouldest require of my hands I shall do, even to the laying down of my life for this cause."2 Immediately, a testimony of the gospel came to him with great power and conviction.

In June 1856, Karl and his family left Germany with plans to immigrate to the United States that year. When they reached England, however, Karl was called to be a missionary to that land and to Scotland. After completing his mission, Karl and his family boarded a seafaring vessel bound for the United States, arriving in July 1857 at Philadelphia, "carrying the shrouded body of their baby, Franklin, who had died two days earlier." Before proceeding to Salt Lake City, Karl was asked to serve another mission, this time in the Southern States Mission. While a missionary in Virginia, Karl was "also engaged as a music teacher to prominent families. . . . This made it possible for Karl's family to survive and he moved them to Virginia."3

It was not until 1860 that Karl and his family arrived in the Salt Lake Valley, more than four years after they had left Germany. To support his family in the valley, Karl opened a school. As his teaching abilities became known, Karl was invited to teach at the Salt Lake 20th Ward schoolhouse. Before long, the fame of Karl's teaching spread throughout Salt Lake City, creating a demand for him to speak to large congregations. Brigham Young employed Karl as a private tutor for his children, and Charles W. Nibley said of him, "I could sit in the dust at the feet of that man."4

At the April 1867 general conference, Karl was surprised when his name was read from the pulpit calling him on a three-year mission to Germany and Switzerland. On his mission, Karl visited and shared the gospel with extended family members and served as the president of the mission. In 1870 he returned to the Salt Lake Valley and again taught school in the Salt Lake 20th Ward. He also occupied the chairs of Pedagogy and German at the University of Deseret, and organized the first normal classes in Utah.

In spring 1876, Brigham Young asked Karl to be the principal of Brigham Young Academy in Provo, Utah. In his instructions to Karl for heading the academy, Brigham Young said, "Brother Maeser, I want you to remember that you ought not to teach even the alphabet or the multiplication tables without the Spirit of God. That is all. God bless you. Good-bye."5

On the first day of school in 1876, twenty-nine students attended the academy. Despite this less than auspicious beginning, enrollment mushroomed under Karl's leadership. For sixteen and a half years, he led the faculty and student body to academic heights. One of Karl's students, George Albert Smith, wrote, "'Not only will you be held accountable for what you do and say, but for what you think,' was stamped indelibly on my mind by Dr. Karl G. Maeser when I was twelve years of age and resulted in a determination to entertain only thoughts that were pure and elevating." Another student, Reed Smoot, wrote, "His undoubted faith in God, his unselfish devotion to and knowledge of his profession, his spirit of self sacrifice, together with a powerful personal magnetism, softened with a true love and a personal interest in every student, [were] characteristics that won my love and admiration for Dr. Karl G. Maeser. His words of counsel were words of wisdom and inspired in me a determination to live for a higher life."6

Karl retired from Brigham Young Academy in 1892 to devote his full time and attention to the duties required of the General Superintendent of Church Schools. During the ceremonies surrounding his retirement, Karl "led his students to the new Education Building constructed on the lower campus, built according to the plan he had received in an inspired dream years earlier, and there delivered his farewell address."

Being superintendent of Church schools was not an easy task, for "forty-two Church schools had now been established and the Sunday School and Religion Classes demanded much of his time requiring that he travel extensively throughout the Church to teach the wards and stakes practical religion."7

In May 1898, Brigham Young Academy invited Karl, his friends, and former students to attend a jubilee celebration in his honor. It was reported that Karl was deeply touched by the honor and the display of affection. In 1899, at age seventy-one, Karl was ordained a patriarch. Of patriarchal blessings, he said, "Our patriarchal blessings are paragraphs from the book of our possibilities." Although Karl expressed much happiness in this calling, he said, "If it pleases my Heavenly Father, I'd like to be a teacher in heaven."8

Karl died on February 15, 1901, in Salt Lake City, the day after the last name on his family genealogy record had been finished. In memory of Karl, his students gave one dollar each to purchase a site for a building to be erected in his honor on Temple Hill in Provo. The Karl G. Maeser Building was completed and dedicated in 1912. In 1958 a statue of Karl was placed near the building.

1   *Karl Gottfried Maeser, 1828–1901: A Character Builder—A Teacher—A Founder of the Brigham Young University He Motivated People to Become Their Better Selves. A Brief Biography.*
2   Ibid.
3   Ibid.
4   Ibid.
5   Ibid.
6   Ibid.
7   Ibid.
8   Ibid.

J. WILLARD MARRIOTT JR.
Hard Work

BILL MARRIOTT IS THE FIRST to admit that living in his father's shadow has been a challenge. Though loving and encouraging, his father was a stern man with high expectations. Bill recalls being assigned the chore of shining his father's shoes on Saturday so they would be clean for church on Sunday. One Saturday, Bill spent most of the afternoon scrubbing his father's shoes, knowing they could only pass inspection if they were absolutely pristine. Reflecting on the memory of his father, Bill said, "Perfection was one notch below the desired result."[1] The lessons of hard work and attention to detail Bill learned from his father carried over into other aspects of his life.

J. Willard "Bill" Marriott Jr., son of John Willard Marriott and Alice Sheets, was born March 25, 1932, in Washington, DC. Bill was born at a time of relative prosperity for the Marriott family. In 1927 his parents had opened a nine-stool root-beer stand that had soon expanded into a restaurant chain called the Hot Shoppes. Bill worked in the family business at a young age, with his first job being to staple invoices for the accounting department.[2]

Hard work and leadership were not difficult characteristics to come by in the Marriott family—they were simply a way of life. Bill was a student at the St. Albans Prep School before attending the University of Utah. While attending the university, Bill was an active participant in the Navy ROTC and an employee of the Hot Shoppe in Salt Lake City. In spite of a rigorous daily schedule, Bill earned academic honors and graduated with a degree in banking and finance from the University of Utah in 1954.[3]

During his senior year at the University of Utah, Bill met and dated Donna Garff, a daughter of one of his professors. Though she was dating someone else at the time, Donna recalls "[Bill] was so fun and friendly. We got along well." Bill and Donna were married June 29, 1955, in the Salt Lake Temple. At the time of his marriage, Bill was serving as a supply officer in the Navy.[4]

When Bill and Donna went east, Bill began to work in the corporate office of his family's restaurant business. In 1956, under the hotel name of Marriott, Bill helped to open the company's first hotel in Arlington, Virginia. During the next three decades, Marriott Corporation emerged as an internationally successful hotel and real estate business. In 1972 Bill became CEO of Marriott Corporation and expanded the lodging division, established new brands, and opened vacation time-share operations.

Following his father's death in 1985, Bill became chairman of the board of Marriott Corporation. *Chief Executive* magazine named him "CEO of the Year" in 1988 and *Fortune* magazine included him on the list of "25 Most Fascinating Business Leaders."[5] Bill has a "hands-on" business style and enjoys working directly with lower-management employees. He travels internationally to show his employees that he values "their work enough to check it out." Checking vacant rooms, looking under beds, and peeking in closets to make sure details are not overlooked are his trademark.[6] Bill believes, like his father, that "a successful company puts its employees first." Bill not only listens to Marriott employees but takes their suggestions and concerns seriously and makes changes where necessary.[7]

Much of the praise showered on Bill comes from his ability to run a successful business while making his first priorities his family and faith. In an interview with a *Forbes* writer, Bill told of his greatest personal achievement being his family. "[My wife and I] have great kids," he observed. "We've got four children, 15 grandchildren, and nine great-grandchildren, and we all get along. Everybody's grandchildren are the best, but mine are even better."[8] Bill spends many hours serving in The Church of Jesus Christ of Latter-day Saints. "My life differs in priorities from other men's and this shows in how I spend my free time," he explains. "I have spent a lot of hours doing church work, anywhere from 10 to 20 hours a week, sometimes more in actual service."[9] Among other callings, Bill has served as a bishop in Maryland. He continues his father's tradition of placing a Book of Mormon with the Bible in every Marriott hotel room.

Bill's leadership of the Marriott Corporation has spanned more than sixty years. In 2012 the family business celebrated its eighty-fifth birthday. "It's amazing to think about what has been accomplished since that root-beer stand was opened so many years ago by my mom and dad in 1927," Bill said.[10]

In March 2012, Bill relinquished his role as chief executive officer of the Marriott Corporation and assumed the role of executive chairman. Though his involvement in the corporation is less noticeable, Bill remains a strong voice for maintaining the values upon which the business was founded. Like his father, Bill believes that "success is never final" and is always searching for ways to improve the corporation.

Between business opportunities, Church service, and family activities, Bill tries to balance his responsibilities and commitments. "No company, institution, or individual is likely to actually *find* the perfect balance," he said. "But in searching for it, you might just discover talents you didn't know you possessed, strength you never imagined, and a dream worth spending a lifetime to build. I certainly have."[11]

1   J. W. Marriott Jr. and Kathi Ann Brown, *The Spirit to Serve: Marriott's Way* (New York: HarperCollins, 1997), 14–15.

2   William Arthur Atkins, "J. Willard Marriott Jr. 1932," *Reference for Business: Encyclopedia of Business*, 2nd ed., 1–4, http://www.referenceforbusiness.com/ biography/M-R/Marriott-J-Willard-Jr-1932.html.

3   Atkins, 4; Dale Van Atta, "A Time to Every Purpose," *Ensign*, Oct. 1982, 26.

4   Van Atta; Atkins, 2.

5   Atkins, 6.

6   Marriott and Brown, 5–6.

7   Ibid., 35.

8   Robyn Meredith, "Bill Marriott's Way," The Good Life, *Forbes*, April 4, 2005, http://www.forbes.com/2005/04/12/cz_rm_0412good.html.

9   Linda Brandi Cateura, *Protestant Portraits: People of Many Cultures Bring New Challenges and Startling Lifestyles to an Old Religion* (Lincoln, NE: Writer's Showcase Press, 2002), 164; Van Atta, 4.

10 J. Willard "Bill" Marriott, Jr., "Changes at the Top (Me)," Marriott on the Move (blog), December 13, 2011, http://www.blogs.marriott.com/marriott-on-the-move/2011/12/changes-at-the-top-me.html.

11 Marriott and Brown, 31, 161.

HELVÉCIO MARTINS

Conviction

Courtesy of the Church History
Library, The Church of Jesus
Christ of Latter-day Saints.

IN 1977 PRESIDENT SPENCER W. KIMBALL presided at the cornerstone-laying ceremony of the São Paulo Brazil Temple. Before the ceremony began, President Kimball asked Helvécio Martins, a member of the LDS Relations Committee in Brazil, to participate in the program. Helvécio was dumbfounded by the request and wondered how he could rise to such an occasion. President Kimball hugged him and said, "Brother Martins, what is necessary for you is fidelity. Remain faithful and you will enjoy all the blessings of the gospel."[1] This was a curious comment, for being a Latter-day Saint of African descent in 1977 meant that Helvécio could not hold the priesthood. But President Kimball's prophetic promise and counsel gave him hope and bolstered his dedication to the gospel of Jesus Christ.

Helvécio Martins, son of Honório and Benedita Martins, was born July 27, 1930, in Rio de Janeiro, Brazil. Due to financial hardships in his family, he left school at age eleven to seek full-time employment picking oranges and digging irrigation ditches. This employment was followed by other menial jobs. Helvécio worked hard and by his twenties was able to secure an office position in Rio de Janeiro. In 1953, Rudá Tourinho de Assis was interviewed for a position at the office where Helvécio worked. When Helvécio saw Rudá, he thought to himself, "[She is] the most beautiful woman I [have] ever seen." He recalled, "I loved her from the moment I first saw her."[2] On their first date, Helvécio asked Rudá to marry him. She promptly said no but continued to see him. She encouraged Helvécio to return to school and prepare for a brighter future.

Determined to win her love, Helvécio entered the College of Finance and Economics of Rio de Janeiro. After dating for several years, Helvécio and Rudá were married on December 7, 1956.

Helvécio graduated from the College of Finance and was hired by the well-known government oil company, Petrobras. He later became director of the financial department of Petrobras. Although he and Rudá now had the financial security for which they had hoped, they felt that something was missing in their lives and "concluded that [they] needed to develop a relationship with God and our Savior, Jesus Christ." To fill the void, Helvécio, Rudá, and their young family attended many different Christian churches but did not feel spiritually satisfied. It wasn't until missionaries from The Church of Jesus Christ of Latter-day Saints left a pass-along card at their front door that Helvécio felt something special. When the missionaries stopped by a few evenings later, they stayed until one in the morning telling Helvécio and Rudá about the gospel of Jesus Christ and bearing their testimony of the truth of the Restoration.[3]

"Within five days of meeting the missionaries in 1972," recalled Elder Neil L. Andersen of the Quorum of the Twelve Apostles, "Brother Martins was at the Church, helping and cleaning, serving in whatever way he could."[4] Many were astonished at Helvécio's conversion and baptism on June 2, 1972, but some "expressed [more] surprise that [they] didn't lapse into inactivity" because of not being able to be ordained to the priesthood. Helvécio's response to the skeptics was simple: "We knew the Church was true, and that was all that mattered."[5]

Helvécio followed the counsel of President Spencer W. Kimball and taught his sixteen-year-old son, Marcus, how to perform priesthood ordinances even though neither could hold the priesthood. When Marcus asked his father why he needed to learn the priesthood ordinances, Helvécio said, "[Just] because you're not [ordained to the priesthood] doesn't mean you're [not] going to do as much as you can."[6] Helvécio taught Marcus that "God would somehow have us in a good place in heaven regardless of whether [we] could hold the priesthood in this life."[7]

After the issuance of Official Declaration 2, which announced that all worthy men regardless of race could hold the priesthood, Helvécio and his son were ordained in 1978. They enjoyed the rewards of conviction and faithfulness just as President Kimball had promised. Helvécio and his wife were sealed for all eternity on November 6, 1978, in the São Paulo Brazil Temple.

Through the power of the priesthood, Helvécio blessed a dying child with full health, intervened in a violent situation to restore peace to a family, and served as mission president of the Brazil Fortaleza Mission in 1990.[8] It was President Thomas S. Monson who extended a call to Helvécio to become a member of the Second Quorum of the Seventy, consequently making him the first General Authority of African descent. Of this Church service Helvécio said, "Only in knowing that the Lord had called me not because of my current qualifications, but because of what I could become, was I able to accept this responsibility."[9] As a Seventy, Helvécio often spoke about race issues in the Church. He emphasized that the "kingdom of God on earth is for all of God's children. The requirement of a calling is not skin color, or the size of your bank account, but your personal honor and integrity and your desire to serve."[10]

In 1995 Helvécio became an Emeritus General Authority. He died ten years later on May 14, 2005. In recalling the greatness of Helvécio's life, Elder Neil L. Andersen said, "Once he believed something was right, he had a steel determination to hold firm and never let go."[11] Due to his strong conviction, Helvécio enjoyed the blessings of the Holy Ghost and the power of the priesthood. As President Kimball promised him, Helvécio enjoyed all the blessings of the gospel.

1   Helvécio Martins and Mark Grover, *The Autobiography of Elder Helvécio Martins* (Salt Lake City: Aspen Books, 1994), 65–66.
2   Ibid., 19.
3   Ibid., 40–41.
4   "Elder Helvecio Martins Dies in Brazil at Age 75," *LDS Church News*, May 21, 2005, 6.
5   Martins and Grover, 57.
6   Marcus H. Martins, "All Are (Really) Alike unto God: Personal Reflections on the 1978 Revelation," June 12, 2001, transcript, Lecture on Video BYU-Television.
7   Marcus H. Martins, "Thirty Years after the 'Long-Promised Day': Reflections and Expectations," *BYU Studies* 47, no. 2 (2008): 83.

8   Martins and Grover, 71–72, 111.
9   Ibid., 110.
10   "Elder Helvécio Martins Dies in Brazil at Age 75," 6.
11   Ibid.

ROBERT J. MATTHEWS
Gospel Scholarship

Courtesy of L. Tom Perry
Special Collections, Harold B.
Lee Library, Brigham Young
University.

ROBERT J. MATTHEWS WAS A PROLIFIC gospel scholar, a beloved teacher, and dean of Religious Education at Brigham Young University. His efforts to build relationships between Latter-day Saint scholars and the Reorganized Church of Jesus Christ of Latter Day Saints (RLDS)—now Community of Christ—are among his many important contributions to the kingdom of God. Robert has the distinction of being the first Latter-day Saint permitted by the RLDS Church to view and to handle Joseph Smith's Translation of the Bible.[1] Through Robert's dedicated efforts to expand understanding and appreciation of the standard works of the Church, much of what is known and understood about Joseph Smith's work with the Bible is now accessible to Latter-day Saints throughout the world.[2]

Robert J. Matthews, the youngest son of Roland Matthews and Elsie Gulliver, was born September 12, 1926, in Evanston, Wyoming. "My father was a student of the scriptures, and my mother knew and loved the scriptures, especially the Book of Mormon," recalled Robert. "There never was a big display about it, but it was always characteristic of our home that we had the scriptures, and we talked about them and read them."[3]His parents encouraged Robert to read the Book of Mormon and to find the truths contained within its pages.

As a teenager Robert could often be found studying the Book of Mormon and one day he received a spiritual witness of its truthfulness.

He described the witness as follows:

> A good friend owned an airplane and he wanted me to go up
> for a ride. . . . I didn't think I ought to go on Sunday. . . . I
> remember as I was walking to church seeing the plane circle
> above. An airplane in Evanston [Wyoming] that long ago
> was a rarity. We hardly ever saw one. I went in to church
> and, when I came out, my sister-in-law met me and said,
> "There's been an airplane crash." I said, "Oh?" I asked
> about my friend who owned the plane. She said, "He was
> badly hurt." But another friend was killed. He was sitting
> where I would have been sitting because, when I didn't
> go, the owner got him to go, and he was killed. That was
> a shock. I went home and I thought, "I wonder where he
> is now?" I remembered that somewhere in the Book of
> Mormon it told where a person went at death. I searched
> until I found it [in Alma 40]. . . . I do know that Alma
> became a real hero to me that day.[4]

As a young man Robert was called to be a missionary in the Western States Mission. After completing an honorable mission, he married Shirley Neves and they became the parents of four. Robert pursued his educational interests at Brigham Young University, earning a bachelor's degree in political science, a master's degree in geography, and a doctorate degree in ancient scripture, all from BYU. His doctoral dissertation was titled *A Plainer Translation: Joseph Smith's Translation of the Bible—A History and Commentary.*

Robert began his career as a teacher by teaching seminary and then institute classes in the Church Educational System. He later became a curriculum writer and editor for the educational arm of the Church. In the late 1960s, Robert joined the Department of Religious Education and Ancient Scripture at BYU, eventually becoming department chair of Ancient Scripture and then dean of Religious Education, a position he held for nearly ten years. He retired from teaching in 1992. His colleagues honored him on his eightieth birthday with a collection of essays titled *A Witness for the Restoration: Essays in Honor of Robert J. Matthews.*

Robert became a noted scholar and author, delivering hundreds of lectures on the scriptures in addition to his extensive work with the Joseph Smith Translation. Robert taught thousands of students and delivered scores of lectures at BYU's Education Week, Know Your Religion series, firesides, and in-service classes for instructors in the Church Educational System. He was instrumental in the creation of the 1979 Bible Dictionary, which was printed and bound with the King James Bible by the LDS Church, and he served as a senior editor of the multivolume *Encyclopedia of Mormonism* published by McMillan and Company of New York.

Robert served in many leadership capacities in the Church, including bishop, high councilman, stake president, and a member of the Church Adult Correlation Committee. After retiring from BYU, he was named the first president of the Mount Timpanogos Utah Temple. At the time of his death, Robert was serving as a stake patriarch. He passed away peacefully in the presence of his family on Sunday afternoon, August 30, 2009, after an extended hospitalization following heart surgery.

"He never ever wanted anything in his life to be about him," Robert's son said at his funeral. "Most of the things that he has done in his life I have learned about from other people." Robert's son also remembered his good friend who took a class from his dad when he was in college. One semester his friend got mono and missed a lot of classes. His friend said, "Your dad was the only teacher that called me on the phone and asked how I was doing and who brought me my coursework."[5]

Robert's legacy of goodness, scholarly contributions, and doctrinal and scriptural insights will be acknowledged for decades to come. More than a brilliant gospel scholar, Robert was a beloved family man, a true believer, and a devoted disciple of Christ.

1   Interview by Alexander L. Baugh, "Teacher, Scholar, Administrator: A Conversation with Robert J. Matthews," *Religious Educator* 5, no. 3 (2004), 125, https://ojs.lib.byu.edu/spc/index.php/RelEd/article/view/2017/1953; see also "Noted LDS Scholar, Educator Robert J. Matthews, Dies at 82," *Open Salon*, Aug. 31, 2009, http://open.salon.com/blog/kathy_riordan/2009/08/31/noted_lds_scholar_educator_robert_j_matthews_dies_at_82.

2   Michael De Groote, "Robert J. Matthews, Key to LDS Edition of Bible, Dies," *Deseret News*, Aug. 31, 2009.

3   Baugh, 120.

4   "A Conversation with Robert J. Matthews," *Journal of Book of Mormon Studies* 12, no. 2 (2003), 88–99, http://maxwellinstitute.com/publications/jbms/?vol=12&num=2&id=326&print.

5   De Groote.

NEAL A. MAXWELL
Discipleship

Courtesy of the Church History
Library, The Church of Jesus
Christ of Latter-day Saints.

As a teenager, Neal Maxwell experienced his share of adolescent rejection and disappointment. He lived on the "wrong side of town," his skin broke out in a severe case of acne, and he was too short to be the star basketball player on the famed Granite High basketball team. Adding to his problems, Neal raised pigs and sold them for a profit, which, he said, "didn't endear me to the social life" at the high school. To make matters worse, although he was a voracious reader, he got a D-minus in English. When Neal told his teacher that he deserved a better grade, she stunned him by saying, "Neal, you are capable of doing 'A' work. Until you do, you are going to continue to get a 'D-minus'." He viewed her words as a challenge instead of a threat. Before high school was over, Neal had become the coeditor of the school paper and was beginning to be recognized as a wordsmith.[1]

Neal Ash Maxwell, son of Clarence Maxwell and Emma Ash, was born July 6, 1926, in Salt Lake City, Utah. He was raised in humble circumstances but had the blessing of a loving and nurturing family who taught him the values of charity and hard work. During the Great Depression, Neal lived in a house that lacked even the convenience of indoor plumbing. "Our family coped with that economic comedown in a way that I knew the family and the Church were what really mattered," Neal said. "I was impressed that my folks could humble themselves and not be bitter and not be cynical."[2]

After graduating from high school, Neal joined the U.S. Army and saw action on the front lines in the infantry in Okinawa, Japan, during World War II. During a fierce battle, Neal prayed earnestly for protection as the enemy had located his position and was exploding shells in his direction. At that moment, he thought of his patriarchal blessing, which promised that his life would not be shortened and that he would not be deprived of fulfilling assignments given to him in the premortal world. At that moment, the shelling stopped. Neal later wrote, "I am sure the Lord answered my prayers. . . . The following night they began to pour [more] shells in [on our position], but almost all of them were duds—either the ammunition had gotten wet or they were not exploding in the very thick, oozing mud. . . . I felt preserved, and unworthily so, but have tried to be somewhat faithful to that [patriarchal] promise."[3]

After World War II, Neal served a mission in eastern Canada. His experiences as a soldier and as a missionary convinced him to seek higher education by enrolling at the University of Utah. In 1952 he graduated with high honors in political science from the University of Utah and later earned a master's degree in the same field. Since that time, he has been awarded five honorary doctoral degrees. In 1998 the University of Utah established the Neal A. Maxwell Presidential Endowed Chair in Political Theory, Public Policy, and Public Service.

Neal married Colleen Hinckley on November 22, 1950, in the Salt Lake Temple; they became the parents of four. Of Colleen, Elder Jeffrey R. Holland said, "[She] is a strong woman—quiet, gentle, but strong. I think Neal has loved that. . . . She's a wonderful mix of velvet and steel."[4] To support his growing family, Neal worked as a legislative assistant to Utah Senator Wallace F. Bennett and as chair of the Utah Constitutional Revision Commission. At the University of Utah, he was employed as an assistant public relations director and eventually became executive vice president.

Neal served in many Church callings, including as bishop of a University of Utah student ward, member of the Young Men's Mutual Improvement Association General Board, member of the Adult Correlation Committee, and a regional representative of the Quorum of the Twelve Apostles. In 1970 Neal was appointed commissioner of education for the Church and given responsibility for supervising seminaries, institutes, elementary schools, high schools, and colleges of the Church, including Brigham Young University. On April 4, 1974,

President Spencer W. Kimball called Neal to be an Assistant to the Quorum of the Twelve Apostles. Eighteen months later, as the First Quorum of the Seventy was being organized, Neal was sustained as one of the seven presidents of the Seventy.

On July 21, 1981, as Neal was in a hospital room recovering from surgery and still groggy from the operation, he was visited by President Kimball. Neal thought the prophet's visit was "just part of his usual attentiveness to those who are ill." Although President Kimball was interested in Neal's well-being, he was at the hospital to inform Neal that Gordon B. Hinckley had just been called as an additional counselor in the First Presidency of the Church and that Neal was being called to fill the vacancy in the Quorum of the Twelve Apostles created by Gordon B. Hinckley's appointment.[5]

As an Apostle of the Lord Jesus Christ, Neal became known worldwide for his extensive vocabulary and distinctive writing style, which were always a challenge for those translating his talks into foreign languages. During one particular general conference, translators categorized each talk to be given by a General Authority according to levels of difficulty. All of the talks fit in levels one through four except Neal's, which was categorized as level five.[6] President Gordon B. Hinckley said that Neal spoke "differently from any of the other General Authorities. He just has a unique style all his own. We all admire it."[7] Neal wrote thirty books and numerous articles, including articles on politics and government for national, professional, and local publications.[8]

After fifteen years of dedicated service as a special witness of Jesus Christ, Neal was diagnosed with leukemia. Through the love and prayers of family, friends, and millions of Latter-day Saints across the world, his ministry was extended. Of coping with adversity, Neal said, "Trials and tribulations tend to squeeze the artificiality out of us, leaving the essence of what we really are and clarifying what we *really* yearn for."[9] After an eight-year battle with leukemia, Neal died on July 21, 2004.

Neal A. Maxwell's life was one of devoted discipleship to the Lord Jesus Christ. Biographer Bruce C. Hafen wrote, "It was not lost on him that he had spoken with increasing frequency, it seemed, about what he has called the postgraduate course in the curriculum of discipleship, teaching the Latter-day Saints that God sometimes gives tutorial afflictions to those who have tried hardest to follow Him."[10]

1   Lawrence Flake, *Prophets and Apostles of the Last Dispensation* (Provo, UT: BYU Religious Studies Center, 2001), 525; Bruce C. Hafen, "Adolescent Disappointments and Directions," in *A Disciple's Life* (Salt Lake City: Deseret Book, 2002), 89–92.

2   Flake, 526.

3   "Elder Neal A. Maxwell: A Devoted Life," *New Era*, Sept. 2004.

4   Hafen, 176.

5   Flake, 527; Hafen, 439–440.

6   "Elder Neal A. Maxwell: A Devoted Life."

7   Hafen, 520.

8   "About Elder Neal A. Maxwell," Neal A. Maxwell Institute for Religious Scholarship, http://maxwellinstitute.byu.edu/about-elder-neal-a-maxwell/.

9   Cory Maxwell, ed., *The Neal A. Maxwell Quote Book* (Salt Lake City: Bookcraft, 1997), 9.

10   Hafen, 12.

BRUCE R. MCCONKIE
Scriptural Understanding

JOSEPH F. MCCONKIE SAID OF his father, Bruce, "Having written ten volumes of scriptural commentary (not including *Mormon Doctrine*) that together number almost six thousand pages, Elder McConkie has become a principal source for virtually every search for scriptural understanding made by Church members." Bruce's sermons, which number in the thousands, were always doctrinal and never biographical, narrative, or said in story form.[1]

Bruce Redd McConkie, son of Walter McConkie and Margaret Vivian Redd, was born July 29, 1915, in Ann Arbor, Michigan. One of his earliest memories was of Monticello, Utah, when he was about seven years old: "[I was] awakened in the middle of the night when people from Blanding knocked at our door to get rifles from my father. They were collecting guns to take back to Blanding for the last Indian war fought in America." Another memory was herding "turkeys in the summer, meaning that we drove the turkeys out in groups where the grasshoppers were and let them eat. There would be about 100 to 150 turkeys in the flock."[2]

But more important, as a young boy, Bruce was preparing for his life's mission. He later said, "I have had a testimony of the divinity of this work from my youth."[3] He was baptized on his eighth birthday and ordained a deacon at age eleven by his father. Of his early ordination, Bruce said, "They were not so hide bound as to years and ages and rules in that day."[4]

Bruce attended Bryant Junior High School and then LDS High School in Salt Lake City, graduating at age fifteen. He completed his junior year of college at the University of Utah before leaving on a mission to the eastern states at age nineteen. Before his mission, Bruce dated Amelia Smith, daughter of Joseph Fielding Smith. Of their first date, Amelia said, "He was fun to talk to, pleasant to be with, and friendly with everyone." Amelia wrote to Bruce on his mission and Bruce looked forward to her letters, for he said, "[My] last image of Amelia [was] an image which will stay with me forever. I was in [the] train door and she on the platform. No words were spoken. We just looked. She was so pathetically sad and beautiful. I shall never forget it. She's so wonderful to me and I love her so much." Although Bruce had initially hoped to serve a mission to England, it was in the eastern states that "the Spirit he came to know in the Sacred Grove, in long hours on the Hill Cumorah, and at the place of the Church's organization in Fayette, never left him."5

When Bruce returned to Salt Lake City, he resumed his schooling at the University of Utah and married Amelia on October 13, 1937, in the Salt Lake Temple; Joseph Fielding Smith performed the ceremony. Bruce and Amelia became the parents of nine. Of their children, Bruce said, "I would never brag about my children. If they are worth bragging about, someone else will do it for me."6

After completing his law degree at the University of Utah in 1939, Bruce ranked third out of seventy-five on the Utah bar exam and gained employment as a city attorney before the advent of World War II. In 1942 he was called into active military duty. Because of his ROTC training at the University of Utah, Bruce was commissioned as a second lieutenant. Regarding his military service, it is known that he briefed "governors and mayors on security matters."7 For his service, Bruce was awarded the American Campaign medal.

After his discharge, Bruce became a reporter and an editorial writer for the *Deseret News*. His employment ended abruptly in May 1946 when he was called to the First Council of the Seventy. Of his call to that council, Bruce said, "I felt the calm and joy of the Spirit of the Lord as I have never felt it." He was challenged by President George F. Richards to be "a work horse, rather than a dog under the wheels." He followed President Richards's advice and concluded, "There is nothing in this world that I would rather do than have the privilege of preaching the gospel and of devoting such time and abilities as the Lord may bless me with to the building up of his kingdom."[8]

At leadership sessions of stake conferences, Bruce avoided speaking of administrative procedures and leadership training, opting instead to teach the doctrines of Jesus Christ. It was at this time that Bruce decided to write a book on Latter-day Saint doctrine. His son Joseph wrote, "The first edition of *Mormon Doctrine*, released in 1958, caused something of a stir by directly identifying Roman Catholicism as the 'great and abominable church' spoken of by Nephi in the Book of Mormon. The authoritative tone of the book was also a concern." Of the criticism Bruce faced for writing and publishing *Mormon Doctrine*, Elder Henry D. Moyle said, "I've never seen a man in the Church in my experience that took our criticism—and it was more than criticism—but he took it better than anyone I ever saw."[9] With the guidance of Spencer W. Kimball, Bruce made changes for the second edition of the book.

Bruce presided over the Southern Australia Mission while still serving in the First Council of the Seventy. "Being a mission president is the best job in the world," he said. Bruce believed his greatest accomplishment in Australia was "the saving of delinquent missionaries, and our next greatest [accomplishment] the delegation of authority to local leaders so as to prepare Adelaide and Perth (and Hobart in due course) to become stakes."[10]

In October 1972, President Harold B. Lee invited Bruce to come to his office and said to him, "The Lord and the Brethren have just called you to fill the vacancy in the Council of the Twelve." Bruce replied, "I know. This is no surprise to me. I have known it for some time." During his apostolic years, "there was never any question where Bruce McConkie stood. He could not be numbered among those who tempered or moderated their tone to accommodate the moment. For him, the course was sure, the response certain." Knowing his message would make some uncomfortable, Bruce enjoyed saying, "Tell them to warm up the tar. I'm coming to speak." When Bruce spoke "in the name of Jesus Christ . . . he had no interest in being cute or funny." For example, in his April 1972 general conference address, he said, "I asked the Lord . . . what he would have me say on this occasion and received the distinct and affirmative impression that I should bear my testimony that Jesus Christ is the Son of the living God and that he was crucified for the sins of the world."[11]

As an Apostle, Bruce was heavily involved in the publication of the LDS edition of the King James Bible in 1979 and new editions of the Book of Mormon, the Doctrine and Covenants, and the Pearl of Great Price in 1981. He "supervised all text and reference matters and wrote the chapter headings and summaries for each of the standard works."[12] He compiled the three-volume *Doctrinal New Testament Commentary*, a six-volume series on the Messiah, and *A New Witness for the Articles of Faith*.

In 1983 Bruce was diagnosed with cancer. At the general conference held on April 6, 1985, Bruce gave his final address. In that address, he stated, "I am one of his [Jesus Christ's] witnesses, and in a coming day I shall feel the nail marks in his hands and in his feet and shall wet his feet with my tears. But I shall not know any better then than I know now that he is God's Almighty Son, that he is our Savior and Redeemer, and that salvation comes in and through his atoning blood and in no other way."[13] Bruce died about two weeks later on April 19, 1985, in Salt Lake City at age sixty-nine.

1   Joseph Fielding McConkie, *The Bruce R. McConkie Story: Reflections of a Son* (Salt Lake City: Deseret Book, 2003), 4.
2   McConkie, 62.
3   Bruce R. McConkie, *Conference Report*, Oct. 1951, 149.
4   McConkie, *Bruce R. McConkie Story*, 66.
5   Ibid., 77, 86, 81.
6   Ibid., 245.
7   Ibid., 130.
8   Ibid., 151, 156, 157.
9   Ibid., 182–183.
10 Ibid., 229, 230.
11 Ibid., 264, 267, 322, 327.
12 Ibid., 382.
13 Ibid., 413–414.

DAVID O. MCKAY

Radiant

Courtesy of the Church
Archives, The Church of Jesus
Christ of Latter-day Saints.

DAVID O. MCKAY TAUGHT, "Man radiates what he is, and that radiation affects to a greater or less degree every person who comes within that radiation."[1] Throughout his life, David developed and maintained a personal character of kindness. His unwavering commitment to high ideals, lifelong missionary work, and the gospel of Jesus Christ was observed and revered by Latter-day Saints and those of other faiths around the world.

David O. McKay, son of David McKay and Jennette Evans, was born September 8, 1873, in Huntsville, Utah. David's father set the standard in his home by serving in the Utah senate and as a bishop of the Eden and Huntsville wards.[2] More importantly, he shared with David his abiding testimony of Jesus Christ.[3] David's mother taught him to respect life, be confident, and maintain personal discipline. David said, "My home life from babyhood to the present time has been the greatest factor in giving me moral and spiritual standards and in shaping the course of my life."[4]

At age seven, David became the man of the house when, over the course of a single year, his father left home to fulfill an LDS mission in the British Isles and his sister died. At age twelve, David served as president of his deacons quorum,[5] and at age thirteen he received his patriarchal blessing. "The eye of the Lord is upon thee," said the patriarch in the blessing to David. "The Lord has a work for thee to do."[6]

While still a teenager, David enrolled in Weber Stake Academy and studied the works of Robert Burns and William Shakespeare. He later attended the University of Utah. During his years at the university, he played on the football team, was a popular pianist, and was elected class president. In 1897 he received a teaching certificate and an offer to teach at the Weber Stake Academy.

Before accepting the offer, David fulfilled a mission to Scotland.[7] On his mission, he received an answer to a prayer that assured him that "sincere prayer is answered 'sometime, somewhere.'"[8] Another answer to prayer concerned his feelings for Emma Ray Riggs, a young woman who wrote to him on his mission. Their courtship blossomed after David returned from Scotland, and on January 2, 1901, David and Emma Ray were married in the Salt Lake Temple, becoming the first couple to be married in that temple in the twentieth century.[9]

On April 8, 1906, David was sustained as a member of the Quorum of the Twelve Apostles. In 1918 he was appointed General Sunday School Superintendent. In that position, he introduced many innovations that have become standard practices throughout the Church today, such as the publication of Sunday School manuals. In 1919 he was appointed Church Commissioner of Education and traveled more than sixty-two thousand miles on a worldwide tour of missions and Church schools.[10] While in the Polynesian Islands, David committed to provide education for the Pacific Saints. This commitment was fulfilled thirty-four years later with the completion of the Church College of Hawaii in the remote community of Laie on the Island of Oahu.

On November 3, 1922, David was appointed president of the European Mission. While fulfilling that assignment, he learned the names of more than five hundred missionaries and coined the phrase, "Every member a missionary."[11] In 1934 he began his service as a counselor in the First Presidency of the Church, a position he held for twenty-seven years. During those years, David helped guide Church members through the turbulence of the Great Depression and World War II.[12]

On April 9, 1951, David was sustained as the ninth President of The Church of Jesus Christ of Latter-day Saints. During his presidency, he defined Church principles, extended Church media options in radio and television, approved the building of additional visitors' centers, sent the Mormon Tabernacle Choir on extended tours, and authorized the organization of international stakes. While fulfilling these heavy responsibilities, David continued to radiate goodwill. "What you sincerely in your heart think of Christ will determine what you are, will largely determine what your acts will be," he taught.[13]

Family was another key touchstone of his presidency. As he spoke of the importance of family, David advised, "No other success can compensate for failure in the home." His was an urgent call for parents to teach their children about character and integrity.[14] "There is no power so potent," he taught, "no power so effective in influencing the lives of others, as *Personality*. It is not just an influence, but many times is an inspiration. . . . *Each of us can become an inspiration to others.*"[15]

David died in his ninety-sixth year on January 18, 1970, the same day the five hundredth stake of the Church was organized. His was a life of inspiration and love to millions throughout the world.

1   *Conference Report*, April 1950, 34.

2   Francis M. Gibbons, *David O. McKay: Apostle to the World, Prophet of God* (Salt Lake City: Deseret Book, 1986), 15; Richard L. Evans, "David O. McKay: Portrait of a President," *The Improvement Era* 54, June 1951, 401.

3   David O. McKay, "Peace through the Gospel of Christ," *The Improvement Era* 24, March 1921, 405–406.

4   Jeanette McKay Morrell, "Boyhood of President David O. McKay," *Relief Society Magazine* 40, no. 10, (Oct. 1953): 656, 656; Richard O. Cowan, *The Latter-day Saint Century* (Salt Lake City: Bookcraft, 1999), 158; Terry W. Call, "David O. McKay," *Deseret News Church Section*, Sept. 25, 1993, 10.

5   Leland H. Monson, "David O. McKay Was a Deacon, Too," *The Instructor*, Sept. 1962, 298–299.

6   Jeanette McKay Morrell, *Highlights in the Life of President David O. McKay* (Salt Lake City, Utah: Deseret Book, 1966), 38.

7   Morrell, *Highlights*, 50.

8   Preston Nibley, *Presidents of the Church* (Salt Lake City: Deseret Book, 1971), 314–315.

9   "Tribute to Emma Ray McKay," International Society of the Daughters of the Utah Pioneers (Salt Lake City, Utah: International Society of the Daughters of the Utah Pioneers).

10 "David O. McKay," International Society of the Daughters of the Utah Pioneers (Salt Lake City, Utah: International Society of the Daughters of the Utah Pioneers).

11 "Tribute to Emma Ray McKay."

12 Richard O. Cowan, *Church in the Twentieth Century* (Salt Lake City: Deseret Book, 1985), 237.

13 David O. McKay, *Conference Report*, April 1951, 93.

14 David O. McKay, *Conference Report*, April 1935, 115–116.

15   David O. McKay, "The Radiation and Influence of a Powerful Personality," *The Instructor*, Aug. 1969, 265.

DALE MURPHY
Gentlemanly

Courtesy of Whitney and Matt
Dellinger.

DALE MURPHY PLAYED EIGHTEEN SEASONS in the majors and became one
of baseball's great players and true gentlemen of the game. Recalling that
he had only one hit in his first season of Little League, he said, "If you
could have seen me play my first season of baseball, you would have never
guessed that I would eventually play in the Major Leagues."[1] But Dale has
left his mark on more than just baseball. In 2005 he started the nonprofit
iWontCheat Foundation to promote ethical behavior and to deter steroid
use and cheating in youth athletics. Since 2008, players at the Little
League World Series have worn the embroidered "I WON'T CHEAT!"
patch above their Little League baseball logo on the left sleeves of their
jerseys.

Dale Murphy, son of Charles and Betty Murphy, was born March
12, 1956, in Portland, Oregon. Dale played baseball and other sports in
high school and was chosen in the first round of the 1974 major league
draft by the Atlanta Braves. He had a long and successful career with the
Atlanta Braves, Philadelphia Phillies, and Colorado Rockies. He won
back-to-back MVP awards in 1982 and 1983 (he is one of only four
outfielders in major league history with consecutive MVP years) and
was a seven-time all-star, a five-time Gold Glove winner, and a four-time
Silver Slugger. Dale also led the major leagues in home runs and runs
batted in from 1981 to 1990. He retired from baseball in 1993, ending

his career with 398 home runs and a .265 lifetime batting average. Dale was one of the most beloved athletes to ever play with the Atlanta Braves. His number (3) was retired by the Braves and now hangs in Turner Field.[2]

It was Dale's teammate, Barry Bonnell, who introduced him to The Church of Jesus Christ of Latter-day Saints. They were playing together on the Braves' farm team when Barry began to ask Dale questions about the importance of baptism and eternal life—gospel concepts that Dale knew little about. "We had many long discussions and then got together with the missionaries," Dale said. "And after receiving the lessons, I knew I wanted to be part of it. Barry baptized me after the 1975 season."[3]

Dale was once asked what he would say if he were invited to give a short "last lecture." Without hesitation, he replied,

> First, I'd talk about my testimony. It wouldn't matter if I was talking to people inside or outside the Church. I'd bear my testimony that the gospel has been restored, that there's a prophet on the earth, that the Savior lives. I would bear my testimony because it is the most precious thing I have—everything from the Hill Cumorah to temple marriage to my family. I would let them know that work is important—nothing is going to come easy— and that circumstances in life do not dictate happiness. Happiness is an attitude. And the best attitude and philosophy of life you can have is found in the gospel of Jesus Christ. I guess I should say something about baseball. I would counsel young people to have fun playing the game. Some days you're going to get a hit, and some days you're going to strike out. Don't let your success days or your failure days, either one, determine your attitude toward the game.[4]

In 1987, *Sports Illustrated* named Dale one of several "Sportsmen of the Year." Dale has received many humanitarian awards, including Who Cares the Most from President Ronald Reagan. He also received the Bart Giamatti Award, the Lou Gehrig Award (given to the player who best fits the image and character of Lou Gehrig on and off the field), and the Roberto Clemente Award (given annually to one major league player in recognition of his character and charitable contributions). Following his retirement from the majors, Dale was inducted into the World Sports Humanitarian Hall of Fame.[5]

Since 2012 Dale has been a guest analyst for the Atlanta Braves television broadcasts. He is in demand as a speaker around the country. Dale divides his time between family, church, and charity work. He and his wife, Nancy, whom he married in the Salt Lake Temple on October 29, 1979, are the parents of seven sons and one daughter. Dale has had many callings in the Church, including president of the Massachusetts Boston Mission from 1997 to 2000.

As to advice for young athletes who enjoy participating in sports, Dale said, "Focus more on the type of person you become through sports than the number of games you win or the trophies you receive. What really matters is your character, not your batting average; your integrity, not your shooting percentage. Do not give the greatest attention to the things which truly do not matter most."

1   Dale Murphy, *The Scouting Report—Youth Athletics* (Dale Murphy, 2007), 13.
2   "Dale Murphy: 3," Dalemurphy.com, http://dalemurphy.com/bio.php.
3   Heber G. Wolsey, "Dale Murphy—MVP," *Ensign*, April 1985, 58.
4   Wolsey.
5   Dalemurphy.com

DAVID NEELEMAN
Innovative

Courtesy of *Deseret News.*

YOUNG DAVID NEELEMAN WAS DESCRIBED as "a handful" and a "window gazer who constantly fell behind on his lessons."[1] Although he was energetic and creative, David did not do well in school. There were times when he wondered if he would make anything of his future. Much of David's hyperactivity has since been attributed to an attention deficit disorder (ADD) that was not diagnosed until he was in his thirties. As an adult, David dealt with entrepreneurial failure, unemployment, and feelings of self-doubt. In spite of these obstacles—or maybe because of them—David has emerged as one of the foremost businessmen in the airline industry. An energetic man with a "bubbling entrepreneurial spirit," much of David's success comes from persevering through trials and turning weaknesses into strengths.[2]

David Neeleman, son of Gary Neeleman and Rose Lewis, was born October 16, 1959, in Sao Paulo, Brazil. David was reared in Brazil while his father worked as the bureau chief for the Latin American United Press International. When David was young he was recognized as having a short attention span, but he was "full of ideas, very, very active, and thinking outside the box all of the time." At age nine, when the family was residing in Utah, David worked at his grandfather's grocery store, where he learned the value of customer satisfaction and hard work.[3]

David graduated from high school with respectable grades and enrolled in the University of Utah to study accounting. He interrupted his university studies to accept a mission call to Rio de Janeiro, Brazil. His mission service to some of the poorest areas of Brazil made a lasting impression. "I saw that the poor and humble were the most wonderful, sweet people," he said. "I realized that everybody is equal and you should treat people the same [and] with respect." Besides gaining love and respect for others on his mission, David became fluent in Portuguese and discovered that he had an unusual knack for sales. Reflecting on his mission experience, David recalled, "It was really the first time I felt like I had some talent."[4]

After completing an honorable mission, David again enrolled at the University of Utah. As a sophomore, he started his first business—a travel agency that packaged inexpensive condos with low airfare rates to Hawaii. As his business flourished, David ended his university studies to focus on the entrepreneurial venture. When his small business collapsed, he assumed that any career for him in the travel industry was over. Such was not the case. In searching for a new job, David found employment with Morris Travel, a successful Utah-based travel agency. Recalling her business relationship with David, June Morris, founder of Morris Travel, said, "David is like a sponge. He listens, he reads, he talks to people, he just soaks everything up. He's very creative coming up with all his ideas. . . . He was just an amazing young fellow."[5]

As an employee David looked for ways to make Morris Travel and travel in general more efficient and profitable. He played a significant role in creating major advances in the airline industry, including e-ticketing. His innovative approaches directly led to the launch of Morris Air, a low-fare charter operation that sold for $129 million to Southwest Airlines in 1994.[6] With that sale, David joined the Southwest team. He was fired five months later due to eccentricity and revolutionary methods.

Over the next five years, David pursued other travel ventures. He cofounded WestJet, a Canadian airline that grew to be one of Canada's leading airlines, and sold his other aviation project (the e-ticketing system Open Skies) to Hewlett-Packard for $20 million. In 2000 he launched his biggest business venture ever, JetBlue Airways. Due to technological advances such as live cable television and David's insistence on customer and employee satisfaction, JetBlue became an instant success. David donated his salary to a fund for JetBlue crew members who had fallen on hard times. He spent time with flight crews, wanting them "to know that their jobs [were] vital and important to the success of JetBlue." He was not above crawling under the seats of a plane to pick up trash. "I've heard it said that a fish stinks from the head, but I guess it also smells good from the head," David joked. "I'm just trying to be as good an example as I possibly can."[7]

David relinquished his position as CEO of JetBlue in 2007 due to an ice storm that stranded hundreds of passengers.[8] The setback was difficult and perhaps added to what he calls his "inferiority complex." But David did not lose momentum. He started another aviation success—Azul Airlines in Brazil. Once again, he surprised the airline industry with his ability to provide great service at low costs.[9]

Remarkably, David has never put his business ventures above his family responsibilities. "The accolades and notoriety that come with his success and his position could easily have him off on cloud nine," said his wife, Vicky. "But around here he's just Dad" to nine children. In spite of their financial success, David and Vicky try to teach their children the value of hard work and family responsibility. "I'm confident the Lord values the family above any other institution," David said.[10]

Though David has often faced feelings of inadequacy and self-doubt, he has not let such feelings hold him back. He even claims that ADD has been the key to his entrepreneurial success. His need to prove himself has given him the drive to succeed where others might not have even tried. Nearly everything about David suggests an innovative spirit, even the effect of the Church on the way he does business. He explains, "I try to live my life the same whether I'm at work or at home or wherever. . . . I feel strongly about being a good example as a businessman and doing things right. I want people to see me . . . as someone who cares deeply about others and is a faithful member of The Church of Jesus Christ of Latter-day Saints."[11]

---

1   James Wynbrant, *Flying High: How JetBlue Founder and CEO David Neeleman Beats the Competition . . . Even in the World's Most Turbulent Industry* (Hoboken, NJ: John Wiley and Sons, Inc., 2004), 10.

2   Ibid., 10–13; Juan Forero, "In Brazil, New Airline Aims to Attract Nation's Growing Middle Class," *Washington Post*, Nov. 23, 2010, http://www.washingtonpost.com/wp-dyn/content/article/2010/11/03/AR2010110304908_3.html?sid=ST2010111905834.

3   Wynbrant, 7–12.
4   Ibid., 13–15.
5   Ibid., 26–27, 33.
6   Ibid., 3–5, 35, 48, 52–53, 55, 60–62.
7   Ibid., 2, 66, 78, 80, 83, 121–125, 146, 221, 155–156.
8   Jeff Bailey, "JetBlue's Leader is Giving Up Chief Executive Title," *The New York Times*, May 11, 2007, http://www.nytimes.com/2007/05/11/business/11air. html?_r=1.
9   Jeff Benedict, *The Mormon Way of Doing Business: Leadership and Success through Faith and Family* (New York: Warner Business Books, 2007), xiii.
10   Benedict, 55–56, 87, 136, 145.
11   Benedict, xiv, 37.

HUGH NIBLEY
Defender of Faith

Courtesy of the Church History
Library, The Church of Jesus
Christ of Latter-day Saints.

OF HUGH NIBLEY, LOUIS MIDGLEY, a Brigham Young University professor
of political science, said, "With the passing of B. H. Roberts, Nibley more
than anyone else has assumed the role of defender of the faith and the
Saints." Hugh defended the Book of Mormon against so-called "Cultural
Mormonism," or those who wanted Church leaders to deemphasize the
significance of the scriptures, and "Sectarian Mormonism," a movement
to align various American middle-class values with gospel principles. As to
the effect of his apologetic defense of the Book of Mormon and his call to
repentance for adopting worldly evidence of God's laws, Hugh observed,
"I have long since learned that my most brash out-speaking leaves the
Philistines untouched, because nobody ever thinks any of the criticism
applies to him, while gleefully recognizing its delicious pertinence to his
neighbors."[1]

Hugh Winder Sloan Nibley, son of El and Sloanie Nibley, was
born March 27, 1910, in Portland, Oregon. When Hugh was eleven
years old, he and his family moved to Los Angeles, California. By then
he knew that there were important matters awaiting his attention.
His grandfather, Charles W. Nibley, wrote to Hugh on his fourteenth
birthday, "We all think you are gifted and talented above many of your
fellows. The Lord has blessed you greatly. . . . Surely you are favored of
the Lord. You must use your ability in His service in all humility and

faithfulness. Do not ever allow yourself to get big-headed. Always be humble, always be prayerful. Do not forget to pray."[2]

At seventeen, Hugh graduated from Los Angeles High School and was "studying hard all the time for his mission." His father said, "[Hugh] is most excellently equipt [sic] and prepared." On November 9, 1927, Hugh was set apart for his mission to Germany by Elder Melvin J. Ballard, who told him, "Tell these people that [unless they repent] they will be destroyed by fire from heaven." On his mission, Hugh received special notice from Elder John A. Widtsoe, who thought Hugh had "all the ear marks of a genius."[3]

After his mission, Hugh rejoined his family in California and enrolled in the University of California at Los Angeles. Hugh graduated *summa cum laude* in history from the university in 1934. From 1934 to 1938 he attended graduate school at Berkeley. He graduated with a PhD after completing a dissertation entitled *Roman Games as a Survival of an Archaic Year Cult.*

Following graduate school, Hugh took various teaching positions, including as a lecturer of history, social philosophy, Greek, and German at Claremont College; a lecturer of modern European history at Pomona College; and a lecturer of humanities at Scripps College. Hugh wrote, "Certainly I can never remain at ease in the stifling atmosphere of the American College, an institution which I hope with all my heart will go the way of the buffalo and the spittoon. It already survives only as a curio." Of his attendance at academic conventions, Hugh wrote, "The one solid comfort I get out of such conferences is the reassurance that if I am a fool there are bigger ones."[4]

In 1942, Hugh enlisted in the U.S. Army and was sent to England with other American soldiers. In preparation for the Normandy invasion, Hugh was asked to compile a list of German general officers and to conduct training sessions on German strategies. On June 6, 1944, he drove a jeep onto Utah Beach during the Allied invasion of France. Letters to his family show the significance of the Book of Mormon at this time to Hugh: "When I can snatch a moment or two off it is devoted to a single engrossing item: at this late date I have discovered the Book of Mormon, and live in a state of perpetual excitement—that marvelous production throws everything done in our age completely into the shadows."[5]

At the end of World War II, Elder Widtsoe asked BYU President Howard McDonald to consider hiring Hugh as a faculty member. Hugh's publication *No, Ma'am, That's Not History: A Brief Review of*

Mrs. Brodie's Reluctant Vindication of the Prophet She Seeks to Expose made President McDonald's decision easy, for in this publication Hugh established himself as a defender of the faith. His only concern was that Hugh was a thirty-six-year-old bachelor. When Elder Widtsoe admonished Hugh to marry, Hugh told him to "work it out with the Lord and 'I would marry the first girl I met at BYU.'" Hugh met Phyllis Draper, a French major and cellist at BYU, and had a whirlwind courtship. Hugh said, "That's why it's called BYWoo, I guess."[6] They were married on September 18, 1946, in the Salt Lake Temple. To their union were born nine children.

Hugh supported his family by teaching Greek, Russian, early Christian history, and world religions at BYU. On his curriculum vitae, he listed a knowledge and understanding of German, French, Arabic, Spanish, Latin, Greek, Russian, Dutch, Italian, Old Norse, Hebrew, Coptic, and Egyptian. In 1957, President David O. McKay invited Hugh to write a manual on the Book of Mormon for Melchizedek Priesthood lessons. In response, Hugh wrote *An Approach to the Book of Mormon*, hearkening back to a journal entry he wrote as a young man, which stated, "The Book of Mormon is giving me greater joy than anything ever did."[7] He later wrote *Lehi in the Desert, Since Cumorah*, and many articles on the Book of Mormon that have been republished by the Foundation for Ancient Research and Mormon Studies.

In 1967, at age fifty-seven, Hugh was ordained a high priest. Eight years later, he retired from BYU but maintained an office and taught a class each semester, teaching his last class in 1994. In his later years, Hugh attacked Sectarian Mormonism, complaining mightily against Latter-day Saints' obsession with wealth. Hugh despised the notion that bigger was better and that more possessions equated with God's love. Elder Neal A. Maxwell saw Hugh's commentary as "a reflection of his deepened discipleship" and felt that Hugh was "so focused on the things that matter, and [was so] spiritually submissive, that he's impatient with mediocrity; he's impatient with irrelevance." Elder Maxwell expressed his gratitude that "the Lord didn't put Hugh in some monastery in the middle ages to plow through the parchments, when, instead, he has been such a rich part of the Restoration's forward movement."[8]

John W. Welch, founder of the Foundation for Ancient Research and Mormon Studies, also recognized Hugh's contribution and said, "We are warned but reassured [by Hugh's works]."[9]

Hugh died at age ninety-four on February 24, 2005, in Provo, Utah. In honor of his memory, the Ancient Studies Reading Room in the Harold B. Lee Library on the BYU campus was renamed the Hugh Nibley Ancient Studies Reading Room.

1   Boyd Jay Petersen, *Hugh Nibley: A Consecrated Life* (Draper, Utah: Greg Kofford Books, 2002), 119, 45, 46.
2   Ibid., 408.
3   Ibid., 85, 87, 86.
4   Ibid., 164.
5   Ibid., 247.
6   Ibid., 231–232, 234.
7   Ibid., 247.
8   Ibid., 44, 408.
9   Ibid., 245.

ROBERT C. OAKS
Zeal

WHEN ROBERT OAKS WAS A FRESHMAN at Brigham Young University, he was recruited to sing and dance in an upcoming talent show. After a few rehearsals, the dance director, Janie Thompson, said to him, "Bob, I like your enthusiasm, but you are not much of a singer." Robert never excelled as a singer, but he has excelled in life, taking to heart the counsel to be zealous as taught in Revelation 3:19.[1] His zeal for the gospel and freedom has been the hallmark of his life.

Robert Charles Oaks, son of Charles E. and Ann Bonnett Oaks, was born February 14, 1936, in Los Angeles, California. Robert grew to manhood in Provo, Utah, where he found joy in the gospel of Jesus Christ and many opportunities to serve others.

After graduating from Brigham Young High School, Robert enrolled in Brigham Young University. At the university he had one goal—playing on the football and basketball teams. When he was cut in the first round of tryouts from both teams, Robert refused to accept the fact that his athletic career was over. A year later, he transferred to the United States Air Force Academy, where he made the football team and competed in collegiate sports until an injury put him on the sidelines. The injury did not prevent Robert from achieving his next goal—flying airplanes.[2] Robert became very proficient in flying planes and graduated with a bachelor's degree in June 1959. That same month, he married his childhood sweetheart, Gloria Mae

Unger—a young woman he had dated for five years—in the Salt Lake Temple.

Robert and Gloria made their first home in Oklahoma, where Robert completed his flight training at Vance Air Force Base. Flying was not always easy for Robert. One of his inspection flights went so poorly "that the instructor pilot . . . said in disgust, 'If we are going to get him down, we will have to shoot him down.'"[3] Nevertheless, Robert refused to give up. He trained harder, and with much persistence he earned his pilot wings in September 1960. He continued to pursue his educational goals and graduated from Ohio State University with a master's degree in business administration in 1967. In 1974, he graduated from a one-year program at the Naval War College.

Robert spent thirty-five years in the military and flew 188 combat missions in Southeast Asia. He received more than twenty military honors and awards for his command of the Air Force squadrons and for leading divisions at the headquarters of the United States Air Force.[4] Robert advanced in rank to a four-star general in 1990.

During his years with the air force, Robert and Gloria moved thirty times with their six children and lived in countries all over the world. In each country, Robert not only attended Church meetings but found ways to give meaningful service to others and never lost sight of the covenants he had made with God. He admitted that "obedience is not always easy. It demands that you humble yourself and acknowledge that someone knows more than you and that there is a better path to follow than the one you might blaze for yourself."[5]

Drawing on his Air Force experiences, Robert enjoys speaking of the parallels between being a pilot and trusting in God:

> I still recall the first rule of instrument flying from my days in pilot training. When you're piloting an aircraft in the clear, cloudless air, you rely on your physical sense of seeing and feeling to maintain your equilibrium. . . . But after you enter the clouds, your physical sense can easily fool you. . . . Hundreds of airplanes and thousands of lives have been lost because pilots have become disoriented while flying in the clouds, unable to see the horizon or their final destination. . . .
>
> The problem is complex, but the solution is simple. The first and most important rule for flying in cloudy weather is to trust your instruments. Believe and follow

their indications even though your physical senses shout something different in your ears.[6]

Robert also said, "By obedience to God's instructions we can take full advantage of his limitless vision and boundless love and thereby avoid many of life's inevitable pitfalls."[7] By trusting in the Lord and not in his own limited vision of life, Robert has been able to accomplish much in his lifetime.

In 2000, Robert was sustained as a member of the Second Quorum of the Seventy. His first assignment was to preside over the Africa Southeast Area. Four years later, Robert was called to the presidency of the Quorums of the Seventy. From 2007 to 2009, he presided over the Europe Central Area. At age seventy-five, as a released General Authority, Robert was appointed chairman of the board for Amendment II, Inc., a company that develops RynoHide™ —"defensive tactical armor material."[8]

Robert understands that God loves him and is making him a better person by giving him experiences to prove his commitment. This knowledge provides an opportunity for him to overcome personal trials, dedicate his life to God and country, learn from mistakes, and to set and accomplish future goals.

1   Robert C. Oaks, "Understand Who You Are," March 21, 2006, *BYU Speeches,* http://speeches.byu.edu/?act=viewitem&id=1534.

2   Robert C. Oaks, *Believe! Helping Youth Trust in the Lord* (Salt Lake City: Deseret Book, 2003), 2–4.

3   Oaks, 3–4.

4   "General Robert C. Oaks," United States Air Force, Aug. 31, 1994, http://www.af.mil/AboutUs/Biographies/Display/tabid/225/Article/106098/general-robert-c-oaks.aspx.

5   Oaks, 64.

6   Ibid., 50–51.

7   Ibid., 64.

8   John Fierro, "Amendment II Names General Robert C. Oaks as Chairman of the Board to Progress the Company's Vision of RynoHide™," PRWeb, Jan. 19, 2012, http://www.prweb.com/releases/2012/1/prweb9119328.htm.

Donny Osmond
Lifting Others

Courtesy of the Church History
Library, The Church of Jesus
Christ of Latter-day Saints.

FOR MORE THAN FIVE DECADES, entertainer Donny Osmond has been one
of the most widely known Mormons in the world. But he has done more
than sing and dance—he has made a difference in the lives of those he
entertains by not being afraid to share his testimony of the gospel of Jesus
Christ. Donny is an acclaimed performer, a compassionate humanitarian,
a man of abiding faith, and, "most importantly a good son, husband, and
father."[1]

Donald Clark Osmond, the seventh son of George and Olive Osmond's
family of nine children, was born December 9, 1957, in Ogden, Utah.
Donny was raised in an active Latter-day Saint home, where he was taught
principles of the restored gospel, the value of hard work, and the importance
of family cohesiveness. "Our religious beliefs influenced everything in our
lives," Donny said. "We grew up knowing that life in this world passes in
the blink of an eye."[2] Donny and his extended family have tried to live by
the guiding principle presented by President David O. McKay: "No other
success can compensate for failure in the home."

Donny's showbiz journey began at age five when he made his television
debut on the *Andy Williams Show* with his brothers Alan, Jay, Merrill, and
Wayne. The Osmonds (also known as "The Osmond Brothers," which
later included youngest brother, Jimmy) were an instant success and soon
became regulars on the *Andy Williams Show*.

By the early 1970s, when Donny was just a teenager, he and his brothers had become an entertainment phenomenon in the United States and the United Kingdom. The Osmond Brothers released hit after hit, taking the United Kingdom by storm and sparking a wave of fandom that became affectionately known as "Osmondmania." When Donny was fourteen, his first debut of a single recording, "Sweet & Innocent," made the Top 10 Hit Parade. He later released hits like "Go Away Little Girl" and "Puppy Love," which sold millions worldwide. With his sister, Marie, Donny sang duets that included more Top 10 hits like "I'm Leaving It All Up To You." Donny and Marie went on to host their own television variety show, *The Donny & Marie Show.*

In his five decades of show business, Donny has sold more than 100 million records and has received thirty-three gold records, eighteen before he was thirteen years old. He also starred in the Broadway production of *Beauty and the Beast* and played the leading role in the North American production of *Joseph and the Amazing Technicolor Dreamcoat*, in which he gave more than two thousand performances. During the 2002 Salt Lake Winter Olympics, Donny, Marie, and their father, George, participated in the official Olympic Torch Relay. Donny and Marie also performed at the closing ceremonies of the Olympics. In 2009, Donny won the ninth season of *Dancing with the Stars.*

Donny is regarded as a living legend in the entertainment world. He is a singer, musician, actor, dancer, radio personality, talk and game show host, record producer, author, and a former teen idol. After all these years in showbiz and the ups and downs that go with being in the entertainment world, Donny knows who he is and what his most important values and priorities are. He has generated millions of dollars for charitable organizations such as the Make-A-Wish Foundation, the Children's Miracle Network, and The One Heart Foundation. In his bestselling book *Life Is Just What You Make It*, Donny reveals his battle with social phobia, a common yet debilitating anxiety disorder that threatened not only his career, but his life. His humility and authenticity in revealing his struggle with this anxiety disorder has helped countless others who face similar struggles.

Donny married Debbie Glenn in the Salt Lake Temple on May 8, 1978, which he describes as "the most joyous day of my life."[3] Donny and Debbie are the parents of five. Reflecting on his marriage, Donny writes, "When I think about how fortunate Debbie and I have been to share the marriage and the family that we have today, I have to credit our families and our faith. . . . That didn't mean that living by our teachings was always easy, and my career certainly put a lot more temptations in my way than I would have faced otherwise. We believe that one important aspect of eternal marriage is the sacred nature of the relationship between husband and wife."[4]

It has been said that the ultimate measure of a man is not where he stands in moments of comfort and convenience but where he stands in times of challenge and tribulation. Donny has experienced both high peaks of success and low valleys and hard times. He credits much of his success and resilience to his parents, George and Olive Osmond, who taught him to live the gospel with devotion, to work hard, and to aim high. Through it all, Donny holds fast to his faith, his principles, and his family values.[5]

1   See "Donny: Through the Years," Donny.com, http://donny.com/donny/.
2   Donny Osmond, *Life Is Just What You Make It—My Story So Far* (New York: Hyperion, 2000), 13–14.
3   Osmond, 182.
4   Ibid., 180.
5   "Donny: Through the Years."

JEROLD OTTLEY
Love of Music

Courtesy of The Mormon
Tabernacle Choir, The Church of
Jesus Christ of Latter-day Saints.

FOR A QUARTER OF A CENTURY, Jerold Ottley (known to most as Jerry) led the Mormon Tabernacle Choir in performing nearly 1300 weekly radio and television broadcasts of *Music and the Spoken Word.* Jerold conducted the choir on more than twenty-two major concert tours throughout the United States and to nations in Europe, Asia, South America, and the Pacific. Additionally, he directed the choir as it sang more than thirty commercial recordings for major labels, including CBS Masterworks, London Decca, Bonneville Classics, and Hallmark Cards. Jerold will long be remembered as the beloved conductor of the Mormon Tabernacle Choir for twenty-five years and for sharing his musical talents in an effort to reach and inspire millions around the world.

Jerold Don Ottley was born April 7, 1934, in Salt Lake City, Utah. As a child, Jerold learned to play the piano and trombone. His interest in music extended into his teenage years when his family moved to New Zealand, where his father was called to serve a mission for The Church of Jesus Christ of Latter-day Saints. From 1953 to 1955, Jerold followed his father's example and accepted a call to also serve a mission in New Zealand.

After completing an honorable mission, Jerold returned to the United States and enrolled in Brigham Young University to study music. Before his freshman year at BYU, Jerold met JoAnn South, a vocal student at the University of Utah. They were married one year later. Before Jerold completed his studies in music, he served his country in the United States Army from 1957 to 1959.[1] After his military stint, Jerold returned to BYU and earned his bachelor's degree in music education in 1961.

For the next seven years, Jerold taught music in the Salt Lake City public schools. After receiving a master's degree in choral conducting from the University of Utah in 1967, he and his wife, JoAnn, who had become a noted soprano, were awarded Fulbright grants to study at the Academy of Music in Cologne, West Germany. After completing their studies in Germany, the Ottleys moved to Oregon, where Jerold pursued a doctorate at the University of Oregon. After Jerold's graduation, the Ottleys returned to Salt Lake City and Jerold joined the music faculty at the University of Utah, eventually becoming the assistant chair of the music department.[2]

Jerold was known throughout Salt Lake Valley as a dedicated choral teacher, "devoted to the art of choir building."[3] But for him, becoming a choral conductor was never in his plans. "I have a bit of chalk dust in my veins," he said.[4] Jerold was also known as a quick wit and irrepressible punster. Although he believed his wit endeared him to his students, Jerold said, "My wife and daughter at one point in time got so disturbed by my constant puns, that they began grading them K through 12. And I didn't very often get up the scale," he lamented. "What I couldn't teach them was the fact that a pun, to be good, has to be just as *bad* as it can be."[5]

In 1974 Jerold was invited by Jay Welch, the new conductor of the Mormon Tabernacle Choir, to be his assistant. Six months later, Welch resigned from the choir and Jerold was appointed the thirteenth conductor of the famed Mormon Tabernacle Choir. "There were questions about what it meant for the Choir and what it meant for me," remarked Jerold. "I sought counsel from my wife who reminded me of past inspirations. I sought counsel and a blessing from my aged father. . . . And I sought counsel from the Lord. All agreed that this was indeed 'my destiny.'"[6] He advised others to "look and listen for those evidences. And finally, be brave! Take some chances—but only if you invite Providence to be your guide when you take those chances." As to his being named the music conductor of the choir, he said, "I didn't have a master plan. I didn't get up one morning and say, 'I'm going to lead the Tabernacle Choir.'"[7]

Jerold's soft-spoken manner and distinguished look—"a great shock of silver hair and a warm, winning smile"—endeared him to choir members and the television viewing audience. Many remarked that "his quiet spiritual strength, his outgoing sense of humor, and his dedication to music and to the Church make him an ideal selection."[8] As music director of the Mormon Tabernacle Choir, Jerold was able to "refine the Choir's sound and its basic musicianship and expand its range of repertoire and performance possibilities."[9]

Retirement from the Mormon Tabernacle Choir seemed unthinkable, but time has a way of changing future plans. After retirement from the choir in 1999, Jerold and his beloved wife became volunteer teachers and administrators of the Mormon Tabernacle Choir Training School at Temple Square. Jerold also served as a Tabernacle Choir staff volunteer, helping to revise the choral library computer database, and he served as an artistic adviser to the Salt Lake Interfaith Roundtable. From 2005 to 2008 he directed the University Chorale at Brigham Young University–Hawaii, where JoAnn also taught vocal music.

Jerold received many deserved honors and awards for his illustrious music career, including the Utah Governor's Commendation, the Presidential Award from Brigham Young University, the University of Oregon's Distinguished Alumnus Award, and the Salt Lake Area Chamber of Honors in the Arts Award. In 1990 Jerold received the Franklin S. Harris Award from BYU, and then in 2012 he returned as the honored alumni speaker for the 2012 homecoming festivities for the BYU College of Fine Arts and Communications.[10] In his speech, Jerold expressed gratitude for the experiences and opportunities that have shaped his destiny, saying, "My life's path is evidence that there are powerful, often unseen forces waiting for *your* arrival on the scene. Look and listen for those evidences."[11]

1   Jerold D. Ottley Oral History, interviews by Gordon Irving, 1983–1990, 2 vols., typescript, 1:3, The James Moyle Oral History Program Archives, Church History Library, Salt Lake City.

2   Lyle Jay Archibald, "Make Haste Slowly—Jerold D. Ottley's Tenure with the Mormon Tabernacle Choir," PhD dissertation, Arizona State University, March 2011, http://repository.asu.edu/attachments/56609/content/Archibald_asu_0010E_10656.pdf, 4–5, 16, 25.

3   Charles Jeffrey Calman, *The Mormon Tabernacle Choir* (New York: Harper & Row, 1979), 107.

4   Calman, 109.

5   "Alumni Achievers," *BYU Magazine*, http://magazine.byu.edu/?act=view&a=3127.

6   Jerold Ottley, "You Want Me to Do What?" College of Fine Arts and Communications, Brigham Young University, Oct. 11, 2012, https://cfac.byu.edu/college/speeches-publications/you-want-me-to-do-what/.

7   "Alumni Acheivers."

8   Calman, 107.

9   Ibid., 109.

10 "Jerold Ottley," College of Fine Arts and Communications, Brigham Young University, http://history.cfac.byu.edu/index.php/Jerold_Ottley.

11 "Alumni Acheivers."

PARLEY P. PRATT
Communication

Courtesy of L. Tom Perry
Special Collections, Harold B.
Lee Library, Brigham Young
University.

"I ALWAYS LOVED A BOOK," wrote Parley P. Pratt. "If I worked hard, a book was in my hand in the morning . . . a book at evening . . . a book at every leisure moment of my life." While preaching in western New York, he visited an old Baptist deacon who told him of a new book, "a VERY STRANGE BOOK!" The next day he read that strange book—the Book of Mormon. "I read all day," wrote Parley. "Eating was a burden, I had no desire for food; sleep was a burden when the night came, for I preferred reading to sleep. . . . I esteemed the Book, or the information contained in it, more than all the riches of the world."[1]

Parley P. Pratt, son of Jared Pratt and Charity Dickinson, was born April 12, 1807, in Burlington, New York. He was baptized in early September 1830 by Oliver Cowdery and ordained an elder shortly thereafter. By October 1830 Parley was called to share the Book of Mormon as a missionary to the Lamanites. With companions Oliver Cowdery, Peter Whitmer, and Ziba Peterson, he traveled to Buffalo and from there to Ohio and then to Missouri. The news Parley and his companions brought about the Book of Mormon caused such excitement in Ohio that Parley recalled, "People thronged us night and day, insomuch that we had no time for rest and retirement."[2]

On February 21, 1835, Parley was ordained an Apostle of the Lord Jesus Christ. In Parley's ordination blessing, the Lord was petitioned to "increase his love for thee and for thy cause; increase his intelligence, communicate to him all that wisdom, that prudence and that understanding which he needs as a minister of righteousness, and to magnify the Apostleship whereunto he is called."[3] As an Apostle, Parley served successive missions to Pennsylvania, New York, New England, and Canada.

Parley was imprisoned with other Church leaders on false charges in Independence and Richmond, Missouri. In November 1838, after listening to the guards in Richmond recount their deeds of rape, murder, and robbery against Latter-day Saints, Parley heard Joseph Smith say, "*SILENCE, ye fiends of the infernal pit. In the name of Jesus Christ I rebuke you, and command you to be still. . . . Cease such talk, or you or I die THIS INSTANT!*" The guards were instantly contrite and begged his pardon.[4]

After a mock trial, Parley was committed to jail for the "alleged crime of murder." On July 4, 1839, he and fellow prisoners, who were now incarcerated in Columbia, Missouri, hung a flag from a window with the word *liberty* written in large letters. Although the flag caused much merriment to the townspeople as the prisoners were deprived of their liberty, they escaped by overpowering the jailor. In the excitement Parley lost contact with his friends and also lost his horse. Yet he felt joyous and exclaimed aloud, "Thank God for this hour, it is the happiest of my life; I am free, although lost in the wilderness, and if I cannot find myself, thank God nobody else can find me." After days of wandering, he arrived among friends in Illinois, where he met Joseph Smith. "Neither of us could refrain from tears as we embraced each other once more as free men," wrote Parley. "He blessed me with a warmth of sympathy and brotherly kindness which I shall never forget."[5]

While serving yet another mission in the United States, Parley was "constrained by the Spirit to start prematurely for home." En route to his home in Nauvoo, Illinois, Parley learned of the deaths of Joseph and Hyrum Smith. "I felt so weighed down with sorrow and the powers of darkness that it was painful for me to converse or speak to any one, or even to try to eat or sleep," wrote Parley. "I really felt that if it had been my own family who had died, and our beloved Prophet been spared alive, I could have borne it. . . . I had loved Joseph with a warmth of affection indescribable." Parley wondered, "How shall I meet the aged and widowed mother of these two martyrs? How shall I meet an entire community bowed down with grief and sorrow unutterable?" His answer came from the Spirit of the Lord: "Go and say unto my people in Nauvoo, that they shall . . . make no movement in Church government to reorganize or alter anything until the return of the remainder of the Quorum of the Twelve."[6] Inspired by the divine answer, Parley was instrumental in comforting Mother Smith and the people of Nauvoo. He later helped those in Nauvoo migrate to the Rockies and establish new settlements in the West.

In describing what would appear to many as a busy life, Parley wrote, "Lest any time should run to waste, I filled up the interstices not otherwise occupied, in the study of the Spanish language." His studying proved beneficial, for Parley was next called on a "General Mission to the Pacific," which led him not only to the Pacific islands but also to South American countries. "Priestcraft reigns triumphant in all these countries," wrote Parley. "I feel as though the Book of Mormon . . . should be translated into Spanish and printed, and then the key be turned to these nations." He had a great desire to translate the Book of Mormon "as soon as I have the language sufficiently perfect."[7]

Parley's final mission was in the United States. On September 7, 1856, he wrote in his journal, "I preached my farewell discourse in the Tabernacle, in which I bore testimony to the Book of Mormon and of the calling of Joseph Smith, and of his Presidency and Apostleship."[8] Fifty-year-old Parley was murdered in May 1857 near Van Buren, Arkansas.

1   Parley P. Pratt, *Autobiography of Parley P. Pratt*, ed. Parley P. Pratt Jr. (Salt Lake City: Deseret Book, 1985), 2, 18, 20, 22.

2   Pratt, 36.

3   Ibid., 97.

4   Ibid., 180.

5   Ibid., 183, 210, 220–221, 253–254.

6   Ibid., 292, 293, 294.

7   Ibid., 342, 363, 369.

8   Ibid., 400.

HARRY REID
Tenacity

"I speak bluntly. Sometimes I can be impulsive. I believe something to be right and I do it," says Harry Reid. "This has not always necessarily served me well, but it is who I am." Harry's determination to follow his conscience has led to a successful political career that included serving as the majority leader of the United States Senate. Speaking of his unlikely rise to national prominence, Harry recalled, "I don't mean this as a boast, but people who come from where I come from generally do not end up in the United States Senate. And in truth, where I've ended up was the furthest thing from my mind as I was getting started."[1]

Harry Reid, son of Harry and Inez Reid, was born December 2, 1939, in Searchlight, Nevada. "The middle of nowhere is a hard place to live," said Harry. "Searchlight never became a ghost town, but it sure tried." The main industry in town was prostitution—there were thirteen brothels and no churches. "There was a local law that said you could not have a house of prostitution or a place that served alcohol within so many feet of a school," Harry recalled. "Once, when it was determined that one of the clubs was in violation of this law, they moved the school."[2]

Of his childhood, Harry said, "I loved my parents very much. They gave life everything they had. But no child should be raised the way I was raised. . . . I've never had much sympathy for people saying,

'The reason I'm so screwed up is because my parents are screwed up.'" Harry believes that "some of the men and women of greatest character that I will ever meet in my life came from this place of hard rocks and inhospitable soil."

From his mother, who worked as a laundress for the brothels, Harry learned "I could handle anything that the world could throw at me, whatever it might be," and from Franklin Delano Roosevelt, he acquired his religion—"We can. We will. We must."[3]

At age thirteen, Harry hitchhiked to Henderson, Nevada, to attend Basic High School. In Harry's freshman year, a friend invited him to attend seminary, promising him that all the best-looking girls went to seminary. "I was really starting to like Mormons. I got good grades and was freshman class president," recalled Harry of his first year at Basic High. But it was Landra Gould who captured his attention. "She was wearing short shorts, I remember that. And she was washing the family car. . . . She looked like she belonged in the movies."[4]

Although Landra was always on Harry's mind, his professed goal was to be an athlete. "It wasn't until college that I'd realize that I wasn't fast enough, big enough, or good enough to be the athlete of my dreams, but in high school I went out for football and baseball." Harry found football practices grueling, but black eyes and soreness were badges of honor. In Harry's senior yearbook, Coach Razmic wrote, "Best of luck to one who never quit." While in high school, Harry also discovered politics. Even though he went on to be student body president, he said, "I really believe that the most important election of my life was junior class treasurer at Basic High."[5]

After graduation, Harry attended the College of Southern Utah at Cedar City on a football scholarship. When an injury forced him to the sidelines, he took up boxing. "I'd go anywhere and fight anybody. I had boxing shoes. I was a full-fledged fighter," Harry said. Harry and Landra corresponded while Harry was at Southern Utah and reached the decision to marry. "Landra was a Jew and I was a nothing," Harry recalled. Landra's father would not give his consent to their marriage, so Harry and Landra were married by an LDS bishop without her father's consent.[6] They then moved to Logan, Utah, where Harry had an academic scholarship to attend Utah State College.

Economics professor Leonard Arrington took Harry "under his wing," while Harmon Judd, his political science professor, told him,

"You obviously have a good mind, but your grammar is atrocious. You really should do something about it." Harry's greatest influence at the university, however, was the Bird family, who lived in the apartment upstairs. Harry recalled, "One evening I needed to use their phone, as we didn't have one, and I knocked on the back door and looked and there they were, all kneeling on the floor. And I thought, What is going on here?"[7] Harry saw unity and love and wanted that for his family. When he and Landra learned the upstairs neighbors were Mormons, they joined the Church in February 1960.

After completing a bachelor's degree at Utah State College, Harry pursued a law degree at George Washington University in Washington, DC. He attended school in the day and worked nights as a United States Capitol policeman. After completing his law degree, Harry returned to Nevada, where he was employed as the town prosecutor for the city council of Henderson. He later joined Singleton, DeLanoy & Jemison, the best law firm in Las Vegas. By the time Harry ended his law career in 1982, he had represented clients in more than a hundred jury trials.

In 1982 Harry was elected to the U.S. Congress as a representative from Nevada. Of his election and place in Washington politics, Harry said, "My arrival in Washington was the culmination of all else that I had done in my life, and brought me to what I have come to think of as my life's work." Harry has served with four U.S. presidents and along the way faced several tough elections. "I've even had to run against God Almighty himself. (This was actually the legal name of my primary challenger in 1992. I defeated him)," said Harry. "And I have learned something about grace in defeat." Of his career, Harry said, "I am . . . proud of the work I've had the pleasure and privilege of doing in Washington, D.C., for the past twenty-five years."[8]

Although some in Congress take offense at Harry's outbursts, he says, "Memory is a kind editor, and a wondrous thing. It tells us our stories differently over time, smoothing out the roughness, removing bitterness, taking away hurt, keeping the people we love young." As to his testimony of the gospel of Jesus Christ, Harry says, "I have knowledge of God's existence and an understanding of His character. I believe faith can be nurtured—faith can be renewed by living the Golden Rule, study, including scriptures, and constant prayer."[9]

1   Harry Reid and Mark Warren, *The Good Fight* (New York: G. P. Putnam's Sons, 2008), 20–21, xii.

2   Ibid., 25, 24, 23.

3   Ibid., 24, 29, 53, 54, 56.

4   Ibid., 99, 108, 117.

5   Ibid., 111, 112.

6   Ibid., 120, 124.

7   Ibid., 127, 129.

8   Ibid., 273, 275, xii.

9   Ibid., 76, 288.

GEORGE REYNOLDS
Sacrifice

Courtesy of the Church History
Library, The Church of Jesus
Christ of Latter-day Saints.

GEORGE REYNOLDS WAS TIMID AND preferred to pray rather than speak.
Yet he was a secretary to the First Presidency of the Church from 1865
to 1909 and a member of the Council of Seventy from 1890 to 1909.
George had the character trait of being "willing to suffer any indignity
or sacrifice to help move forward the cause of Zion." He was recognized
by Latter-day Saints as a "living martyr to the cause of Zion" and "a
representative prisoner suffering for the conscientious faith of the whole
people."[1]

George Reynolds, son of George Reynolds and Julia Ann Tautz,
was born January 1, 1842, in Marylebone, England. At age seven, he
felt disgusted after overhearing men in his father's tailor shop speak
disparagingly about religious matters. At age nine, he attended an
LDS meeting, listened to gospel truths, and immediately wanted to be
baptized.[2] His father refused to give him permission. It was not until
1856, when George was fourteen years old, that he was baptized. By
1861 George was serving the first of two missions in England.

In 1865 George immigrated to America and trekked to the Salt Lake
Valley. Five months after arriving in the valley, he was hired as a secretary
to the First Presidency of the Church. George worked for five Presidents
of the Church—Brigham Young, John Taylor, Wilford Woodruff,
Lorenzo Snow, and Joseph F. Smith. George told a colleague, "I fancy

that when I am entering the pearly gates someone will call out here comes Brother Reynolds, let's make him secretary."[3]

George lived the principle of plural marriage and was the husband of Mary A. Tuddenham and Amelia Jane Schofield. George's plural marriages and the court cases that followed propelled him into the national spotlight. He wrote, "In October 1874 it was agreed between the U.S. Prosecuting Attorney [William Carey] and the Presidency of the Church that a case should be gotten up, to test the constitutionality of the law of 1862 (the Anti-Polygamy Act) and that other prosecutions should be stayed in the mean time. I was asked to step to the front. I willingly complied."[4]

George was set apart as a sacrifice in behalf of Israel before being indicted for bigamy on October 23, 1874. On October 26, "George pleaded not guilty and was released on a twenty-five-hundred-dollar bond provided by Salt Lake City businessmen." He was later found guilty. His case, *Reynolds v. United States*, was appealed to the "Utah Territorial Supreme Court in the June term [of 1874]. After hearing arguments from both sides on 13 June, the Court sustained the guilty verdict." The case was next appealed to the United States Supreme Court. "Arguments were heard over two days"—November 14 and 15, 1878.[5] On January 6, 1879, justices of the U.S. Supreme Court voted unanimously against Reynolds.

Petitions with more than thirty-two thousand signatures were sent to U.S. President Rutherford B. Hayes asking him to pardon George "on the grounds that his was a test case." George was not pardoned. Instead, he was incarcerated for eighteen months—one month in the Nebraska State Penitentiary in Lincoln, Nebraska, and the remaining months in the Utah Territorial Penitentiary in Sugar House, Utah. From prison, George wrote, "Be assured there are many worse places in the world than in prison *for conscience' sake*. It cannot take away the peace which reigns in my heart." But he added, "The day of deliverance, however soon it may come, will be gladly welcomed, with exceeding joy."[6]

During George's confinement, Church members prayed for him. George Teasdale, a railroad executive, wrote the following to George: "I do not think there is a man in Israel for whom prayer is offered up, that receives more fervent prayers offered up for him than yourself."

George did not idle away his time in prison. He wrote about "eighty articles, which appeared in the *Juvenile Instructor*, the *Woman's Exponent*, the *Contributor*, the *Millennial Star*, the *Deseret News*, and the Provo *Enquirer*." But he is best remembered for his writings on the Book of Mormon. By January 1881, George had written twenty-five thousand entries in what became a Book of Mormon concordance, a work he considered "his greatest contribution to the work of the kingdom."7 That same month, he was released from prison and invited to report on his mission at the Assembly Hall on Temple Square in Salt Lake City.

George gave his last public address at the October 1906 general conference. In that address, he said, "I hope that all through my life I shall ever consider the Kingdom of God and His righteousness first, last, and all the time."

George died of meningitis on August 9, 1909, in Salt Lake City. Of George's sacrifice, President Lorenzo Snow said,

> I suppose that a great number of people will obtain their salvation and some kind of glory without making very little, if any, what is called personal sacrifice. But to gain a Celestial crown and be exalted to the fulness of the Godhead, I believe one and all will have to pay one time or another, a big price, all he is able or capable of paying. . . . It has fallen your lot in the progress of the work of God to be cast into a penitentiary: which may be considered your part to fulfill as you move forward in your path to the fulness of the Godhead.8

1   Bruce A. Van Orden, *Prisoner for Conscience' Sake: The Life of George Reynolds* (Salt Lake City: Deseret Book, 1992), 91, 93.
2   Ibid., 3–5.
3   Ibid., 119.
4   Ibid., 61.
5   Ibid., 62, 79, 85.
6   Ibid., 89, 97.
7   Ibid., 105, 108, 201.
8   Ibid., 218, 112.

LEGRAND RICHARDS
Longevity

Courtesy of the Church History
Library, The Church of Jesus
Christ of Latter-day Saints.

OF LEGRAND RICHARDS, PRESIDENT GORDON B. Hinckley said, "Few men in our generation have done more to advance the work of the Lord than has Elder LeGrand Richards. To have served so long and so ably in a variety of capacities, and particularly as a General Authority of the Church, and to have done so with vitality and enthusiasm, is a remarkable accomplishment, in many ways unique."[1]

LeGrand Richards, son of George F. Richards and Alice Almira Robinson, was born February 6, 1886, in Farmington, Utah, and raised on a ranch in Tooele, Utah. Three significant events in LeGrand's childhood had great bearing on his later years. The first was seeing President Wilford Woodruff. Impressed by the prophet's appearance, LeGrand said, "I looked around for angels, but I didn't see any!"[2] The second was his baptism in Coleman's Pond in Tooele. The third was receiving a patriarchal blessing from his father, a patriarch. Although LeGrand joked that his father practiced giving blessings on him, he cherished that blessing, which read in part, "Thou hast not come here upon earth by chance, but in fulfillment of the decrees of the Almighty to accomplish a great work."[3]

Unfortunately, at age nine a bone disease in LeGrand's hip was not properly treated, leaving him permanently disabled, with one leg an inch and a half shorter than the other. The malady caused him to limp and be in constant discomfort and pain.[4] But the affliction did not stop LeGrand from wanting to live in such a manner that he could claim the promises contained in his patriarchal blessing. When he was offered a beer by a young girl at a party, he refused. The girl asked, "What's the matter? Are you too good to drink a little beer?" He responded, "I guess I am. And I thought you were too." He later said, "I resolved that no friend of mine would ever be able to accuse me of befouling his mind with dirty stories." He proudly declared, "I can go back to the town where I was raised as a boy and can tell parents how to raise their children, and I don't need to worry about old women my age sitting down in the back saying, 'Yes, but you should have known him when we knew him as a boy.'"[5]

After graduating from Tooele High School in 1901, LeGrand attended the Salt Lake Business College for eighteen months. Although he enjoyed aspects of college life, he deeply desired to be a missionary. In answer to his earnest prayers, LeGrand was called in 1905 on a mission to Holland, the first of four missions he would serve. In Rotterdam, Holland, LeGrand saw a city "of dog-carts, wooden shoes, and speech that sounded like 'one long unbroken word.' Yet he felt confident that if the dogs, whose barks sounded familiar, could understand Dutch, so in time could he."[6] On that mission, LeGrand mastered the Dutch language and gained a deep love for the people he served.

After returning to the United States, LeGrand met Ina Jane Ashton and said it was "love at first sight." When proposing to Ina, LeGrand said, "I had such a wonderful experience in the mission field, I almost feel that I walked and talked with the Lord. My duty to him and his Church will have to come first. If you want second place, it is yours."[7] LeGrand and Ina were married May 19, 1909, in the Salt Lake Temple.

From this point on LeGrand's life was filled with Church work and family matters. To support his growing family, LeGrand entered the real estate and investment field. Yet he willingly interrupted his business dealings to accept Church callings, such as president of the Netherlands Mission, president of the Southern States Mission, bishop, and so on. In many ways, his most impressive service was in 1926 in response to President Heber J. Grant's call for a thousand "men of mature years and sound judgment who have had experience in the preaching of the gospel . . . who are financially able to go forth and labor in the mission fields."[8] LeGrand left a very successful real estate and investment company and volunteered to serve.

When President Grant asked him to move to California to serve as president of the Hollywood Stake, LeGrand immediately left his company and holdings in Utah to settle in Southern California.

In 1938, at age fifty-two, LeGrand was called to be the Presiding Bishop of the Church. Under his leadership, "all tithes and contributions, Churchwide, came to the Presiding Bishop's Office first, and expense monies were then dispersed back to the local units of the Church according to their size and needs."[9] In addition, LeGrand gathered Church membership records and housed them permanently in the Church Office Building. Although these were sweeping and long-lasting changes in his era, his most remembered contribution is his book *A Marvelous Work and a Wonder*, which is still read and shared by missionaries throughout the world today.

On April 6, 1952, after serving fourteen years as the Presiding Bishop of the Church, LeGrand was called to be an Apostle of the Lord Jesus Christ. Of his new calling, LeGrand said, "I have been trying to figure out how I could measure up and not disappoint you people, and not disappoint the Lord. . . . I pledge you all the strength and ability that the Lord has given me to continue to help build up his kingdom on earth."[10] Of LeGrand's years of apostolic service, President Thomas S. Monson said, "He has traveled the world, lifting his quick-paced voice like a clarion in proclaiming the gospel which he so much loves."[11]

LeGrand died January 11, 1983, at age ninety-six. Of his tireless service to the Lord's kingdom, President Gordon B. Hinckley said, "His example in never permitting physical limitations to restrict his service has given courage to thousands of others who suffer from handicaps. Lame from childhood, and seldom without pain, he has kept up a demanding regimen of travel, speaking, and administrative duties. . . . His capacity for remembering scripture, stories, and the experiences he has had is remarkable. His power of recall is, I think, an absolute miracle."[12]

1   Lucile C. Tate, *LeGrand Richards: Beloved Apostle* (Salt Lake City: Bookcraft, 1982), foreword.

2   Richard Neitzel Holzapfel, "Oxen, Temple Stones, and a Playground," *Friend*, April 1993, 14.

3   LeGrand Richards, "A Constructive Life," *New Era*, June 1976, 8.

4   D. Michael Quinn, "They Served: The Richards Legacy in the Church," *Ensign*, Jan. 1980, 29.

5   Tate, 18, 21.

6   Ibid., 37.

7   Ibid., 55, 56.

8   Ibid., 122.
9   Ibid., 211.
10   "Elder LeGrand Richards Dies: Beloved Apostle, Missionary, Friend," *Ensign*, Feb. 1983, 6.
11   Tate, 263.
12   Ibid., foreword, 263.

LEROY ROBERTSON

Originality

Courtesy, of L. Tom Perry
Special Collections, Harold B.
Lee Library, Brigham Young
University, Provo, UT.

"HAS THE LATTER-DAY SAINT CULTURE produced a truly great composer whose works are definitely Mormon?" editors of the *New Era* asked Lowell M. Durham. After naming several prominent Latter-day Saint musicians, Durham said, "It is conceivable that one hundred years from now another name—Leroy Robertson—will loom above these others."[1]

Leroy did rise above the others named in national and international prominence, but it didn't take him a hundred years. In 1947 his photograph, depicting him as a "fiddle-playing, sheep-herding" composer, made the national news and weekly magazines with the announcement that Leroy had won $25,000, the "largest prize in musical history." The prize was presented to him at a nationwide broadcast of his symphony *Trilogy*, performed before a live audience in Detroit, Michigan.[2] More recognition followed for this talented composer and music educator, whose compositions are now enjoyed by audiences throughout the world.

Leroy Jasper Robertson, son of Jasper Robertson and Alice Adams, was born December 21, 1896, in Fountain Green, Utah. Leroy was a descendant of hardworking, faithful pioneers who settled the raw frontiers of central Utah. Leroy left Fountain Green at age fifteen to improve his educational opportunities. He moved in with his grandparents in Utah County so that he could attend Pleasant Grove

High School. After graduating from high school, Leroy taught violin before being drafted into the United States Army. It was not the battles that raged in World War I but the flu epidemic that sent him home to recover from health issues.

Following his recovery, Leroy attended the New England Conservatory of Music in Boston. He interrupted his studies at the conservatory to accept a short-term mission assignment (mid-July to mid-September) to the New England States to perform, arrange, and direct music for the Church. In 1923 Leroy graduated from the conservatory with a certificate in public-school music and diplomas in composition, violin, and piano. That same year, he received the coveted Endicott prize for his *Overture in E Minor*.

After leaving Boston, Leroy returned to Utah, where he taught music in many academic settings. He first taught at North Cache High School in Richmond and then at his alma mater, Pleasant Grove High School, where he supervised music instruction for the entire Alpine School District. Before joining the music faculty at Brigham Young University, Leroy married Naomi Nelson on September 1, 1925. They became the parents of four.

From 1925 to 1948, Leroy was a professor of music and the chair of the department of music at BYU. He was largely responsible for expanding the music curriculum at BYU and for building the first nationally recognized symphony orchestra in the Intermountain West.[3] To further his musical talents and abilities as a teacher, Leroy studied with the famed Ernest Bloch at the San Francisco Conservatory of Music (1930) and in Roveredo Capriasca, Switzerland (1932). In 1933 he studied with Hugo Leichtentritt, the "Father of Musicology," in Berlin, Germany. From 1948 to 1952 Leroy was the chair of the department of music at the University of Utah. In 1954 he earned his PhD degree from the University of Southern California.

Leroy turned down several impressive offers in the field of music because he wanted to live near the mountains of Utah. Although colleagues questioned his decision, Leroy was confident that if his compositions were good enough, they would extend his influence beyond the environs of Utah. Major artistic groups—including the Utah Symphony, Philadelphia Orchestra, Berlin Philharmonic, and the Mormon Tabernacle Choir—performed his compositions in virtually every musical form. Leroy's compositions—including *Songs from the Shadow, Fantasia for the Organ, Quintet, String Quartet,* and *Passacaglia*—have been performed before audiences on every continent.

Leroy is perhaps best known for his monumental composition *Oratorio from the Book of Mormon,* which premiered with the Utah Symphony in 1953. Critics called the *Oratorio* "undoubtedly one of the finest [works] ever to be presented in recent times" and "one of the musical masterpieces of the twentieth century."[4] For thirty-six years, Leroy was a member of the General Music Committee of the Church.

On July 25, 1971, Leroy, who had been struggling with the effects of diabetes for years, died of a heart condition. His daughter lamented his death and described him as "a man with the greatest of hearts who ironically died of heart failure; a visionary who embodied both imaginative idealism and unsentimental practicality; a determined soul of uncompromising integrity and great humanity."[5]

As a testament to his musical genius, Leroy's compositions are well represented in the 1985 Latter-day Saint hymnal, comprising the hymns "On This Day of Joy and Gladness," "Let Earth's Inhabitants Rejoice," "Great King of Heaven," "God of Our Fathers, Known of Old," "I'm a Pilgrim, I'm a Stranger," "Upon the Cross of Calvary," "We Love Thy House, O God," and "Go Ye Messengers of Glory."[6]

1   Lowell M. Durham, "Q&A: Questions and Answers," *New Era,* Nov. 1972, 17–18.
2   Ibid.
3   "Leroy Robertson and the *Oratorio from the Book of Mormon*: Reminiscences of a Daughter," FARMS, Brigham Young University, http://farms.byu.edu/publications/jbms/8/2/S00003-Leroy_Robertson_and_the_iOratorio_from_the_Book_of_Mormoni_R.html.
4   Marian Robertson Wilson, *Leroy Robertson—Music Giant from the Rockies* (Salt Lake City: Blue Ribbon Publications, 1996), 204.
5   Ibid., 311.
6   See Karen Lynn Davidson, *Our Latter-day Hymns* (Salt Lake City: Bookcraft, 1988), 432.

ORRIN PORTER ROCKWELL
Loyalty

Courtesy of the Church History
Library, The Church of Jesus
Christ of Latter-day Saints.

SEPARATING FACT FROM FICTION, LEGEND, and Mormon folklore is nearly impossible for historians studying Porter Rockwell—who has been heralded as both hero and villain. Lacking personal writings because of Porter's illiteracy, historians are left to rely on eyewitness accounts and reminiscences. Was Porter the "Destroying Angel" of Mormonism, a notorious religious zealot, or a committed Latter-day Saint? Fictional narratives portray him as infamous and controversial as lawmen Pat Garett and Wyatt Earp, while faith-based writers depict Porter as the faithful bodyguard to two LDS prophets. Unraveling the truth leaves both camps unsatisfied.

Orrin Porter Rockwell, son of Orin Rockwell and Sarah Witt, was born on June 28, 1813 (or it may have been 1815), in Belchertown, Massachusetts. Although Porter was eight years younger than Joseph Smith, they are referred to as boyhood friends. As a youth Porter showed not only friendship to Joseph but belief in the Book of Mormon when Porter picked berries and hauled wood so that he could contribute to the publication of the first edition of that book in Palmyra, New York. At age sixteen, Porter was baptized in April 1830, becoming the youngest person to accept baptism after the Church was organized.

Porter migrated with other Church members from western New York to Ohio and then to Jackson County, Missouri. On February 2,

1832, he married Luana Beebe, the first of his three wives. In Jackson County, Porter became "a crack marksman with a gun" and identified himself with those who would come to the defense of the Latter-day Saints against the rising tide of antagonistic anti-Mormons.[1] Ever loyal to the Prophet Joseph Smith, Porter risked his life to take food to him and others wrongly incarcerated in Liberty Jail. Joseph said of Porter, "Orrin Porter Rockwell, who is now a fellow-wanderer with myself, [is] an exile from his home, because of the murderous deeds, and infernal, fiendish dispositions . . . and unrelenting hand of the Missourians. He is an innocent and a noble boy. May God Almighty deliver him from the hands of his pursuers. . . . Let the blessings of salvation and honor be his portion."[2]

When Lilburn W. Boggs, former governor of Missouri, was shot in May 1842 at his home in Independence, Missouri, Porter was charged with the assassination attempt. Without evidence to support the charge, Porter was taken prisoner in Missouri. After nine months, Porter was freed with no indictment issued against him. After being freed, he hurried to Nauvoo, Illinois, arriving at Joseph's home on Christmas Day of 1843, just as the Prophet and others were sitting down to dinner. "During the festivities," Joseph recounted, "a man with his hair long and falling over his shoulders, and apparently drunk, came in and acted like a Missourian. I requested the captain of the police to put him out of doors. A scuffle ensued, and . . . to my great surprise and joy untold, I discovered it was my long-tried, warm, but cruelly persecuted friend, Orrin Porter Rockwell."[3] Joseph told Porter that "as long as [Porter] remained loyal and true to his faith, he need fear no enemy: 'Cut not thy hair and no bullet or blade can harm thee!'"[4]

Following these prophetic words, Porter's enemies sought his life and those of his friends. From the Nauvoo Exodus to the settlements in the Utah Territory, Porter was ever ready to defend the defenseless. In 1849 he was appointed deputy marshal of the provisional state of Deseret. When government troops threatened Utah, Porter was sent with the "Mormon Raiders" to harass the troops. During the Civil War, U.S. Colonel P. E. Connor hired Porter as a scout for his infantry in a military action against the Shoshone Indians in 1863. Porter ran the Hot Springs Hotel and Brewery near the Point of the Mountain in the Salt Lake Valley. The site of the hotel, now the land on which the Utah State Prison is located, is commemorated by a stone marker.

Porter died on June 9, 1878, in Salt Lake City. At his funeral, Joseph F. Smith said, "He had his little faults, but Porter's life on earth, taken altogether, was one worthy of example, and reflected honor upon the Church. Through all his trials he had never once forgotten his obligations to his brethren and his God."[5] The inscription on his tombstone reads, "He was brave and loyal to his faith. True to the Prophet Jos. Smith. A promise made him by the prophet. Through obedience it was fulfilled." Folk musicians and former LDS Church members Peter and Mary Danzig wrote a song entitled "Porter Rockwell," which includes the following lyrics:

Have you heard of Porter Rockwell
He's the Mormon triggerite
They say he hunts for horse thieves
When the moon is shining bright,
So if you rustle cattle
I'll tell you what to do,
Get the drop on Porter Rockwell
Or he'll get the drop on you.

They say that Porter Rockwell
Is a scout for Brigham Young—
He's hunting up the unsuspects
That haven't yet been hung
So if you steal some Mormon girl
I'll tell you what to do,
Get the drop on Porter Rockwell
Or he'll get the drop on you.

1   Lawrence Cummins, "Orrin Porter Rockwell," *Friend*, May 1984, 42.
2   *History of the Church*, 5:125.
3   *History of the Church*, 6:134–135.
4   Harold Schindler, "Orrin Porter Rockwell," *Utah History Encyclopedia*, ed. Allan Kent Powell (Salt Lake City: University of Utah Press, 1994), 473.
5   Cummins, 44.

MARION G. ROMNEY
Humility

Courtesy of the Church History
Library, The Church of Jesus
Christ of Latter-day Saints.

AT THE APRIL 1983 GENERAL CONFERENCE, Marion G. Romney spoke on
the power of unity and how to become unified. "The way to unity is for
us to learn the will of the Lord and then to do it," he said. "The power of
the Church for good in the world depends upon the extent to which we,
the members thereof, observe this principle."[1] With his strong stance on
the importance of unity, it came as no surprise that Marion was selected
to lead the welfare program of the Church. His dedication to the principle
and practice of Church welfare and his love for those who struggled
to earn the necessities of life became legendary. Through meaningful
charitable acts, Marion received the respect of people throughout the
world.

Marion George Romney, son of George S. Romney and Artemesia
Redd, was born September 19, 1897, in the Mormon colony of Colonia
Juarez, Mexico.[2] Eight days after Marion's birth, his father left Mexico to
fulfill a mission call to the northern states. Due to his father's example of
service, at a young age Marion developed the habit of looking for ways to
serve others.

Marion attended Ricks Academy, where he met and fell in love with
Ida Jensen, an English teacher at the academy. Although serious about
his interest in Ida, Marion felt unworthy to be her husband, even though
he had been promised in his patriarchal blessing that he had "faith

similar to that enjoyed by the Brother of Jared."[3] After graduating from the academy in 1920, Marion planned to attend the University of Idaho, play on the university's basketball team, and become a professional coach after receiving his diploma. His plans changed, however, as he listened to Melvin J. Ballard of the Quorum of the Twelve bear testimony of the Savior. During Elder Ballard's speech, Marion had a strong spiritual impression that he should serve a mission like his father.[4] He advised Ida "to get married" while he served a three-year mission to Australia.[5]

When Marion returned from the mission, much to his delight he found that Ida was still single and thinking of him. Marion and Ida were married September 12, 1924, and settled in Salt Lake City, where Marion attended the University of Utah and graduated with a bachelor's degree in history and political science. He then attended the University of Utah College of Law and graduated in 1932 with a jurisdoctorate degree.

Marion practiced law for eleven years. As an attorney, he never assumed that he knew everything about a subject and tried to learn as much as he could from authorities on the subject before entering a case. F. Burton Howard, a member of the First Quorum of the Seventy, said of Marion, "He would privately indicate that he did not know many things; but when he spoke, after meticulous research and thoughtful preparation, he was seldom wrong."[6]

In 1934 Marion was elected to the Utah State Legislature. Other positions of trust soon followed. In 1941 he was appointed assistant managing director of the Church's welfare program. In October 1951, he was called to the Quorum of the Twelve Apostles. From 1959 to 1963 he was general chairman of the welfare program of the Church. Among his associates, Marion was known as "Mr. Welfare." He believed that "people must work for what they receive, and that compassion is needed for those who suffer misfortune."[7]

After being released as chairman of the welfare program, Marion accepted the call to be a counselor in the First Presidency of the Church. He served as a counselor to Presidents Harold B. Lee and Spencer W. Kimball from 1972 until his death in 1988. Throughout his life, Marion was a force for good in his profession, in his service to the Church, and to those in need.

1   Marion G. Romney, "Unity," *Ensign*, May 1983, 17.

2   Richard O. Cowan, "Marion G. Romney," in *Counselors to the Prophets*, comp. Michael K. Winder (Salt Lake City: Eborn Books, 2001), 449.

3   Spencer W. Kimball, "President Marion G. Romney: A Symbol of Righteousness," *Ensign*, Nov. 1972, 20.

4   F. Burton Howard, *Marion G. Romney: His Life and Faith* (Salt Lake City: Bookcraft, 1988), 62–64.

5   "Pres. Marion G. Romney, 90, Dies at His S.L. Home," *Deseret News*, May 20, 1988, http://www.deseretnews.com/article/5111/PRES-MARION-G-ROMNEY-90-DIES-AT-HIS-SL-HOME.html?pg=all.

6   Howard, 2.

7   Lee Davidson, "LDS Leaders Eulogize President Romney as a Man Who Knew and Served the Lord," *Deseret News*, May 24, 1988, B1.

MITT ROMNEY
Integrity

SINCE SPENDING HIS EARLY DAYS in Michigan as the son of an automotive executive and governor, Mitt Romney has graduated with honors from Brigham Young University, earned two graduate degrees from Harvard University, climbed to the top of the management consulting and venture capital world, lost a hard-fought Senate campaign, rallied the troubled Salt Lake Olympics, and served a term as governor of Massachusetts. With his eye on the United States presidency, Mitt endured "the buffetings of media scrutiny and garnered equal measures of derision and devotion from across the political spectrum. He won the nomination of a major party—a first for a BYU alum or a Mormon—but eventually lost his bid for the presidency in a narrow popular defeat."[1]

Willard Mitt Romney, son of three-term Michigan Governor George W. Romney and Lenore LaFount, was born March 12, 1947, in Detroit, Michigan. His parents named Mitt in honor of their good friend J. Willard Marriott and after his cousin Milton "Mitt" Romney, a former quarterback for the Chicago Bears. Mitt's father came from humble beginnings, apprenticing as a plaster carpenter and selling aluminum paint before beginning a career that propelled him to president of American Motors Corporation, the forty-third governor of Michigan, United States Secretary of Housing and Urban Development, and a candidate for president of the United States in 1968.

Reflecting on his father's legacy, Mitt said, "On my father's eightieth birthday, I asked him what had brought him the most satisfaction in his life, what was his greatest accomplishment. He had been a three-term governor, a United States Cabinet member, presidential candidate, CEO, multimillionaire, and prominent Church leader. His answer was immediate: 'My relationship with your mother and with my children and grandchildren is my greatest accomplishment and satisfaction.'"[2]

Upon graduating from high school, Mitt attended Stanford University before leaving the country to serve a thirty-month mission to France for The Church of Jesus Christ of Latter-day Saints. While Mitt was serving as assistant to the mission president, an oncoming vehicle ran into the car he was driving, seriously injuring him and killing one of his passengers. Although Mitt was not at fault, the tragic accident was a sober reminder to him of the preciousness of life.

Upon his return to the United States, Mitt married his high school sweetheart, Ann Lois Davies. Mitt and Ann have been married since 1969 and have five sons. Of her experience as a mother, Ann said, "When I consider the joy my sons have brought me, when I experience their strength of character and devotion to God, I silently weep with gratitude. I am so thankful for scriptures and prophets and a church that encouraged my choice of having children and devoting myself to teaching and caring for them."[3]

Mitt enrolled in Brigham Young University, graduating in 1971 with a bachelor's degree in English. He then moved to Boston, where he attended Harvard Law and Harvard Business School, graduating with honors in 1975. Mitt worked as a management consultant, helping businesses grow and improve their operations until 1984, when he founded Bain Capital, one of the nation's most successful venture capital and investment firms. He also ventured into politics as the Massachusetts Republican nominee for the U.S. Senate in 1994, losing the race to Democrat Ted Kennedy.

In the run up to the 2002 Winter Olympics, Mitt left the private sector to become president and CEO of the Salt Lake Organizing Committee and was given the task of turning around an Olympics mired in controversy and saddled with debt. When the 2002 Winter Olympics ended, Mitt returned to Boston, where he was elected the seventieth governor of Massachusetts. As governor, Mitt presided over an economic turnaround, balanced the state budget without raising taxes, and created tens of thousands of new jobs. In 2006 he was elected chairman of the Republican Governors Association and raised a then record-breaking $27 million for candidates running in state house contests across the country. Mitt ran for president of the United States on the Republican ticket in 2008 but did not become the party's nominee. In 2012 he was the Republican Party's nominee but was defeated in the general election by the Democrat nominee, Barack Obama.[4]

While running for president of the United States, Mitt compared his religious position to that of John F. Kennedy:

> Like him, I am an American running for President. I do not define my candidacy by my religion. A person should not be elected because of his faith nor should he be rejected because of his faith. . . . There are some for whom these commitments are not enough. They would prefer it if I would simply distance myself from my religion, say that it is more a tradition than my personal conviction, or disavow one or another of its precepts. That I will not do. I believe in my Mormon faith and I endeavor to live by it. My faith is the faith of my fathers—I will be true to them and to my beliefs. Some believe that such a confession of my faith will sink my candidacy. If they are right, so be it. But I think they underestimate the American people. Americans do not respect believers of convenience. Americans tire of those who would jettison their beliefs, even to gain the world.[5]

Throughout his life Mitt has been deeply involved in community and civic affairs, serving in the Church in a variety of callings, including home teacher, bishop, and stake president in Boston. He has also been involved in many charities and philanthropic efforts, including City Year, the Boy Scouts, and the Points of Light Foundation.

Mitt's life of service has been based on core values. "Unless you purposefully hold fast to living first by your innermost values, you will not succeed," Mitt said. "I have watched people of great worldly accomplishments who lived first with integrity for love, family, service, and devotion. In the words of Jacob, 'and ye will seek them for the intent to do good' [Jacob 2:19]. I have also watched some such people lose their money and their worldly esteem without it eroding their lives, happiness, or their measures of success, for their lives were built on the unshakeable foundation of personal integrity, of pursuit of values the world cannot corrupt or disappoint. . . . A decision to live with integrity will make all the difference."[6]

1   W. Mitt Romney, "Forty Years On," *BYU Magazine*, Winter 2013: 30.
2   Jennifer Melody Murdock and Joseph D. Ogden, *Business with Integrity* (Provo, UT: Brigham Young University Press, 2005), 165–166.
3   *Why I Believe* (Salt Lake City: Deseret Book, 2002), 282.
4   "Mitt Romney," Race 4 2016, http://race42016.com/mitt-romney/.
5   "Romney's 'Faith in America Address,'" December 6, 2007, http://www. nytimes.com/2007/12/06/us/politics/06text-romney.html?pagewanted=print&_ r=0.
6   Murdock and Ogden,168–169.

AL ROUNDS
Imagery

To ARTIST AL ROUNDS, "the world is a series of passing images trying out for a painting." Echoing the words of famed American artist Edward Hopper, Al says, "If you could say it in words, there'd be no need to paint it." Initially Al had no intention of becoming a landscape watercolor painter, in part due to the technical difficulty of reworking and correcting mistakes made in watercolor. "Watercolors are totally unforgiving," he says. As to Al's success using this medium, Jay Todd, former editor of the *Ensign*, said, "[Al Rounds] is the premier landscape painter of LDS historic sites. . . . He's made a great contribution to the Utah art community and to Latter-day Saints. His name will be permanent in the LDS community."[1]

Although Alan G. Rounds was born in Utah, he was raised in the small community of Walnut Creek in California. His parents recognized his desire to draw but they also had rules about when he could draw, especially during church. "My parents had a rule that we could not draw until the sacrament was over, but I could never wait that long," Al recalled. One of his earliest memories was of a classmate in third grade pointing to him and saying, "There is the artist in class." But it was not until a high school English teacher encouraged him to paint instead of coming to class that Al concluded that he was a gifted artist. The teacher said to Al, "If you do anything with your life except paint, you will be wasting your life."[2]

After graduating from Del Valle High School in Walnut Creek, Al attended Dixie College before transferring to Brigham Young University and ultimately graduating from the University of Utah, where he earned a bachelor's degree in art in 1977. Following his university studies, Al pursued a full-time career as an artist. *Deseret News* senior writer Doug Robinson wrote, "[Al] sold his paintings by the square inch at malls and art shows. He sold them out of his house for 15 years because he couldn't afford a gallery, which takes half the profits in commission. His former professors told him he was squandering his talent by selling rapid-production paintings in malls." Yet it was worth it to make ends meet.

Al painted everywhere in his house, from the kitchen table to the basement laundry room. "I wanted to get better, not faster," he recalled, "but to make money you have to be faster. . . . I couldn't do three paintings a day in oil (they don't dry fast enough, for one thing). I tried. I started doing watercolors just because I could sit on location and do two or three [a] day. At night I'd go home and work on oils. I did watercolors so I could make a living. But the more I did, the better I got, and I started enjoying it. I started doing things with watercolors that hadn't been done before. I experimented with washes and papers. I knew the techniques before I knew the words for them."[3]

Now Al paints about twelve watercolor landscapes a year, which requires much time and travel. Robinson writes, "He'll be driving down a highway and suddenly pull off to the side of the road. His family knows the routine. He reaches under the seat for his camera and bounds out of the car to take pictures." Al has walked through the Nauvoo countryside when the temperature was so cold his camera froze. Always in search of the right vantage point or look for a future painting, Al "has climbed out on tree limbs, fallen into lakes and streams with his camera, scaled no-trespassing fences, risked land mines, dodged rock-throwing Palestinians, ventured onto a single-lane train trestle over the Washington, D.C., beltway . . . and hiked a mountain in thigh-deep snow for several hours."[4]

Al later sorts through hundreds of photographs taken during his travels to find exactly what he wants to paint before he starts to draw. After selecting an image, he first "draws every detail—every shadow, every branch, every rock—on the canvas in pencil so that it looks like a paint-by-number kit." He then begins to paint with watercolors. "It's horrible," said Al of working with watercolors. "I spent one month on a painting recently and threw it away. You can mess up a painting with just one stupid stroke or one thing that gets away from you. You can't save it. You just have to start over."[5]

Al is now the premier artist of Utah landscapes and Latter-day Saint historical sites. His artistic renderings have appeared in the *Ensign*, the Salt Lake City and County Building, Abravanel Hall, and the Church Office Building. Many of his works can also be seen in Latter-day Saint homes, proudly displayed in a prominent place.

As to why Al has chosen to create such a large collection of landscapes and historical sites, he says, "I love it. It's what I live for."[6] Art dealer Steevun Lemon asked Al, "What will people say of Al Rounds in the next 50 years?" Al replied, laughing, "He is still short and bald." On a more serious note, he added, "I hope they say I tried. Every day I tried. . . . When I think of the paintings and my life I pray that the Lord is pleased with me and that my sacrifice is enough."[7]

1   Doug Robinson, "Al Rounds: Utah Painter's 'Calling' Is a Stroke of Wonder," *Deseret News*, Oct. 28, 2002, http://www.deseretnews.com/article/340008040/ Al-Rounds-Utah-painters-calling-is-a-stroke-of-wonder.html?pg=all.

2   Steevun Lemon, "Window to Our Past: An Interview with Al Rounds," *Meridian Magazine*, April 27, 2009, http://ldsmag.com/article/1258.

3   Robinson.

4   Ibid.

5   Ibid.

6   Ibid.

7   Lemon.

ALEXANDER SCHREINER
Creativity

FOR MORE THAN FIFTY YEARS, Alexander Schreiner was a Mormon
Tabernacle organist and one of the world's most noted organists and
composers. His remarkable musical legacy and extensive concertizing
reached millions of listeners and influenced generations of organists.
"With his reputation," said a former conductor of the Mormon Tabernacle
Choir, "[Alexander] could have done anything, but he chose to remain in
the Tabernacle."[1]

Alexander Schreiner, son of Johann and Margarethe Schreiner, was born
on July 31, 1901, in Nuremberg, Germany. His parents were converted to
The Church of Jesus Christ of Latter-day Saints in 1903 and were the only
members in their small branch to own a piano. As a result, choir rehearsals
and congregational meetings were often held in their home. When meetings
went long, four-year-old Alexander resisted efforts to put him to bed,
preferring to watch the pianist. The next few days, he would attempt to
reproduce what the pianist had done. By age eight, Alexander was playing
for choir rehearsals, Sunday School, and sacrament meetings.[2]

When Alexander was eleven years old, he and his family immigrated
to America and settled in the Salt Lake Valley. Alexander took piano and
organ lessons from John J. McClellan, the Mormon Tabernacle organist
and composer of the hymn "Sweet Is the Work."[3] At age sixteen, Alexander
gave his first organ performance at the American Theater in Salt Lake

City. In 1920, after graduating from high school and with plans to study electrical engineering in college, he accepted employment as a theater organist at the Rialto Theatre in Butte, Montana, and then at the Star Theatre in Portland, Oregon.

At age twenty, Alexander returned to Salt Lake City to prepare for a mission to Southern California. To his surprise, he was asked by the Presiding Bishop of the Church to participate in a daily noon organ recital series on Temple Square before leaving on his mission. This was the first time that Alexander performed on the famed Tabernacle organ. In the fall of 1921, Alexander began his mission service using the money he had saved from playing the organ for motion pictures. On his thirty-month mission, he served in leadership capacities, performed at many organ recitals, and accompanied the Southern California Mormon Choir. Alexander's mission "provided [him] with important spiritual, musical, and leadership experiences that equipped him for future endeavors, while Southern California's multifaceted music community provided a nourishing environment that continued to beckon him for many years."[4] At the April 1924 general conference, just a few weeks after Alexander returned from his mission, he was appointed an assistant Tabernacle organist. On April 14, 1924, he played his first recital in the Tabernacle as an official member of the organ staff. Six months later, he was granted a leave of absence so that he could study organ performance with renowned organists Charles Marie Widor and Louis Vierne in Paris, France. In France, Alexander courted a cellist and high school friend who also studied music in Paris—Margaret Lyman, daughter of Richard R. and Amy Brown Lyman. Alexander returned to his post as Tabernacle organist two years later and married Margaret on June 7, 1927, in the Salt Lake Temple. They became the parents of four.

Alexander earned a bachelor's degree and later a doctorate degree from the University of Utah, and was the first person awarded a PhD in music from the university, studying under Leroy J. Robertson. He was later awarded four honorary doctorate degrees.[5]

Over the next few years, in an effort to make a living and expand his concertizing outreach, Alexander traveled widely and played the organ for many different organizations. For example, he was an organist at the Grauman's Metropolitan Theatre in Southern California and at the First Methodist Episcopal Church in Los Angeles, the largest Methodist congregation in the world. He also played the organ at the University of

California at Los Angeles (where he was university organist and lecturer in music), the Jewish Wilshire Boulevard Temple, and the Capitol Theatre in Salt Lake City. While in Southern California, he became a member of the Hollywood California LDS Stake high council and later was named stake music director.[6]

In the summer of 1938, Alexander met with President Heber J. Grant and was invited to return to Salt Lake City on a permanent basis as soon as possible. Alexander accepted the invitation and served as fulltime Tabernacle organist from 1939 to 1977. He also took a leading role in the rebuilding of the Tabernacle organ in the late 1940s.[7] Beginning in 1943, Alexander performed concert tours in nearly every state in the United States. He also became widely known for his recordings and radio performances.

Alexander's beloved wife, Margaret, died of cancer on May 13, 1985, just a few weeks short of their fifty-eighth wedding anniversary. She set aside her own musical ambitions early in her marriage to devote her time and energy to raising children and furthering her husband's career. Losing his beloved wife was difficult for Alexander. His health steadily declined after her death and on Margaret's birthday, September 15, 1987, Alexander died at age eighty-six, leaving a musical legacy that few can match.[8]

Alexander is remembered today in Latter-day Saint congregations throughout the world for composing nine hymns in the 1985 LDS hymnbook; among them are "Truth Eternal," "Lead Me Into Life Eternal," "Thy Spirit, Lord, Has Stirred Our Souls," "God Loved Us, So He Sent His Son," "While of These Emblems We Partake," and "In Memory of the Crucified."

1   Daniel F. Berghout, *Alexander Schreiner: Mormon Tabernacle Organist*, PhD dissertation, Brigham Young University, 2001, 159.
2   Berghout, 3–4.
3   "Golden Anniversary for Alexander Schreiner," *Ensign*, April 1974.
4   Berghout, 11.
5   Donald Q. Cannon, Richard O. Cowan, and Arnold K. Garr, *Encyclopedia of Latter-day Saint History* (Salt Lake City: Deseret Book, 2001), 1079; see also Karen Lynn Davidson, *Our Latter-day Hymns* (Salt Lake City: Bookcraft, 1988), 435–36; see also Berghout, 126.
6   Cannon, Cowan, and Garr, 1079; see also Davidson, 435–436; see also Berghout, 53–77.
7   Ibid., 72, 101–122.
8   Ibid., 159.

W. CLEON SKOUSEN
Liberty

Courtesy of L. Tom Perry
Special Collections, Harold B.
Lee Library, Brigham Young
University.

CLEON SKOUSEN, A FAITH-BASED POLITICAL theorist and ultraright constitutionalist, created quite a stir in American society with his publications *The 5,000 Year Leap* and *The Naked Communist*. Radio and television commentator Glenn Beck embraced the political theories found in Cleon's writings, as did supporters of the John Birch Society. The other side of the political spectrum denounced Cleon's work as fragmented figments of imagination and unfortunate rhetoric. Regardless of the heated and diverse opinions Cleon's speeches and writings evoked, neither his supporters nor his antagonists disputed the fact that Cleon provided an alternate voice for solving America's problems. His was a plan to cleanse the United States of communism, conspirators, and laws outside the scope of the United States Constitution.

Willard Cleon Skousen, son of Royal Pratt Skousen and Margarita Bentley, was born January 20, 1913, in Raymond, Alberta, Canada. Cleon, whose name means "one to take the place of," lived on a dry-land farm in western Canada until age ten, when his family moved to California and, a few years later, to Colonia Juarez in Mexico.

In 1930 Cleon returned to California, graduated from high school, and was honored to represent his fellow seniors at the graduation ceremony by speaking on "The Molding of an American." After graduation, Cleon served a mission for The Church of Jesus Christ of

Latter-day Saints to Great Britain. Upon returning to the United States, he attended San Bernardino Junior College in 1935, where he was elected student body president. In 1936, he married Jewel Pitcher in the Salt Lake Temple. Cleon and Jewel became the parents of eight.

Cleon attended the George Washington University School of Law and received his LLB degree in 1940. After passing the Washington, DC, bar exam, he joined the Federal Bureau of Investigation. Although it has been suggested that he was a personal assistant to J. Edgar Hoover, it appears his work was more clerical than administrative. Cleon left the FBI at the request of Ernest L. Wilkinson, president of Brigham Young University, and moved to Provo, Utah, where he worked as the director of the Alumni Association for BYU.

In 1956 Cleon was appointed the chief of police in Salt Lake City. After four years in law enforcement, Cleon was dismissed by Governor J. Bracken Lee for raiding an illegal poker club in which the governor was in attendance. Cleon's supporters protested his dismissal and burned crosses in the governor's lawn. Cleon kept his fingers in law enforcement by editing the journal *Law and Order* and by serving as the field director for the American Security Council.

Perhaps more important to his life story, Cleon founded the All-American Society—an exemplar of ultra-far-right philosophy. He affiliated with the John Birch Society, lecturing across the nation at society events. In his lectures, Cleon denounced what he perceived as communist attacks on the John Birch Society and characterized criticism of the society as communism. At that time, Cleon was accused of promoting "anti-communism for obvious financial purposes" by the FBI.[1] His exposé on the "Red Menace" was published in book form and titled *The Naked Communist*, a title suggested by movie producer Cecil B. DeMille. The book was an immediate success and thrust Cleon into prominence among far-right speakers. When Cleon was asked how he became such an authority on communism, he spoke of his work with the FBI and his being privy to inside information.

In 1971 Cleon founded the nonprofit Freeman Institute, taking the name *freeman* from the Book of Mormon. The ostensible purpose of the institute was to provide students with political documents to read; however, some claimed its purpose was to uncover a superconspiracy led by the Rockefellers and the Rothschilds. In 1982 the name of the institute was changed to the National Center for Constitutional Studies.

Cleon served as president of the center for sixteen and a half years before resigning in 1988 on his seventy-fifth birthday. Latter-day Saint support for the center was impressive until 1979, when the First Presidency of the Church issued a letter to wards and stakes warning members not to promote Cleon or the center in Church-owned facilities or at Church meetings.

By 1988, Cleon had been appointed to the Council for National Policy by the Reagan Administration and had written *The 5,000 Year Leap*. Glenn Beck rescued this work, one of forty-six books authored by Cleon, "from the remainder pile of history, and introduced [Cleon] to a receptive new audience." By March 2009, *The 5,000 Year Leap* was number one in sales on Amazon.com. When this book and others of Skousen's were prominently displayed on high school library shelves, school board officials asked government officials whether the book was a reliable source. The FBI, which had compiled more than two thousand pages on Cleon, responded that it was not.[2] Yet ultraright admirers sided with Cleon, a man they cheered as being unafraid to express constitutional principles and to decry the evils of communism.

Cleon died on January 9, 2006, in Salt Lake City at age ninety-two. Utah Senator Orrin Hatch eulogized him by saying, "Shortly before I announced that I would be running for the U.S. Senate in 1976 as a political novice and virtually unknown candidate—Cleon was one of the first people of political significance and substance who agreed to meet with me and discuss my candidacy. . . . We found in each other at that first meeting many areas of common ground and a shared love for the principles that make America the strongest bastion of freedom on Earth."[3]

1   Sean Wilentz, "Confounding Fathers: The Tea Party's Cold War Roots," *The New Yorker*, Oct. 18, 2010, http://www.newyorker.com/ reporting/2010/10/18/101018fa_fact_wilentz.

2   Alexander Zaitchik, "Meet the Man Who Changed Glenn Beck's Life," Salon Media Group, Sept. 16, 2009, http://www.salon.com/2009/09/16/beck_ skousen/.

3   Senator Orrin Hatch, "Tribute to W. Cleon Skousen," *Congressional Record*, 109th Congress, Jan. 25, 2006, S114.

GEORGE ALBERT SMITH

Love

Courtesy of the Church
Archives, The Church of Jesus
Christ of Latter-day Saints.

WARD MEMBERS WHO HAD KNOWN George Albert Smith as a boy described him as the "terror to the 17th ward," a "horrid boy," and a boy "frightened children needed protection from." "Girls would run blocks rather than meet him alone," they said. Even his school teachers "breathe[d] a sigh of relief" if George was absent from school. How many Latter-day Saints would be surprised to know that "the worst boy" neighbors and teachers knew became a prophet who is remembered for his Christlike love?[1]

George Albert Smith, son of John Henry Smith and Sarah Farr, was born April 4, 1870, near Temple Square in Salt Lake City. George descended from a long line of faithful leaders—his father, grandfather, and great-grandfather all served in leading quorums of the Church. George's patriarchal blessing suggested that he would follow in his forebears' footsteps and also become a Church leader.

At age ten, George fell in love with his future wife, Emily Lucy Woodruff. He "expected to marry her"[2] although she showed much disdain for his boyish pranks. At age twelve, George attended Brigham Young Academy, where he learned from Professor Karl G. Maeser that he would be held accountable for his actions and thoughts. This teaching had a lifelong effect on him.

On May 25, 1892, George and Emily were married in the Manti Temple.[3] Soon after their marriage, George accepted a mission call to the southern states, where intense prejudice threatened to destroy the work of God. George was a successful missionary because of an unusual ability to love all people. After completing his mission, George returned to his family in Salt Lake City. To support his family, he worked as a salesman for ZCMI department store and as a receiver for the United States Land Office.

In 1903, George was called to the Quorum of the Twelve Apostles, serving in the same quorum with his father. As an Apostle of the Lord Jesus Christ, George felt inspired to write a personal creed regarding how he wanted to live the remainder of his life. The creed included the following statements:

> I would be a friend to the friendless and find joy in min-
> istering to the needs of the poor. I would visit the sick
> and afflicted and inspire in them a desire for faith to be
> healed. I would teach the truth to the understanding and
> blessing of all mankind. I would seek out the erring one
> and try to win him back to a righteous and happy life.
> I would not seek to force people to live up to my ideals
> but rather love them into doing the thing that is right. I
> would live with the masses and help to solve their prob-
> lems that their earth life may be happy. . . . I would not
> knowingly wound the feeling of any, not even one who
> may have wronged me, but would seek to do him good
> and make him my friend. . . . I would not be an enemy
> to any living soul.[4]

Using the creed as his guide, George became known throughout the world for his kindness to children, his succoring of those in need, and his concern for the handicapped, sick, and poor.

After serving as an Apostle for six years, George became very ill. Although there was never a definitive diagnosis of his health problem, many attributed his illness to a serious case of *la grippe*, a type of influenza.[5] The illness left him with emotional, mental, and physical problems.[6] A three-year bout of depression, discomfort, and discouragement followed. A turning point in his health was a dream in which George saw his grandfather, George A. Smith, and told him of his continuing faithfulness to the Smith name.[7] Although health problems continued and public speaking remained a struggle, George put his trust in God and fought his emotional and physical problems with faith.

In 1945 George was sustained as President of The Church of Jesus Christ of Latter-day Saints. During his administration, he encouraged Latter-day Saints to love all men and to be kind. One public act of remembered kindness was when George authorized the sending of supplies to war-torn Europe to help survivors of World War II.

On his birthday, April 4, 1951, George died at age eighty-one. He is no longer remembered as the little boy who terrorized neighbors but as the prophet who demonstrated Christlike love on a daily basis.

1   A Member of the YLMIA, "A Brief Biography Written for the Present Occasion," George A. Smith Papers, Box 151, Fd 6, 1–7.

2   Francis M. Gibbons, *George Albert Smith: Kind and Caring Christian, Prophet of God* (Salt Lake City: Deseret Book, 1990), 9.

3   Gibbons, 21.

4   "President George Albert Smith's Creed," *Improvement Era*, April 1950, 262.

5   George Albert Smith Journal, February 24–25, 1909, George A. Smith Papers, Marriott Library, University of Utah, Salt Lake City.

6   George Albert Smith Journal, Jan. 24, 1909.

7   George Albert Smith, "Your Good Name," *The Improvement Era*, March 1947, 139.

Hyrum Smith
Watch Care

Courtesy of Religious Education
Image Project, Brigham Young
University.

"HYRUM, I MUST DIE," SAID HIS BROTHER Alvin in November 1823. "Take care of [our parents] in their old age, and do not any more let them work hard."[1] True to his brother's trust, Hyrum Smith cared for his parents. He also exercised special watch care over his younger brother Joseph. When a dispute arose between his brothers Joseph and William, Hyrum interceded. Joseph recognized his peaceful mediation and wrote of him, "I could pray in my heart that all my brethren were like unto my beloved brother Hyrum, who possesses the mildness of a lamb, and the integrity of a Job, and in short, the meekness and humility of Christ; and I love him with that love that is stronger than death, for I never had occasion to rebuke him, nor he me."[2]

Hyrum Smith, son of Joseph Smith Sr. and Lucy Mack, was born February 9, 1800, in Tunbridge, Vermont. He was one of Eight Witnesses to the Book of Mormon and helped preserve the printer's copy of the Book of Mormon manuscript. According to typesetter John H. Gilbert, "Hyrum Smith brought the first installment of manuscript, of 24 pages, closely written on common foolscap paper—he had it under his vest, and vest and coat closely buttoned over it. At night Smith came and got the manuscript, and with the same precaution carried it away. . . . This was kept up several days."[3] In June 1829 Hyrum was baptized in Seneca Lake by his brother Joseph. On April 6, 1830, he became one of the original six members of the Church.

Hyrum served on the Church finance committee, the Kirtland Temple building committee, and the Kirtland high council. He became Assistant Counselor to the First Presidency and later Second Counselor in the First Presidency. While faithfully serving in these capacities, he endured religious persecution and incarceration. "We endeavored to find out for what cause [we were imprisoned]," recalled Hyrum. "But all we could learn was, that it was because we were 'Mormons.'"[4] Hyrum endured imprisonment in Liberty Jail from December 1838 to April 1839. "Many call to see us out of curiosity to view us as they would an Elephant," he wrote.[5] After his escape from jail, Hyrum settled with his family in Nauvoo, Illinois.

Hyrum is perhaps best remembered as Patriarch to the Church, a calling to which he was sustained on January 24, 1841. As a patriarch, Hyrum was promised that "whoever he blesses shall be blessed, and whoever he curses shall be cursed; that whatsoever he shall bind on earth shall be bound in heaven; and whatsoever he shall loose on earth shall be loosed in heaven. And from this time forth I appoint unto him that he may be a prophet, and a seer, and a revelator unto my church, as well as my servant Joseph."[6]

On June 27, 1844, Hyrum died a religious martyr when a mob attacked Carthage Jail, where he and Joseph were incarcerated. When a ball struck him on the left side of the nose, Hyrum fell backward, exclaiming, "*I am a dead man!*" As he fell to the floor, another bullet entered his left side. At the same instant a bullet from the door grazed his breast and entered his head by the throat. A fourth ball entered his left leg. John Taylor, a witness to this barbaric scene, wrote that Hyrum and his brother Joseph "will be classed among the martyrs of religion. . . . They lived for glory; they died for glory; and glory is their eternal reward. From age to age shall their names go down to posterity as gems for the sanctified."[7]

Of his brother Hyrum, Joseph wrote, "O may the Eternal Jehovah crown eternal blessings upon your head, as a reward for the care you have had for my soul! O how many are the sorrows we have shared together; and again we find ourselves shackled with the unrelenting hand of oppression. Hyrum, thy name shall be written in the book of the law of the Lord, for those who come after thee to look upon, that they may pattern after thy works."[8]

1   Lucy Mack Smith, *The Revised and Enhanced History of Joseph Smith by His Mother*, ed. Scot Facer Proctor and Maurine Jensen Proctor (Salt Lake City: Bookcraft, 1996), 115, 116.
2   *History of the Church*, 2:338.

3   Wilford Wood, *Joseph Smith Begins His Work* (Wilford Wood, 1958), as cited in
     Pearson H. Corbett, *Hyrum Smith—Patriarch* (Salt Lake City: Deseret Book,
     1963), 54.

4   *History of the Church*, 3:420.

5   Hyrum Smith, "A Daily Record of H. Smith," October 29, 1838–April 18,
     1839, as cited in Davis Bitton, *Guide to Mormon Diaries and Autobiographies*
     (Provo: Brigham Young University Press, 1977), 321.

6   D&C 124:93–94.

7   D&C 135:1, 6.

8   *History of the Church*, 5:108.

Joseph Smith Jr.
Wisdom

Joseph Smith © William
Whitaker, oil on canvas.

IN THE EARLY NINETEENTH CENTURY in western New York, religious revivalists shouted, "Lo here, . . . lo there." The contest that ensued led young Joseph Smith to say to himself, "What is to be done? Who of all these parties are right; or, are they all wrong together? If any one of them be right, which is it, and how shall I know it?" One day while reading in the Epistle of James, first chapter and fifth verse, Joseph read, "If any of you lack wisdom, let him ask of God, that giveth to all men liberally, and upbraideth not; and it shall be given him." He later wrote, "Never did any passage of scripture come with more power to the heart of man than this did at this time to mine."[1]

Joseph desired wisdom, and so, on a beautiful clear day in the spring of 1820, he asked God in prayer which church he should join. In answer to his prayer, he saw "two Personages, whose brightness and glory defy all description," and was told to join none of the churches, "for they were all wrong." After sharing his answer, he was treated with contempt by many and was told that all visions and revelations had "ceased with the apostles." Despite the persecution that followed, Joseph declared, "I had actually seen a light, and in the midst of that light I saw two Personages, and they did in reality speak to me. . . . I knew it, and I knew that God knew it, and I could not deny it."[2]

Joseph Smith Jr., son of Joseph Smith Sr. and Lucy Mack, was born December 23, 1805, in Sharon, Vermont. Three and a half years after Joseph's first vision, Moroni, an ancient prophet who had once lived in

America, appeared to Joseph as an angel. Moroni told Joseph of a book "written upon gold plates, giving an account of the former inhabitants of this continent."[3] In 1829 Joseph was privileged to receive and translate the ancient writings, known as the Book of Mormon. The contents of this book were shared with family, friends, and newfound acquaintances from New England to the frontiers of the United States.

On April 6, 1830, a few believers gathered in Fayette, New York, to organize a church, today known as The Church of Jesus Christ of Latter-day Saints. The Church established in Fayette was "like to a grain of mustard seed, which a man took, and sowed in his field: . . . when it is grown, it is the greatest among herbs."[4] The newly baptized declared the truth of the Book of Mormon and accepted mission calls to spread the gospel of Jesus Christ and bring souls unto Him. The young and the old, the learned and the illiterate listened and embraced the teachings of the new church.

From small beginnings, the Church grew rapidly despite mounting persecution against Joseph and his followers in New York, Ohio, Missouri, and Illinois. The growth of the Church led Josiah Quincy, mayor of Boston from 1845 to 1849, to write, "It is by no means improbable that some future textbook . . . will contain a question something like this: What historical American of the nineteenth century has exerted the most powerful influence upon the destinies of his countrymen? And it is by no means impossible that the answer to that interrogatory may be thus written: Joseph Smith, the Mormon Prophet."[5]

Joseph did not seek for fame but sought to do the will of God. The Lord blessed his quest. Revelations, translations, covenants, and eternal truths were the fruits of his life's labor. "I could lean back and listen [to the Prophet]. Ah what pleasure this gave me," penned Wandle Mace. "He would unravel the scriptures and explain doctrine as no other man could. What had been mystery he made so plain it was no longer mystery. . . . I ask, who understood anything about these things until Joseph being inspired from on high touched the key and unlocked the door of these mysteries of the kingdom?"[6]

During these gospel conversations, Joseph explained the covenants and ordinances made in holy temples. He assured his followers that through participating in temple ordinances they would become more committed to a Christlike life and have a greater love for God. He taught, "The pleasing joys of family ties and associations . . . contribute to the happiness, power and dominion of those who attain to the celestial glory."[7]

Joseph's devotion to God was noted by faithful contemporaries such as John Taylor. After the martyrdom of the Prophet on June 27, 1844, in Carthage, Illinois, John wrote that Joseph "left a fame and name that cannot be slain."[8] He also wrote, "I think [Joseph] was one of the greatest Prophets that ever lived, Jesus himself excepted."[9] Millions who remember the life of Joseph Smith with gratitude belong to The Church of Jesus Christ of Latter-day Saints, a church that "shine[s] forth fair as the moon, clear as the sun" and beckons all to come unto Christ.[10]

1   JS—H 1:5, 10–12.
2   JS—H 1:17, 19, 21, 25.
3   JS—H 1:34.
4   Matthew 13:31–32.
5   B. H. Roberts, *Comprehensive History of the Church of Jesus Christ of Latter-day Saints* (Provo, UT: Brigham Young University Press, 1965), 2:349–350.
6   Wandle Mace, Autobiography, typescript, 94, L. Tom Perry Special Collections, Harold B. Lee Library, Brigham Young University, Provo, Utah.
7   B. H. Roberts, *Outlines of Ecclesiastical History*, 3rd ed. (Salt Lake City: Deseret News, 1902), 394.
8   D&C 135:3.
9   *Journal of Discourses*, 18:327.
10 D&C 109:73.

JOSEPH F. SMITH
Clarity

Courtesy of the Church
Archives, The Church of Jesus
Christ of Latter-day Saints.

THE MOST DIFFICULT PERSONAL EXPERIENCE in Joseph F. Smith's administration occurred in 1918 with the death of his forty-two-year-old son, Hyrum M. Smith, a member of the Quorum of the Twelve Apostles. "My soul is rent asunder," Joseph said. "My heart is broken, and flutters for life! O my sweet son, my joy, my hope! O I love him still."[1] Perhaps to console the bereaved father, on October 3, 1918, the Lord gave Joseph a vision of the Savior's visit to the spirits of the dead. This vision was submitted to the counselors in the First Presidency, the Council of the Twelve, and the Presiding Patriarch. It was unanimously accepted by them on October 31, 1918, and is now D&C 138.

Joseph Fielding Smith, son of Hyrum Smith and Mary Fielding, was born November 13, 1838, in Far West, Missouri. When Joseph was two months old, a mob ransacked the family home while his mother was visiting his father in Liberty Jail. "I, being an infant, and lying on the bed, another bed being on the floor, was entirely over looked . . . during the fright and excitement," wrote Joseph. "So when the mob entered the room where I was, the bed on the floor was thrown on to the other completely smothering me up."[2] Miraculously, he survived. A few days later Joseph was taken by his mother to Illinois. After the assassination of his father, Joseph and his mother journeyed to the Salt Lake Valley.

At age fifteen, Joseph was called to labor as a missionary in the Hawaiian Islands—the first of five missions he would serve over the next thirteen years. While on his first mission, Joseph penned, "I well know that I am young and inexperienced at present, therefore I wish to be humble, prayerful before the Lord, that I may be worthy of the blessings and love of God to protect me at all times."[3] After an absence of nearly four years, Joseph returned to Salt Lake City.

On July 1, 1866, Brigham Young said to Joseph, "I always feel well to do as the Spirit constrains me. It is my mind to ordain Brother Joseph F. Smith to the Apostleship, and to be one of my counselors."[4] At the age of twenty-seven, Joseph joined the Quorum of the Twelve Apostles and the First Presidency. He served as a counselor to Brigham Young, John Taylor, Wilford Woodruff, and Lorenzo Snow. During these years, he was also active in civil affairs. He was elected to the Utah House of Representatives for seven consecutive years. He acted as president of the Constitutional Convention in 1882 and served on the Salt Lake City Council for several terms.

Joseph's civil service ended when a federal government crusade against the doctrine of plural marriage forced him into exile. From 1884 to 1891 he hid from federal officers and polygamy hunters who sought his arrest. Joseph wrote of the frustrations of living in exile: "I cannot conceive of anything more contemptible or more execrable than the present and continued attempts of the Federal Officials to blast the peace and break up the sacred relationship of husbands and wives, parents and children!"[5]

From 1901 to 1918 Joseph served as President of The Church of Jesus Christ of Latter-day Saints. During his administration, two declarations were issued by the First Presidency—"The Origin of Man," which contains the official doctrine of the Church concerning man's origin and purpose, and "The Role of the Father and the Son," which outlines the nature of the Godhead.

Joseph was subpoenaed to appear before a United States Senate investigation committee in 1903, when Reed Smoot was elected to the U.S. Senate. Though Joseph declared that he received "scandalous treatment from the public press on account of my testimony given before the Committee," his testimony clarified much about the behavior of which Reed Smoot and the Church had been wrongly accused.[6]

Joseph died shortly after an attack of pleurisy and just nineteen days after the unanimous affirmation of his vision of the Savior's visit to the spirits of the dead. Bishop Charles W. Nibley eulogized Joseph by saying,

"As a preacher of righteousness, who could compare with him? He was the greatest that I ever heard—strong, powerful, clear, appealing."[7]

1   Joseph Fielding Smith, comp., *Life of Joseph F. Smith: Sixth President of the Church of Jesus Christ of Latter-day Saints*, 2nd ed. (Salt Lake City: Deseret Book, 1969), 474.
2   Smith, 124.
3   Ibid., 180–181.
4   Ibid., 227.
5   Ibid., 258.
6   Joseph F. Smith to Reed Smoot, April 9, 1904, in Smoot papers, L. Tom Perry Special Collections, Harold B. Lee Library, Brigham Young University, Provo, UT.
7   Smith, 433.

JOSEPH FIELDING SMITH
Gospel Scholarship

Courtesy of the Church
Archives, The Church of Jesus
Christ of Latter-day Saints.

JOSEPH FIELDING SMITH'S PUBLIC ADDRESSES and scholarly works were concise and exacting. He always presented with clarity where he stood on gospel principles and doctrine. As a result, his public persona was that of a serious and somber man.[1] His wife Ethel said,

> When [Joseph] is gone people will say, "He is a good man, sincere, orthodox, etc." They will speak of him as the public knows him; but the man they have in mind is very different from the man I know. The man I know is a kind, loving husband and father whose greatest ambition in life is to make his family happy, entirely forgetful of self in his efforts to do this . . . The man I know is most gentle, and if he feels that he has been unjust to anyone the distance is never too far for him to go and, with loving words or kind deeds, erase the hurt. . . . He enjoys a good story and is quick to see the humor of a situation, to laugh and to be laughed at, always willing to join in any wholesome activity. The man I know is unselfish, uncomplaining, considerate, thoughtful, sympathetic. . . . That is the man I know.[2]

Joseph Fielding Smith, son of Joseph F. Smith and Julina Lambson, was born on July 19, 1876, in Salt Lake City, Utah. As a child, Joseph loved to read the scriptures. "From my earliest recollection," Joseph said, "from the time I could first read, I have received more pleasure and greater satisfaction out of the study of the scriptures . . . than from anything else in all the world."[3] He would rather read the Book of Mormon than play baseball with neighborhood friends.

In 1894 Louie Shurtliff of Ogden moved into the Smith household while she attended the University of Utah. Joseph fell in love with Louie and they were married on April 26, 1898, in the Salt Lake Temple. Less than a year later, Joseph was called to serve a mission in Great Britain. Missionary service proved difficult for Joseph—he did not baptize anyone—as he was naturally reserved and quiet.[4] After returning to his family in Salt Lake City, Joseph obtained employment in the Church Historian's office. He enjoyed his employment so much that he found occasions to be associated with that office for the next seventy years.

After ten years of marriage and the birth of two daughters, Louie died from complications of pregnancy. Joseph was devastated. Later he met eighteen-year-old Ethel Georgina Reynolds at the Church Historian's office. They were married on November 8, 1908. Their marriage was blessed with nine children and much happiness until Ethel died at age forty-seven. Once again, Joseph was devastated. He eventually married a third time to Jessie Ella Evans, a woman twenty-six years his junior. Jessie and Joseph were married for thirty-three years[5] until Jessie passed away on August 3, 1971. At age ninety-five, Joseph was once again a widower.

In 1910, Joseph was called to the Quorum of the Twelve Apostles. For the next sixty-two years, he was known as the Apostle who clarified important doctrines and published gospel scholarship. His public addresses and more than twenty-five scholarly books focused on the importance of maintaining doctrinal purity.[6] His capacity to clearly write about the principles and doctrines of the gospel became the hallmark of his ministry, especially his writings on the Atonement of Jesus Christ, the necessity of repentance, and the Restoration of the gospel through Joseph Smith.

After the death of President David O. McKay on January 23, 1970, Joseph became the tenth President of The Church of Jesus Christ of Latter-day Saints. At age ninety-six, Joseph was the oldest man ever to become President of the Church.

During his two-and-a-half-year administration, Joseph consolidated Church magazines into three publications—the *Ensign*, the *New Era*, and the *Friend.* He designated Monday night as family home evening and authorized the formation of LDS Social Services. In a testimony given in 1972, Joseph prayed for the Latter-day Saints, saying, "O God our Heavenly and Eternal Father, look down in love and in mercy upon this thy church and upon the members of the church who keep thy commandments. Let thy Spirit dwell in our hearts forever; and when the trials and woes of this life are over, may we return to thy presence, with our loved ones, and dwell in thy house forever."[7]

Joseph died on July 2, 1972, in Salt Lake City.

1   Joseph Fielding Smith, "That the Fulness of My Gospel Might Be Proclaimed," *Improvement Era*, Dec. 1970, 4.

2   Bryant S. Hinckley, "Greatness in Men—Joseph Fielding Smith," *Improvement Era*, June 1932, 459.

3   Joseph Fielding Smith, Conference Report, April 1930, 91.

4   Blair G. Van Dyke, "Joseph Fielding Smith," in *Presidents of the Church: The Lives and Teachings of the Modern Prophets*, ed. Craig K. Manscill, Robert C. Freeman, and Dennis Wright (Springville, UT: Cedar Fort, 2008), 260.

5   Van Dyke, 261–262.

6   Smith, "That the Fulness of My Gospel Might Be Proclaimed," 2.

7   Joseph Fielding Smith, "A Prophet's Blessing," *Ensign*, July 1972, 130.

REED SMOOT
Leadership

Courtesy of L. Tom Perry
Special Collections, Harold B.
Lee Library, Brigham Young
University.

REED SMOOT SERVED AS A United States Senator from 1903 to 1933, longer than any other Utah Senator at that time and was the first Apostle in this dispensation to distinguish himself in this manner. His thirty years in the Senate were filled with controversial issues, none more so than the Smoot-Hawley Tariff Act that Reed cosponsored. The act raised tariffs on twenty thousand dutiable items to record-breaking levels and exacerbated the Great Depression. But through controversial issues and popular elections, Reed maintained an abiding faith in the truthfulness of The Church of Jesus Christ of Latter-day Saints.

Reed Owen Smoot, son of Abraham Smoot and Anna Kirstine Mouritsen, was born January 10, 1862, in Salt Lake City, Utah. Reed grew to manhood in Provo, Utah, where his father served as a stake president, town mayor, and president of Brigham Young Academy. Reed was one of twenty-nine students in the first class to graduate from the academy. After graduation, he became an employee of the Provo Woolen Mills, a manufacturing company his father founded, and an employee of the Provo Co-operative Institution. Before long, Reed was the manager of the mills and superintendent of the institution.[1]

Although Reed received a mission call in 1880, the call was rescinded when Church leaders learned of his position in the cooperative institution. In 1884 a second mission call was changed to a five-year call to serve as manager of the Provo Woolen Mills. In these positions, Reed became very prosperous, leading some to wonder whether his interest in financial success was leading him to abandon his religious roots. Such wonderings were put to rest in 1890 when he accepted a mission call to Europe, where he served as a bookkeeper and emigration clerk in the mission office in Liverpool.[2]

A year later, Reed returned to Provo in response to a telegram sent by Wilford Woodruff informing him of the serious illness that had befallen his father. He immediately began managing his father's financial affairs, including the Provo Lumber Manufacturing and Building Company, and again assumed the managerial position at the Provo Woolen Mills. Reed became president of the Provo Commercial and Savings Bank, vice president of the Grand Central Mining Company, and director of the Clark-Eldredge Company of Salt Lake City. Civically, Reed served as the director of the Territorial Insane Asylum and as a member of the Semi-Centennial Commission. In ecclesiastical matters, he was a counselor in the Utah Stake of Zion before receiving a call to the Apostleship on April 8, 1900.[3]

Two years after being ordained as an Apostle, Reed was elected to the United States Senate. Before he was seated as a Senator-elect, lengthy hearings over the allegation of his being a polygamist were heard by the Senate Ways and Means Committee. Although Reed was not a polygamist and had married only Alpha May Eldredge, opponents contended that he could not uphold the United States Constitution while serving as a leader in The Church of Jesus Christ of Latter-day Saints. Opponents purported that the Church still sanctioned plural marriage. "Outraged Christians gathered more than 3 million signatures on a petition against seating Smoot and the Senate launched an investigation into every aspect of Mormon belief and practice."[4] The Smoot Hearings, held from 1903 to 1907, were highly publicized and in many ways were a trial against the Church: "Investigators probed into past and present polygamous relationships of leaders and lay members alike. They raised questions on points of doctrine that affected how Church members and their leaders interacted with American society at large."[5]

The Senate Ways and Means Committee—which had investigated Reed and interviewed hundreds of witnesses, including President Joseph F. Smith—voted seven to five to not allow Reed to take his seat in the Senate. On February 20, 1907, the full Senate voted to defeat the committee's recommendation and welcomed Reed as an elected Senator. Reed served in the United States Senate for five terms. During his terms, he served for ten years on the Senate Appropriations Committee and was regarded by those in and out of the Senate as an expert on finance. He also took a leading role in the Republican Party as chairman of the Resolutions Committee and chairman of the Senatorial Campaign Committee.

In 1932 Reed was defeated for a sixth Senate bid by Democrat Elbert D. Thomas. Following his unsuccessful bid for reelection, Reed no longer took an active role in business or political pursuits. He dedicated the remainder of his life to his role as an Apostle.

Reed died on February 9, 1941, in St. Petersburg, Florida. Although he is best remembered for his role in the Senate's investigation of polygamy, it was his testimony and character that "shaped the positive national image the Church was to enjoy throughout the twentieth century."[6]

1   Andrew Jenson, *LDS Biographical Encyclopedia* 1:178–179.
2   Ibid., 179.
3   Ibid., 179–180.
4   Peggy Fletcher Stack, "LDS Leader Guided Church's Evolution from 'Menace' to Mainstream," *The Salt Lake Tribune*, April 3, 2004.
5   Harvard S. Heath, "Smoot Hearings," *Encyclopedia of Mormonism*, 3:1363.
6   Heath, 3:1364.

LORENZO SNOW

Grace

Courtesy of the Church
Archives, The Church of Jesus
Christ of Latter-day Saints.

In 1899, a casual acquaintance said of Lorenzo Snow, "President Snow is a cultured man, in mind and soul and body. His language is choice, diplomatic, friendly, scholarly. His mannerisms show the studied grace of schools. The tenor of his spirit is as gentle as a child. You are introduced to him. You are pleased with him. You converse with him, you like him. You visit with him long, you love him. And yet, he is a 'Mormon!'"[1]

Lorenzo Snow, son of Oliver Snow and Rosetta Leonora Pettibone, was born April 3, 1814, in Mantua, Ohio. In 1832 Lorenzo first met the Prophet Joseph Smith in Kirtland. After their brief meeting, Lorenzo said to his sister Eliza, "Joseph Smith is a most remarkable man. I want to get better acquainted with him. Perhaps, after all, there is something more to Joseph Smith and to Mormonism than I have ever dreamed."[2]

In June 1836 Lorenzo was baptized in the Chagrin River by John F. Boynton, yet he was dissatisfied with his baptism for he had not felt the promptings of the Holy Ghost. Retiring to a secluded wooded area, Lorenzo spoke to the Lord in prayer about the matter. While in prayer, Lorenzo heard the sound of "'rustling of silk robes.' Immediately the Holy Ghost descended upon him, enveloping his entire person and permeating his body from the crown of his head to the soles of his feet. He was as completely immersed in the spirit of the Holy Ghost as he had been immersed in the water."[3]

After his baptism, Lorenzo received a patriarchal blessing from Joseph Smith Sr. in which he was told, "Thou hast a great work to perform in thy day and generation. God has called thee to the ministry. Thou must preach the gospel of thy Savior to the inhabitants of the earth."4

Following the counsel given in his patriarchal blessing, Lorenzo devoted himself to the Lord's work, preaching the gospel in Ohio, Missouri, Kentucky, and Illinois. He said of the work, "The Lord was with me, and I was greatly blessed in performing my arduous labors." Under the direction of the Quorum of the Twelve Apostles, Lorenzo was asked in 1840 to preside over the missionary work in London, England. Of London, Lorenzo said, "Though surrounded with high-handed wickedness of every description, Zion begins to break forth, and, I trust, ere long will become a shining lamp in this city."5

By 1843 Lorenzo had returned to the United States, bringing with him two hundred fifty Latter-day Saint converts from England bound for Nauvoo, Illinois. Lorenzo did not stay long in Nauvoo due to his desire to campaign for Joseph Smith's bid for president of the United States. After the martyrdom of the Prophet Joseph and his brother Hyrum, Lorenzo returned to Nauvoo a brokenhearted man.

In 1846 Lorenzo fled from persecution in Nauvoo to Iowa, where he presided over the temporary LDS settlement at Mount Pisgah before leading a group of Saints to the Salt Lake Valley. In February 1849 Lorenzo was ordained an Apostle and welcomed into the Quorum of the Twelve Apostles. As an Apostle, he served a mission to Italy, where he supervised the publication of the Book of Mormon in Italian and published the pamphlet *The Voice of Joseph*.

After returning to the United States in 1852, Lorenzo was elected to the Utah State Legislature, a position he held for about thirty years. In 1853, he was called to preside over the Latter-day Saints in Brigham City, Utah.

From March to May 1864, Lorenzo served a short mission to the Hawaiian Islands. On that mission, he boarded a small boat heading to the Lahaina Harbor. "The first inkling Lorenzo had that the boat was in peril came when the captain shouted to the oarsmen, 'Hurry up! Hurry up!' in an apparent attempt to catch the crest of a wave and ride it to the safety of the beach. Glancing backward, Lorenzo saw what had provoked the captain's urgent command: 'I saw an immense surf, thirty or forty feet high,' he later reported, 'rushing toward us swifter than a race horse.'" The boat capsized and Lorenzo was tossed into the surf. According to Elder Cluff, when Lorenzo was rescued, "his body was stiff, and life apparently extinct. . . . But we did not feel like giving him up, and still prayed and worked over him, with an assurance that the Lord would hear and answer our prayers."[6] The Lord answered their prayers, for Lorenzo survived the near-drowning accident.

Lorenzo was next assigned to tour Europe and the Middle East. This was followed by a mission assignment to the American Indians. Lorenzo's assignments ended when he was arrested and imprisoned for "unlawful cohabitation" (plural marriage). After being freed from prison, Lorenzo gave the dedicatory prayer for the Manti Temple in 1888 and was sustained as President of the Quorum of the Twelve Apostles in 1889. Four years later, Lorenzo became the first president of the Salt Lake Temple on May 19, 1893. In the temple, Lorenzo received a divine manifestation in which he "saw the Savior . . . and talked with Him face to face."[7] The Lord Jesus Christ instructed Lorenzo "to move forward with the reorganization of the First Presidency" following the death of President Wilford Woodruff.[8]

Lorenzo accepted the Lord's call to the presidency "with the same sense of diffidence that had characterized his demeanor throughout life. 'If I had had the power to escape it honorably . . . I would never have been found in my present position.'"[9] During his administration, the issue of Church indebtedness weighed heavily on him. Abraham Owen Woodruff said, "President Snow is a Prophet of God; he now carries a heavy load—the indebtedness of the Church, for which he was not responsible. This grave responsibility has killed one Prophet. It is my sincere belief that my father [Wilford Woodruff] would now be living if it were not for the great responsibility which rested upon him. President Snow is in his 86th year."[10]

In May 1899, on his travels to St. George, Utah, Lorenzo received a revelation to solve the problem of indebtedness by recommitting the Saints to live the law of tithing. Of Lorenzo's revelation, his son LeRoi wrote, "I was sitting at a table reporting the proceedings, when all at once father paused in his discourse, complete stillness filled the room. When he commenced to speak again his voice strengthened and the inspiration of God seemed suddenly to come over him."[11] Lorenzo promised the Latter-day Saints that if they were to pay an honest tithing, the Church would be "relieved of its great indebtedness, but through the blessings of the Lord this would also be the means of freeing the Latter-day Saints from their individual obligations."[12]

Of his life's labors, Lorenzo said, "I never desired but one thing, one office in this Church, and that was to be an Elder, and that I received under the direction of Joseph Smith, the Prophet. I have gone along from one thing to another, with much fear, knowing my inability. I devoted myself wholly to discharging my duties and the Lord has helped me through, and he will continue to help me."[13]

Lorenzo died on October 10, 1901, of pneumonia.

1   *Millennial Star* 61, no. 37 (Sept. 14, 1899), 579.

2   Dr. Thomas C. Romney, *The Life of Lorenzo Snow, Fifth President of The Church of Jesus Christ of Latter-Day Saints* (Salt Lake City: Sugarhouse Press, 1955), 11.

3   Romney, 15.

4   Francis M. Gibbons, *Lorenzo Snow: Spiritual Giant, Prophet of God* (Salt Lake City: Deseret Book, 1982), 10.

5   Eliza R. Snow, *Biography and Family Record of Lorenzo Snow* (Salt Lake City: Deseret News Company, 1884), 19, 58.

6   Gibbons, 93, 95.

7   LeRoi C. Snow, "An Experience of My Father's," *Improvement Era* 36, no. 11 (Sept. 1933), 677; Andrew Jenson, *LDS Biographical Encyclopedia*, 1:26; Spencer J. Condie "Lorenzo Snow," *Heroes of the Restoration* (Salt Lake City: Deseret Book, 1977), 176–178.

8   *Teachings of Presidents of the Church: Lorenzo Snow* (Salt Lake City: The Church of Jesus Christ of Latter-day Saints, 2012), xii.

9   Gibbons, 214–215.

10   Romney, 425.

11   Ibid., 430.

12   LeRoi C. Snow, "The Lord's Way Out of Bondage," *Improvement Era*, July 1938, 439.

13   Romney, 439.

SIDNEY SPERRY
Unshakeable Faith

Courtesy of L. Tom Perry
Special Collections, Harold B.
Lee Library, Brigham Young
University.

OF SIDNEY SPERRY, SCHOLAR HUGH NIBLEY said, "In a world where it was fashionable to deny the literalness of the Bible and revelation, Brother Sperry, almost alone, played a crucial role in defending the Bible, the Book of Mormon, and other revelations given to Joseph Smith."[1]

Sidney Branton Sperry, son of Harrison Sperry and Josephine Titcomb, was born on December 26, 1895, in Salt Lake City, Utah. As a teenager at the LDS High School in Salt Lake City, Sidney heard that Reverend Franklin S. Spalding was trying "to discredit the Book of Abraham" in the Pearl of Great Price. Sidney's thought was that one day in the future he would "defend the latter-day scriptures he saw under attack."[2]

In 1917 Sidney graduated with his bachelor's degree in chemistry from the University of Utah. He was employed as a chemist at the United States Bureau of Metallurgical Research until receiving a mission call to the Southern States Mission in 1919. During his mission, Sidney served as president of the South Carolina District. After completing a successful mission, he returned to Utah and married Eva Lila Braithwaite in September 1921. They became the parents of eight.

To support his family, Sidney accepted employment as a seminary and institute instructor in the Church Educational System. Wanting to further his education in religious matters, he spoke with Elder James

E. Talmage, who encouraged him to learn languages of antiquity that had bearing on the scriptures.[3] Sidney accepted his encouragement and by 1926 had earned a master's degree in Old Testament languages and literature from the University of Chicago. After becoming the director of the Institute of Religion at the University of Idaho, he completed his dissertation and was awarded a PhD in biblical languages from the University of Chicago in 1931, becoming the first Latter-day Saint to receive a doctorate in ancient languages. Next, Sidney conducted postdoctorate research in archeology at the American School of Oriental Research in Jerusalem.

While in Jerusalem, Sidney weighed the professional options available to him at prestigious universities in the eastern states. He said, "I didn't really think I would ally myself with Brigham Young University because it was still so small and so far from other great universities and libraries. I was thinking that perhaps I could be a Mormon scholar 'out in the world,' and thereby have an influence for good among non-Mormons."[4] One night, however, Sidney had a dream:

> I was up high, looking down on the foothills of Y mountain, but it was a time farther in the future. The campus I saw was not the tiny cluster of buildings I had known, but a great array of many, many buildings. I was amazed at Brigham Young University, and I thought, "How much is going on in those buildings, with thousands of students and teachers, and much research. What a power for good it is!"
>
> Then I scanned the foothills and saw that the university spread northward, with many more buildings, and most of the structures were white. They reached the point where they adjoined a white temple, and I thought, "So we will have a temple!"[5]

Sidney joined the Brigham Young University faculty in 1932, just as the Great Depression was taking its toll on university funds. When faculty members expressed fear that BYU would close its doors, Sidney related his dream and expressed confidence that "the Lord would somehow change things. [Sidney] simply said, 'BYU will not close its doors. The Church [is] not going to give up BYU.'" Doors remained opened and Sidney became the "father of religious education" at the university. Of Sidney, scholar Ellis Rasmussen said, "'It was he who really persuaded the administration and the Brethren that there needed to be a core of people that were trained' at the highest academic levels in matters of the Old and New Testaments (as well as an understanding of the milieu out of which all of the standard works came and their doctrines)." Hugh Nibley agreed with Rasmussen's assessment and said that Sidney was "the 'Grand Old Man' of religious education who had the rare attribute of unshakable faith."[6]

From 1948 to 1954, Sidney served as the director of the Division of Religion and from 1954 to 1959 as the director of Graduate Studies in Religion at BYU. Although the titles and work were rewarding, he had to supplement his income to support his family. Colleague Keith Meservy recalled that several times Sidney entered "a race sponsored in Provo. . . . The object of the race was to use the least amount of gas, and Brother Sperry in his Volkswagon won this race [and its corresponding financial award] at least twice." Colleague David Yarn told of Sidney earning money by driving "a truck at Geneva Steel while the plant was being constructed."[7]

Sidney is credited with being the "first to suggest that the Book of Mormon—with its heroes and villains, its beautiful, poetic passages, and its theology centering on God's love and our Savior's redemptive sacrifice—amply qualifies as truly great literature."[8] In addition, Sidney was the pioneer of the BYU Study Abroad program, played a key role in founding the BYU Department of Archaeology, and was a popular speaker in the BYU Know Your Religion and Education Week programs. In 1962 Sidney received the prestigious Karl G. Maeser Teaching Award. He retired from academia in 1971.

Sidney's most enduring contributions to religious scholarship are his written works. "In the course of his productive career, he produced one book each on the Pearl of Great Price, the Doctrine and Covenants, and the New Testament, and four books and many articles on the Old Testament."[9] In total, Sidney authored eighteen books, including *Our Book of Mormon, The Voice of Israel's Prophets, Paul's Life and Letters, Doctrine and Covenants Compendium*, and *Book of Mormon Compendium*.

In giving advice to future generations of Latter-day Saints, Sidney said, "We are living in a time when men doubt that Christ is the very Son of God, the Redeemer and Savior of the world, who was literally raised from the dead and who, by the shedding of His blood, wrought out an atonement for all mankind. . . . Without this testimony there is little reason to study [the words of holy prophets]."[10] Sidney died at age eighty-two on September 4, 1977. His funeral services were held in the Joseph Smith Auditorium on the BYU campus. The Sidney B. Sperry Symposium is held annually at BYU in his honor.

1   "Sidney B. Sperry: The Man, Scholar, and Teacher," *Journal of Book of Mormon Studies* 4, no. 1 (1995): xii.

2   Ellis T. Rasmussen, "Sidney B. Sperry: Student of the Book of Mormon," *Ensign*, July 1986, 24.

3   V. Wallace McCarlie, "Sidney B. Sperry: Father of Religious Education at BYU," *BYU Religious Education Review*, Winter 2009, 11.

4   Carma deJong Anderson, "Sidney B. Sperry: Memories," *Journal of Book of Mormon Studies* 4, no. 1 (1995): xix.

5   McCarlie, 12.

6   Ibid.

7   "Sidney B. Sperry: The Man, Scholar, and Teacher," xiv–xv.

8   Rasmussen, 25.

9   Ibid., 24.

10   McCarlie, 13.

EVAN STEPHENS
Ambition

Courtesy of the Church History
Library, The Church of Jesus
Christ of Latter-day Saints.

WHILE LATTER-DAY SAINTS MAY KNOW the name of Evan Stephens as the man who composed sixteen hymns in the LDS hymnal, they might not know that Evan was also a brilliant music teacher and a longtime director of the Mormon Tabernacle Choir. At Evan's funeral, Elder Anthony C. Lund said, "Evan Stephens has done more than any other one person toward musical progress of the Church and this state [Utah]."[1] Though circumstances in his life could have prevented his musical contribution, "step by step" Evan rose "from obscurity to the highest position in the realm of music within . . . his Church."[2]

Evan Stephens, son of David Stephens and Jane Evans Stephens, was born June 28, 1854, in Pencader, South Wales. On the day of Evan's birth, his mother was working in a potato field despite intense heat and the heavy weight of her unborn child.[3] His father, a common farm laborer, also worked under adverse conditions. By age twelve, Evan was helping to support his family by working as a sheepherder.[4]

It was not until Evan and his family members were introduced to The Church of Jesus Christ of Latter-day Saints that they began to rise above abject poverty. They migrated to America in hopes of joining other Latter-day Saints residing in the Rockies. Of his trek across the plains, Evan recalled, "I was too elated to walk, so I would run ahead and then would stop and wait for the crowd."[5] In 1866, after arriving in the Salt

Lake Valley, Evan and his family settled in Willard, Utah, where Evan worked as a farmer, a teamster, a builder on the railroad, and a common laborer carrying rock and mortar. During this intense period of hard labor, Evan wrote, "I seemed to be bubbling over with musical thoughts. . . . The world became a new creation, and rhythm began to manifest itself in everything. I walked in rhythmic motion through the fields and behind the cows, and music was felt everywhere."[6]

Due to his passion for music, Evan decided to join the Willard Ward choir. When his older brother, Thomas, brought a small organ to their home, Evan spent hours playing hymns on the organ. Before long, Evan was named ward choir leader, Sunday School organist, and glee club director. Close neighbors referred to him as a "musical genius."[7] His unique musical talents eventually came to the attention of Professor Alex Lewis, who offered Evan a position as an organist with the Logan choir. After two years of playing for the choir, Evan moved to Salt Lake City in the hope of instructing choirs and supervising music at the University of Utah. To improve his own musical skills, Evan studied under the guidance of renowned musician Joseph J. Daynes and later at the New England Conservatory of Music in Boston.

In October 1890, Evan was appointed director of the Mormon Tabernacle Choir, a position he held for twenty-six years.[8] Six months after his appointment, the choir increased in number from 125 members to more than six hundred members. In 1893 Evan took members of the Mormon Tabernacle Choir to the World's Fair in Chicago and entered the choir in a musical competition. President Wilford Woodruff said of Evan's ambition for the choir, "A shepherd boy came down from the mountains and is here today to contest in this great competition."[9] The choir won second place in the World's Columbian Exposition.

The choir made seven national tours under Evan's direction, including a performance at Madison Square Garden in New York City and a concert at the White House for President William Howard Taft and his guests. To Church leaders, under Evan's leadership the choir had become the "foremost public relations representative to the world."[10]

Though Evan was greatly blessed for his work with the choir, his personal life was one of solitude. Several incidents, including the death of a fiancée, led to him to choose the life of a bachelor. He found solace in the "stillness of mountain[s]" and inspiration in "flowers, trees, mountain streams, rocky peaks and pine-clad hills."[11] For example, after listening to a sermon by President Joseph F. Smith, Evan went to the canyon and wrote the lyrics to the hymn "True to the Faith."[12] Of his music, Evan said, "Music should be a consistent and faithful servant to the Church and neither its master nor its slave, but always consistently harmonious with its aims, sentiments, and spiritual emotions and feelings."[13]

After resigning from the choir in 1916, Evan served on the General Music Committee of the Church. As a committee member, he was expected to compose musical arrangements and Church hymns, a task that he enjoyed very much. Evan died on October 26, 1930, at age seventy-six. At his funeral, prominent Salt Lake musician Dale Johnson said, "The music of Evan Stephens is a reflection of his character. It is rugged, indeed, almost primitive at times. It makes one think of craggy peaks and wide valleys. But at other times it breathes a spirit of tenderness that goes straight to the human heart."[14] Latter-day Saints still sing Evan's compositions, which tell of "joy and peace, of triumph and thanksgiving, of faith in the God of Israel and redemption for all mankind."[15]

1   Preston Nibley, *Stalwarts of Mormonism* (Salt Lake City: Deseret Book, 1954), 206.

2   George D. Pyper, "The Story of Our Hymns," *Improvement Era*, 1937, 297.

3   Ray L. Bergman, *The Children Sang: The Life and Music of Evan Stephens with the Mormon Tabernacle Choir* (Salt Lake City: Northwest Publishing Inc., 1992), 26.

4   George D. Pyper, "Evan Stephens," *Improvement Era*, 1933, 573.

5   Bergman, 41.

6   Dale A. Johnson, "The Life and Contributions of Evan Stephens," master's thesis, Brigham Young University, Dec. 1951, 4.

7   Nibley, 202; John Henry Evans, "Some Men Who Have Done Things," *Improvement Era*, 1910, 268.

8   Johnson, 22–23; Nibley, 205.

9   Karen Lynn Davidson, *Our Latter-day Hymns: The Stories and the Messages* (Deseret Book Company: Salt Lake City, 1988), 442.

10 Bergman, 129.

11 Joseph E. Richards, "Evan Stephens," *Improvement Era*, 1931, 584; Pyper, 573.

12 J. Spencer Cornwall, *Stories of Our Mormon Hymns* (Salt Lake City: Deseret Book Company, 1963), 173.

13 Bergman, 98.

14 Johnson, 71.

15 Richards, 584.

JAMES E. TALMAGE

Assurance

Courtesy of L. Tom Perry
Special Collections, Harold B.
Lee Library, Brigham Young
University.

JAMES E. TALMAGE SAID OF his faith in the Lord's work,

Since reaching the years that bring with them the powers of
judgment, I have never been without an assurance of the divinity of this cause, and therefore I claim no honor for having gained such knowledge. I regard it as the greatest gift of
God to me on earth. . . . [My faith] is like a greenhouse plant
nourished through artificial culture, and alive only because
protected from the blasts that wither and the frosts that destroy. . . . Sophistry, doubt, and the craft of misbelief have
surged in threatening torrents about the delicate roots of the
feeble plant of my faith; yet, through the protecting care of
the All Merciful, these dark rivers have been made to yield
nutriment and impart strength to the rising stem and its
sprouting branches.[1]

James Edward Talmage, son of James Joyce Talmage and Susannah
Preater, was born on September 21, 1862, in Hungerford, England. James
spent his youthful days in England, where he was baptized in 1873 at age
ten by his father. Of his conversion to the gospel of Jesus Christ, James
later said, "I set about investigating the claims of the Church and pursued

the investigation by prayer, fasting, and research. . . . After months of such inquiry, I found myself in possession of an assurance beyond all question that I was in solemn fact a member of the Church of Jesus Christ."[2]

In 1876 James and his family emigrated from England to the United States and settled in Provo, Utah, where James attended Brigham Young Academy. In 1881 he was awarded the first collegiate diploma from the academy's scientific department. At the request of Professor Karl G. Maeser, James taught at the academy from 1884 to 1888 and served on the academy board of trustees. James's interest in chemistry and geology led him to pursue advanced degrees at Lehigh University in Bethlehem, Pennsylvania, and John Hopkins University in Baltimore, Maryland. In 1896 James earned his PhD from Illinois Wesleyan University at age twenty-one.

While pursuing his educational goals, James was "so busy that he hadn't had a chance to do anything to look for a wife, but he knew he should. So he went into the mountains after fasting and praying that he would be able to know whom he should marry. He felt that the Lord had the big picture. There he had a clear impression in his mind of a girl who lived in a nearby small town. So he went to her home. When she came to the door he knew she was the one."[3] James married Mary Booth, the beautiful girl from the small town, on June 14, 1888, in the Manti Temple. To their union were born eight children.

To support his family and contribute to scientific academia, James served as president of the University of Deseret from 1894 to 1897 and as a professor of geology at the University of Utah from 1897 to 1907. By 1909 he was the director of the Deseret Museum. James was highly recognized as a geologist and for his travels throughout the nation and Europe in pursuit of scientific research. Of his professional work, Orson F. Whitney said, "Professionally a scientist and a preceptor, with gifts and powers equaled by few . . . his well stored mind, capacious memory, quick recollection and remarkable readiness of speech render him a beau-ideal instructor, in public or in private."[4]

James was a "Fellow of the Royal Microscopical Society (London), Fellow of the Royal Scottish Geographical Society (Edinburgh), Fellow of the Geological Society (London), Fellow of the Geological Society of America, Fellow of the Royal Society of Edinburgh, Associate of the Philosophical Society of Great Britain, or Victoria Institute, and Fellow of the American Association for the Advancement of Science."[5] In addition, James was the author of many scientific works, such as *First Book of Nature*

(1888) and *The Great Salt Lake, Present and Past* (1900). His religious works include *The Articles of Faith* (1899), *The Great Apostasy* (1909), *The House of the Lord* (1912), and *Jesus the Christ* (1915). Adding to his religious works, James headed a Church committee to arrange the Pearl of Great Price in verse format and add scriptural references.

On December 7, 1911, at age forty-nine, James was called to be an Apostle of the Lord Jesus Christ. The remainder of his life was devoted to Church service, which included a three-year stint as president of the European Mission. Of his missionary service, James wrote, "We trust that in the summing up of our labors during the last 38 months the Lord will graciously take note of our desires and intentions—for we have meant to do right, and have tried to do our best, though that best should have been better."[6]

At age seventy James died of inflammation of the heart on July 27, 1933, in Salt Lake City. Of his passing, Melvin J. Ballard said, "He takes with him the things that are worthwhile—a marvelous knowledge, his faith, his well-trained mind, and . . . his right to the holy Apostleship."[7] In honor of James, the Mathematics and Computer Sciences Building on the Brigham Young University campus and a similar building on the University of Utah campus are named for him. To future generations of budding scientists and Church leaders James advised, "We may not know what lies ahead of us in the future years, nor even in the days or hours immediately beyond. But for a few yards, or possibly only a few feet, the track is clear, our duty is plain, our course is illumined. For that short distance, for the next step, lighted by the inspiration of God, go on!"[8]

1   James E. Talmage, "How I Gained My Testimony of the Truth," *Young Woman's Journal* 4, no. 6 (March 1893): 259.

2   James E. Talmage, *The Parables of James E. Talmage*, comp. Albert L. Zobell, Jr. (Salt Lake City: Deseret Book, 1973), 66.

3   "James E. Talmage: Teacher, Mining Geologist, Engineer, University President, Writer and Apostle," Brigham Young Academy and Brigham Young High School Alumni Association, 2013, http://abc.eznettools.net/byhigh/History/Presidents/UofU/Talmage-JamesE.html.

4   Andrew Jenson, *LDS Biographical Encyclopedia*, 3:789.

5   Ibid., 3:788.

6   James E. Talmage, Personal Journal, 1926, 1927, Dec. 31, 1927, MSS 229, L. Tom Perry Special Collections, Harold B. Lee Library, Brigham Young University.

7   Melvin J. Ballard, "Dr. James E. Talmage," *Improvement Era*, Sept. 1933, 648.

8   James E. Talmage, "Three Parables: The Unwise Bee, the Owl Express, and Two Lamps," *Ensign*, Feb. 2003, 12.

N. Eldon Tanner

Integrity

Courtesy of Religious Education
Image Project, Brigham Young
University.

THOUGH BORN IN SALT LAKE CITY on May 9, 1898, Nathan Eldon Tanner was Canadian. His parents, Nathan William Tanner and Sarah Edna Brown Tanner, had settled near Cardston, Alberta, several years earlier, and Sarah had returned to Utah for the birth.[1] Apostle Hugh B. Brown of the Quorum of the Twelve later recalled that as a boy he had been present during the baby's labor and delivery, as his mother was there to assist. Remarking that he had heard Eldon's first cry, Brown later said, "Ever since that time there has been a bond between us, as I instinctively recognized a child of promise."[2] Above all, Brown admired his friend and fellow Apostle's integrity, the quality for which Eldon would be known throughout his life.

Young Eldon worked hard on his family's farm in Alberta alongside his seven younger brothers and sisters. His father once left for the day to attend to his responsibilities as a bishop, and he left Eldon in charge of his brothers, all of whom were given several responsibilities. The boys instead spent the day riding calves, and their father was deeply disappointed when he returned. Rather than punishing them, he simply told Eldon, "My boy, I thought I could depend on *you*."[3] Eldon spent the rest of his days ensuring that he met the expectations of both his earthly father and his Father in Heaven.

Eldon completed school through the eleventh grade in Aetna and Raymond before enrolling in Calgary Normal School for twelve months and qualifying to teach. All the while, he remained firm in his integrity, placing morals, family, and religion above personal gain. Turning down a better-paying job in a distant area, Eldon began teaching and acting as principal in a three-room school in Hill Spring, near where his family lived. Initially teaching seventh and eighth grades, he taught an additional grade level each year so that he could continue instructing the same group of students through graduation. He shared his moral code with his students, and the boys he taught began to participate in Scouts and sports, eventually becoming the best mannered in the stake. Eventually, Eldon and his six graduates went to Cardston to attend twelfth grade together. He then returned to Hill Spring as a teacher.[4]

While in Hill Spring, Eldon met and married Sara Isabelle Merrill. In 1923, four years after their wedding, they were sealed in the newly dedicated Alberta Temple. Together they had five daughters. His daughter Ruth recalled that her father's stern looks were deterrent enough to keep them from doing wrong, but the girls also fondly recalled his gentleness and praise.[5] One of his daughters later said, "All through Daddy's life he has found time for us and has always made us feel important."[6]

To earn extra money, the couple opened a general store and post office, which became so successful that Eldon stopped teaching for a time. He later moved to Cardston to teach high school and served as a Scoutmaster, bishopric member, deacons quorum adviser, and bishop there. He also became involved in politics, working as a member of the town council. In 1935, he ran for office and was elected to the Provincial legislature in Edmonton. His integrity earned the respect of his fellow public servants, and they soon selected him as Speaker of the House.

In 1936, the premier of Alberta, William Aberhart, invited Eldon to join his cabinet as minister of Lands and Mines. In this position, Eldon organized a conservation program, introduced successful legislation, helped keep Alberta debt free, and met with international dignitaries, including Queen Elizabeth. He worked in this position until 1952, when he resigned, moved to Calgary, and became president of Merrill Petroleums of Canada. Because of Eldon's reputation for integrity, Trans-Canada Pipelines Ltd. asked him two years later to head a $350 million, two-thousand-mile pipeline-building project between Alberta and Montreal. Though initially reluctant, Eldon agreed after the premier of Alberta and the national minister of Trade and Industry encouraged him. Extensive complications existed, but when Eldon left the position in 1959, the project was profitable and thriving thanks to his reputable business practices.[7] He even earned the nickname "Mr. Integrity."[8]

Throughout his life, Eldon served faithfully in the Church as a branch president, ward teacher, high council member, and stake president. Though he had no sons of his own, he particularly supported Boy Scouts and acted as provincial Scout commissioner and part of the Canadian Scout Committee. When asked why he felt such commitment to the organization and regularly wore a Scout pin, he replied, "Well, I want to help boys to be worthy of my daughters."[9] Just as he had as a teacher in Hill Spring, Tanner remained committed to teaching youth about virtue, honesty, and honor.

Hoping to enjoy retirement, Eldon and Sara built their dream home in Calgary near their friends, children, and grandchildren. In the fall of 1960, however, he was called as an Assistant to the Council of the Twelve. He and his wife moved to Utah, and in October general conference of that year, he declared, "I shall do my best and am prepared to dedicate my life and my best to the work of the Lord."[10] Shortly afterward, he was named president of the West European Mission. Then, in 1962, he was called as a member of the Quorum of the Twelve. The next year he began serving as president of the Genealogical Society and then as Second Counselor in the First Presidency. In 1972, he became First Counselor to President Harold B. Lee. Despite Parkinson's disease, failing strength and eyesight, and increasing age, he served faithfully in this position until his death from a heart attack on November 27, 1982.[11]

Hugh B. Brown said of his fellow Apostle,

> President Tanner is a man whose life is one of constancy amidst change, whose life testifies that there must be a reorientation around the hard core of spiritual values if individual and national integrity are to be saved. He knows that man, being a child of God, has a divine purpose in life. Spiritual values can be wrought only in the hearts of men, and this he exemplified in his own life.
>
> Here is a man of outstanding executive ability, unquestioned integrity, who has been known throughout his public career, even by his political opponents, for his rugged and undeviating honesty.[12]

1   "President N. Eldon Tanner Dies," *Ensign*, Jan. 1983, 6.
2   Hugh B. Brown, "President N. Eldon Tanner: A Man of Integrity," *Ensign*, Nov. 1972, 13–14.
3   Ibid., 14.
4   Ibid., 14–15.
5   Ibid., 15–16.
6   Marvin J. Ashton, "N. Eldon Tanner: An Example to Follow," *1977 Devotional Speeches of the Year* (Provo, UT: Brigham Young University Press, 1978), 192.
7   Brown, 16–17.
8   Ashton, 190.
9   Brown, 17.
10   N. Eldon Tanner, *Conference Report*, Oct. 1960, 46.
11   "President N. Eldon Tanner Dies," *Ensign*, Jan. 1983, 13, 6.
12   Brown, 19.

JOHN TAYLOR
Champion of Liberty

Courtesy of the Church
Archives, The Church of Jesus
Christ of Latter-day Saints.
Photographer: Hansen & Savage.

WHEN JOHN TAYLOR WAS A small boy, he saw a vision of an angel in the heavens holding a trumpet to his mouth and sounding a message to the nations. Although he would not understand the vision until later in life, it led him on a quest for greater truth.[1] John's growth from an obscure boy in England to a champion of liberty in America has everything to do with his commitment to The Church of Jesus Christ of Latter-day Saints.

John Taylor, son of James and Agnes Taylor, was born November 1, 1808, in Milnthorpe, England. At age fourteen, John became an apprentice to a cooper in Liverpool and later took up the turner's trade in Penrith, England. In England, he was introduced to the Methodist faith and joined that sect in 1824. A year or so later, John became a Methodist exhorter or teacher, a distinction he continued when he migrated to Canada. His unusual perceptions of the Methodist faith led to his dismissal as an exhorter and to his formation of Bible study classes.

John was introduced to Mormonism by Parley P. Pratt; as he carefully compared Parley's teachings with the scriptures, John wrote, "I made a regular business of it for three weeks, and followed Brother Parley from place to place." On May 9, 1836, John was baptized by Parley. Of his confidence in the gospel, John said, "I have never doubted any principle of Mormonism since."[2] His testimony for the work was evident in his ordinations as an elder, a high priest, and an Apostle.

Of his apostolic appointment, John said, "I felt my own weakness and littleness; but I felt determined, the Lord being my helper, to endeavor to magnify it."[3]

As an Apostle, John crossed the ocean to Great Britain, where he was instrumental in taking the gospel to Ireland, assisting migrating Saints to Nauvoo, and baptizing hundreds. After his return to Nauvoo, John became prominent in civic affairs as he was elected to the Nauvoo City Council and was named a regent of the University of Nauvoo. He was also the editor of the *Times and Seasons*, the *Wasp*, and the *Nauvoo Neighbor*. In the Nauvoo era, John is best remembered for being with the Prophet Joseph Smith and his brother Hyrum in Carthage Jail on June 27, 1844. On that afternoon in the loathsome jail, he sang "A Poor Wayfaring Man of Grief" before being severely wounded by four bullets that penetrated his body.

Although John was a victim of religious bigotry, his faithful obedience endured. He said, "I expected when I came into this Church, that I should be persecuted and proscribed. I expected that the people would be persecuted. But I believed that God had spoken, that the eternal principles of truth had been revealed, and that God had a work to accomplish which was in opposition to the ideas, values, and notions of men, and I did not know but it would cost me my life before I got through."[4]

John followed the leadership of the Quorum of the Twelve Apostles from Nauvoo to the Salt Lake Valley. From 1857 to 1876 he served in the Utah Territorial Legislature as speaker of the House of Representatives for the first five sessions. From 1868 to 1870 he was the probate judge of Utah County, and he served as superintendent of the district schools in 1877.

Following the death of Brigham Young, John's civic service ended as he became President of the Church. As the leader of the Latter-day Saints, John pushed forward the building of temples and holding of regular priesthood meetings and conferences in the stakes of Zion. In 1880 he held a Jubilee year to commemorate the fiftieth anniversary of the organization of the Church. Following an Old Testament tradition, John forgave one-half of the debt owed to the Perpetual Immigration Fund and one-half of the delinquent tithing of the poor.

John took a firm stance in defense of plural marriage when Senator Edmunds of Vermont began pushing legislation in the U.S. Congress to curtail the religious practice. John explained that "his argument was not against his country, but against those who would use its power to abuse the rights of others."[5] On February 1, 1885, John preached his last public sermon: "You will see trouble! *trouble!* TROUBLE enough in these United States. . . . *I tell you in the name of God, WOE! to them that fight against Zion, for God will fight against them!*"[6] That same night he went into self-imposed exile to escape the ruthless persecution aimed at him by unrelenting enemies of the Church. While in hiding, John wrote, "We are engaged in a great work, and laying the foundation thereof—a work that has been spoken of by all the holy prophets since the world was."[7]

President John Taylor died at age seventy-eight. Engraved on a silver plate on his coffin are the words, "Holiness to the Lord. Rest in Peace."

1   B. H. Roberts, *The Life of John Taylor* (Salt Lake City: Bookcraft, 1963), 28.
2   Ibid., 38.
3   Ibid., 48.
4   *Journal of Discourses*, 25:91.
5   Paul Hyde and Dennis Wright, "John Taylor," in *Presidents of the Church: The Lives and Teachings of the Modern Prophets*, ed. Craig Manscill, Robert Freeman, and Dennis Wright (Springville, UT: Cedar Fort, 2008), 63.
6   Roberts, 383–384.
7   Ibid., 394.

PETER VIDMAR
Hard Work

Courtesy of Peter Vidmar.

BEFORE PETER VIDMAR ENTERED HIS first national gymnastics training camp, Coach Makoto Sakamoto told him, "I don't care if you learn any new skills, just tell me when you return that you worked harder than anyone else on the national team." Taking this advice to heart, Peter was the last gymnast to leave after practice each night. He avoided eating unhealthy food and exercised in his room after other teammates had gone to bed. When the training camp ended, Peter was "proud to tell his couch, 'Yes, I worked harder than everyone else.'"[1] Peter won three medals at the 1984 Los Angeles Summer Olympic Games.[2] He held the record for being the highest-scoring United States male gymnast in Olympic history.

Peter Vidmar, son of John Vidmar and Doris Neely, was born June 3, 1961. He credits his parents with teaching him "the fundamental lessons that helped shape his character and life." Although his father was afflicted with polio, Peter does not recall that he complained about his infirmities. Of his father, Peter said, "He never quit, and that became our family motto. He taught us to finish what we start."[3]

Peter's parents also taught him to keep the Word of Wisdom, which made it easier for Peter to say no when during the victory ceremony after winning a gold medal he was offered wine at a gymnastics competition in Germany. "I felt a bit embarrassed, but I felt proud that it was easy to say no," said Peter. "I believe that if we make proper decisions before we are faced with [them], we will find it much easier to resist."[4] Peter wrote, "As a member of The Church of Jesus Christ of Latter-day Saints, I have been taught from my youth to live a certain way that seems outdated to many people. But I don't feel hemmed in or burdened by rules. I feel free." Of his attending early-morning seminary, Peter said, "The lessons I learned about Jesus Christ . . . had a tremendous impact on me. I wanted to have the peace that came from trying to live a Christlike life."[5]

Peter's parents introduced him to gymnastics at age eleven by responding to a newspaper advertisement about an experimental gymnastics program offered by Makoto Sakamoto, an international gymnastics champion. Of Sakamoto's coaching ability, Peter said, "[He] never compromised, trained hard, and believed in always doing what you say you're going to do."[6] When Sakamoto asked Peter to train on Sundays, Peter told him that he could not. Peter remembered, "I did a poor job of explaining this to him, and he was very disappointed. . . . He asked me to leave. I was devastated." When Sakamoto learned that Peter's reason for not practicing on Sunday was his commitment to religious principles, Sakamoto allowed Peter to return to the gymnasium, believing that "[Peter] could channel that discipline to gymnastics."[7]

While training for the Olympics, Peter learned "the key to getting through the tough spots is to *have a plan and to stick to it.*"[8] Training with five other competitive gymnasts proved an incentive, for as Peter later explained, "If they were working hard and I was tired, that picked me up, and I worked a little harder. If I was working hard, and they were tired, then I helped to pick them up." Peter also learned that a little extra work made all the difference. "If one gymnast is training six hours a day, I can't train twelve," he said. "That's impossible—my body would fall apart. But I can train six hours and fifteen minutes a day—just a little bit more."[9]

Peter's "little bit more" paid off when he was named captain of the 1984 United States Men's Gymnastics Team. His was the first U.S. Gymnastics team to win a gold medal at the Olympics. "To win the team medal was the most exhilarating 'up' I have ever experienced," recalled Peter.[10] As for his individual performance, Peter won a gold medal for scoring a perfect 10 on the pommel horse. He also won a silver medal in the men's all-round individual gymnastics competition.

In addition to Olympic success, Peter has "numerous NCAA and international titles, an economics degree from UCLA, and experience as a television announcer for CBS."[11] He has been chairman of the Board of USA Gymnastics and served in many capacities with the Olympic movement.

Today, Peter is a popular motivational speaker for audiences across the nation. What he values most, however, is his relationship with his family. Peter married UCLA gymnast Donna Harris. Peter and Donna have five grown children and live in California. Of his family life, Peter says, "I've learned life isn't about accomplishing things—it's really about building relationships. What I treasure most is the relationship I have with my wife and children, with family and friends. . . . That's what makes life full and enriching." In a recent interview, Peter stated, "I don't know if children are an accomplishment, but my greatest joy in life comes from seeing my [five] children find joy."[12]

1   Peter Vidmar, "Pursuing Excellence," *Ensign*, May 1985.

2   Trent Toone, "Beyond Gymnastics with Peter Vidmar," *Deseret News*, March 22, 2012, http://www.deseretnews.com/article/865552605/Beyond-gymnastics-with-Peter-Vidmar.html?pg=all.

3   Ibid.

4   Vidmar.

5   "Peter Vidmar," in *Why I Believe* (Salt Lake City: Deseret Book, 2001).

6   Karen Owoc, "An Interview with Peter Vidmar," http://www.usa-sports.org/PeterVidmar.pdf.

7   *Why I Believe.*

8   Owoc.

9   Peter Vidmar, *Go for the Gold! Excerpts from the Addresses Given at a Fireside of the Salt Lake Institute of Religion on February 3, 1985* (Salt Lake City: Deseret Book, 1985), 2, 6.

10   Kit Poole, "Athletes Pursue Excellence at Olympics," *Ensign*, Oct. 1984, 78.

11   *Why I Believe.*

12   Toone.

David Whitmer
Truth

IN 1828 DAVID WHITMER HEARD rumors of a gold Bible, and letters from a young schoolmaster named Oliver Cowdery confirmed these rumors. David first met Joseph Smith when he conveyed the Prophet, his wife, Emma, and Oliver Cowdery by team and wagon from Pennsylvania to the Whitmer home in Fayette, New York. David readily accepted Joseph's prophetic calling and was privileged to be one of Three Witnesses to see the plates and behold "a dazzlingly brilliant light that surpassed in brightness even the sun at noonday and . . . a personage clothed in white and near him a table containing . . . ancient artifacts."[1]

One of the first baptized in this dispensation, David is numbered among the six original members of the Church and was ordained an elder on the day the Church was organized. Although he did not remain with the Church, he was always true to his testimony of the Book of Mormon.

David Whitmer, son of Peter Whitmer Sr. and Mary Musselman, was born on January 7, 1805, in Harrisburg, Pennsylvania. During his infancy David's family moved to a wooded farmland adjoining Seneca Lake in western New York. There David grew to manhood. At age twenty he was elected sergeant in the Seneca Grenadiers, a newly organized militia company. After his marriage to Julia Ann Jolly in January 1831, he moved with his young bride to Ohio and then to the frontier of Missouri to be with the Saints.

On July 3, 1834, David was appointed president of the Clay County high council. His leadership was laudatory, yet, after becoming a general agent for the Church's Literary Firm in September 1835 and attending the Kirtland Temple dedication in March 1836, he began to doubt the leadership of Joseph Smith and aligned himself with apostate sentiments in Kirtland. He declared that under Joseph Smith's leadership the Church had "drifted into error and spiritual blindness" and had "departed in a great measure from the faith of the Church of Christ as it was first established."[2] For these reasons, as well as for violating the Word of Wisdom and possessing the same spirit as dissenters, he was excommunicated in April 1838 at Far West, Missouri.

Feeling betrayed by the verdict, David turned for support to his extended family. The Whitmers joined David and left the Church, most settling in Richmond, Missouri. In that community, David was elected to the city council several times and filled the unexpired term of mayor from 1867 to 1868. For nearly a quarter of a century, he operated the "Livery and Feed Stable" of "D. Whitmer & Son" or "Whitmer & Co." of Richmond. His advertisements promised, "Customers may rely on promptness, good turnouts, safe horses, and moderate charges."[3]

The *Richmond Conservator* reported that "the forty six years of private citizenship on the part of David Whitmer, in Richmond, [was] without stain or blemish. . . . If a life of probity, of unobtrusive benevolence and well doing for well nigh a half century, marks a man as a good citizen, then David Whitmer should enjoy the confidence and esteem of his fellow men."[4]

In the 1870s David organized the Church of Christ, whose congregation consisted of his extended family and a handful of friends. In 1887 he wrote and published a pamphlet titled *An Address to all Believers in Christ*, which earnestly expressed his religious views and his rejection of Mormonism as defined by Brigham Young. In spite of rejecting the Church, David tenaciously held to his testimony of the Book of Mormon. He was widely known as the last surviving witness and was interviewed far more extensively than any other witness.

Just before his death, David said to his attending physician, "Dr. Buchanan, I want you to say whether or not I am in my right mind, before I give my dying testimony." The doctor answered, "Yes, you are in your right mind." David then bore his testimony: "I want to say to you all, the Bible and the record of the Nephites (Book of Mormon) is true, so you can say that you have heard me bear my testimony on my death-bed."[5]

David died on January 25, 1888, in Richmond at the age of eighty-three. The *Richmond Democrat* eulogized his life: "[N]o man ever lived here, who had among our people, more friends and fewer enemies. Honest, conscientious and upright in all his dealings, just in his estimate of men, and open, manly and frank in his treatment of all, he made lasting friends who loved him to the end."[6]

1   Lyndon W. Cook, ed., *David Whitmer Interviews: A Restoration Witness* (Orem, UT: Grandin Book Co., 1991), xiv.

2   David Whitmer, *An Address to All Believers in Christ* (Richmond, MO: David Whitmer, 1887), 59, 4.

3   *Richmond Conservator*, September 10, 1863, as cited in Richard Lloyd Anderson, *Investigating the Book of Mormon Witnesses* (Salt Lake City: Deseret Book, 1981), 72.

4   *Richmond Conservator*, Jan. 9, 1885, as cited in Anderson, 74.

5   Andrew Jenson, *LDS Biographical Encyclopedia*, 1:270.

6   *Richmond Democrat*, Jan. 26, 1888, as cited in Anderson, 76.

NEWEL K. WHITNEY
Friendship

Courtesy of the Church History
Library, The Church of Jesus
Christ of Latter-day Saints.

BELIEVING HIMSELF INCAPABLE OF HOLDING the office of bishop, Newel
Whitney said to the Prophet Joseph Smith, "Brother Joseph, I can't
see a Bishop in myself." Joseph answered, "Go and ask the Lord about
it." Newel asked the Lord and heard a voice from heaven proclaim,
"Thy strength is in me."[1] On October 7, 1835, the Lord said of Newel,
"Blessed of the Lord is Brother Whitney, even the Bishop of the Church
of Latter-day Saints, for the Bishopric shall never be taken away from him
while he liveth. . . . He shall deal with a liberal hand to the poor and the
needy, the sick and the afflicted, the widow and the fatherless."[2]

Newel K. Whitney, son of Samuel Whitney and Susanna Kimball, was
born on February 5, 1795, in Marlborough, Vermont. At age nineteen
he entered the merchandising business in the village of Plattsburg, New
York. Due to the War of 1812 and subsequent battles fought in Plattsburg,
Newel lost most of his possessions.

After the war, Newel moved from Plattsburg to Green Bay on Lake
Michigan, where he became an Indian trader, buying and selling furs for
eastern markets. A skirmish with an enraged, drunken Indian led him
to abandon his Indian trade. He next moved to Kirtland, Ohio, where
he once again entered the mercantile business. His business success in
Kirtland was described by his wife, Elizabeth, who said, "We prospered in
all our efforts to accumulate wealth, so much so, that among our friends

it came to be remarked that nothing of Whitney's ever got lost on the lake, and no product of his exportation was ever low in the market; always ready sales and fair prices."[3]

Yet Newel and his wife didn't enjoy the same success with religious creeds of the day. One evening about midnight, as they were praying to know how to receive the Holy Ghost, Elizabeth recalled, "The Spirit rested upon us and a cloud overshadowed the house. It was as though we were out of doors. The house passed away from our vision. . . . A solemn awe pervaded us. We saw the cloud and felt the Spirit of the Lord. Then we heard a voice out of the cloud saying, 'Prepare to receive the word of the Lord, for it is coming.'"[4]

On or about February 1, 1831, Joseph Smith arrived at the Whitney store. "Newel K. Whitney! Thou art the man!" Joseph exclaimed as he extended his hand. "You have the advantage of me," replied Newel. "I could not call you by name, as you have me." Joseph said, "I am Joseph, the Prophet. You've prayed me here; now what do you want of me?"[5] Elizabeth wrote of this meeting, "I remarked to my husband that this was the fulfilment of the vision we had seen of a cloud, as of glory, resting upon our house."[6]

Joseph and his wife, Emma, resided with the Whitneys for several weeks in 1831. Joseph wrote of Newel, "He is Chearfull [*sic*] and patient and a true Brother to me."[7] Newel was also a true brother to many. For example, he held a three-day feast in January 1836 for the poor Saints residing in the Kirtland vicinity. "Attended a sumptuous feast at Bishop Newel K. Whitney's," wrote Joseph. "This feast was after the order of the Son of God—the lame, the halt, and the blind were invited, according to the instructions of the Savior."[8] Joseph later wrote of Newel's continual service to the poor: "Thou art a faithful friend in whom the afflicted sons of men can confide, with the most perfect safety. Let the blessings of the Eternal also be crowned upon his head. How warm that heart! how anxious that soul!"[9]

In 1848 Newel was called as the Presiding Bishop of the Church. Less than two years later, he died on September 21, 1850, in Salt Lake City. A tribute in the *Deseret Weekly News* read, "One of the oldest, most exemplary, and most useful members of the Church fallen suddenly. . . . He has gone down to the grave, leaving a spotless name behind him, and thousands to mourn the loss of such a valuable man."[10]

1   Roy W. Doxey, *Latter-day Prophets and the Doctrine and Covenants*, 4 vols. (Salt Lake City: Deseret Book, 1978), 2:406.

2   *History of the Church*, 2:288.

3   Edward W. Tullidge, *The Women of Mormondom* (New York: Tullidge and Crandall, 1877), 34.

4   Andrew Jenson, *LDS Biographical Encyclopedia*, 1:223.

5   Orson F. Whitney, "Newel K. Whitney," *Contributor* 6, no. 4 (Jan. 1885): 125.

6   Jenson, 1:224.

7   Dean C. Jessee, *The Personal Writings of Joseph Smith* (Salt Lake City: Deseret Book, 1984), 239.

8   *History of the Church*, 2:362.

9   *History of the Church*, 5:108.

10   Jenson, 1:227.

JOHN A. WIDTSOE
Love of Learning

Courtesy of the Church History
Library, The Church of Jesus
Christ of Latter-day Saints.

AT AGE SIX JOHN WIDTSOE stood near his father's open grave and heard a priest utter, "Dust thou art, to dust thou returnest." As John tossed a rose on his father's casket, he promised to carry on his father's high ideals and to follow him as a role model.[1] Reflecting on his father's life, John said, "He had served his generation well. He was gifted, capable, farseeing, and wise, and was much beloved among the people. In my childish appreciation of him, I pledged, as his grave was filled, to keep his good work going."[2] Throughout his life, John strove to bring honor to his father's name through academics, hard work, and faithful service to God.

John Andreas Widtsoe, son of John Andersen Widtsoe and Anna Karine Gaarden, was born January 31, 1872, on an obscure island in Norway. At John's birth, his right wrist was attached to the right side of his head. An operation to correct the deformity was performed. John's loss of blood after the operation made his survival nothing short of miraculous.

John's parents instilled in him a love of learning in his childhood. "At five years of age I read easily," he recalled. "My father had an unusually well stocked library. My parents held me closely to the Bible; but I spent much time browsing among my father's books."[3]

After her husband's death, John's mother became acquainted with Latter-day Saint missionaries. After two years of investigating

Mormonism, his mother joined The Church of Jesus Christ of Latter-day Saints and made plans to immigrate to America to be with the Saints. By 1883, the Widtsoe family resided in Logan, Utah, where John learned to speak English and found employment to supplement his family's income. Despite the potential he demonstrated at work, John's objective was to further his education. "From my earliest youth," he wrote, "education became my objective. . . . There was a real relish for learning in my soul."[4]

At age seventeen John entered Brigham Young College in Logan and received what he described as "food to my soul." He next enrolled in Harvard and studied chemistry. At Harvard in 1893, John met Leah Eudora Dunford, a granddaughter of Brigham Young and resident of Utah. After graduating *summa cum laude* from Harvard in 1894, John accepted a professorship at the Agricultural College of Utah in Logan so that he could continue to court Leah.[5]

In 1898 John and Leah were sealed for time and eternity in the Salt Lake Temple by President Joseph F. Smith. Of his wife, John observed, "Leah . . . was blessed with an attractive personality, an excellent intelligence, and a clear understanding of problems. . . . Her help added much to whatever success I may have attained in life." John and Leah's successful marriage was not without heartache. Though they both desired to rear a large family, five of their seven children died at a young age. "There were lights and shadows in our lives," John wrote. "We had to face many changes. Our love, however, was not affected. . . . May I borrow Mark Twain's phrase and say that wherever Leah is there is Eden."[6]

John continued his education in Germany at the Gottingen University and earned a PhD in chemistry.[7] After completing this degree, John returned to Logan, where he pursued agricultural research at Utah State University. He received national and international recognition for his research on irrigation, dry farming, and other agrarian subjects. Officials of the United States Department of Agriculture and the Office of Experiment Stations often called on him for consultation. John authored many articles, books, and manuals, and was a major contributor to and editor of the *Improvement Era*. John also served as president of Utah State University and president of the University of Utah.[8]

John's professional success by no means undermined his devotion to the gospel of Jesus Christ. He magnified his callings in the priesthood and made important contributions to Church auxiliaries, especially the Young Men's Mutual Improvement Association.[9] He became known for his teachings on the harmony that exists between correct science and religion, claiming that the study of one need not diminish a belief in or focus on the other. His writings and theories on science and religion are still referenced today.

In 1921 John was called to the Quorum of the Twelve Apostles. Of this calling, he said, "I had never refused a call by the priesthood. It was too late to begin now."[10]

John died on November 29, 1952, after serving in the Quorum of the Twelve for thirty-two years. To family, friends, and Latter-day Saints throughout the world, John fulfilled the pledge he had made at his father's grave "to live unselfishly, to serve God and help my fellow man, and use my time and talents industriously for the advancement of human good."[11]

1   Alan K. Parrish, *John A. Widtsoe: A Biography* (Salt Lake City: Deseret Book, 2003), 18.

2   John A. Widtsoe, *In a Sunlit Land: The Autobiography of John A. Widtsoe* (Salt Lake City: Deseret News Press, 1952), 3.

3   Ibid., 4–5.

4   Parrish, 23, 28, 45; Widtsoe, 19.

5   Parrish, 50, 61, 76, 83.

6   Widtsoe, 233, 235–239.

7   Robert L. Miller, "Science and Scientists," in *Encyclopedia of Mormonism*, ed. Daniel H. Ludlow (New York: Macmillan, 1992), 3:1274.

8   Parrish, 128–131, 195, 226.

9   Alan K. Parrish, "Joseph F. Smith and John A Widtsoe: Reaching the Young Men through the *Improvement Era*," in *Times of Transition*, ed. Thomas G. Alexander (Salt Lake City: Joseph Fielding Smith Institute for Latter-day Saint History at Brigham Young University, 2003), 33–38.

10 Widtsoe, 156.

11 Parrish, 662; Widtsoe, 244.

MACK WILBERG

Beauty of Music

Courtesy of The Mormon
Tabernacle Choir, The Church
of Jesus Christ of Latter-day
Saints.

AFTER SERVING AS AN ASSOCIATE music director of the Mormon Tabernacle
Choir for nine years, noted composer and conductor Mack Wilberg
was named the musical director of the choir in March 2008. Mack is
internationally recognized for his choral compositions and arrangements
published exclusively with Oxford University Press. His biography on
the Oxford University Press website states, "Wilberg's arrangements
and compositions are performed and recorded by choral organizations
throughout the world. With their grandeur, energy, and craftsmanship,
they inspire performers and audiences everywhere."[1] Whether composing
or conducting a rousing rendition of a popular American folk tune, an
orchestrated hymn, or a gentle Christmas carol, Mack willingly shares his
musical talents with old and young throughout the world.

Mack Wilberg, son of LaMar Wilberg and Helen McNeil, was born
on February 20, 1955, in the small town of Castle Dale, Utah. His father,
a coal miner, was killed in a mining-related accident when Mack was nine
years old. His mother, a second-grade school teacher, taught Mack and
his older sister, Julie, small-town values of hard work and integrity and
helped both to develop their God-given talents. From an early age, Mack
demonstrated a love of music and began playing the piano by ear when
he was four years old. By age six, he was taking piano lessons; by age nine,
he was playing the organ for Church meetings. It was at this time that

Mack began to compose music and learned how to play other musical instruments.

Through his formative years in rural Utah, Mack came to deeply appreciate both music and his small-town heritage. He said of his musical upbringing, "I have always been aware of what bringing the joy of music does to people. Music has the power to unite people from all walks of life, to soften hearts, and to bridge socio-economic, educational, and religious barriers."[2] With the help of good teachers and mentors, Mack began to formulate plans for a career in music.

After returning from a mission to South Korea in 1976, Mack went to Brigham Young University. He earned a bachelor's degree in music in 1979, followed by a master's and doctorate degree from the University of Southern California, where he was named the outstanding student in his doctoral class. While working toward his doctorate degree, Mack met his wife-to-be, Rebecca, on a blind date. Rebecca, also a gifted musician, was pursuing a doctorate degree in music at Brigham Young University and doing research in Southern California. Mack and Rebecca married and became the parents of four.

In 1984 Mack joined the music faculty at Brigham Young University, where he became well-known as the conductor of the Brigham Young University Men's Chorus and Concert Choir. He was also a member of the American Piano Quartet, for whom he arranged many works. Mack taught at BYU for fifteen years before joining the Mormon Tabernacle Choir in 1999 as an associate music director. Of being asked to direct the famous choir in 2008, Mack said, "I feel it an honor and privilege to be a part of this historic and beloved organization and tradition. I never imagined as a small-town boy that someday I would have the opportunities I've had and I'm grateful to the many—past and present—who have made these experiences possible."[3]

As the director of the choir, Mack has oversight of the musical and creative aspects of the Mormon Tabernacle Choir, the Orchestra at Temple Square, the Temple Square Chorale, and the Bells on Temple Square. In rehearsals, concerts, tours, recordings, and in the creative direction of the weekly *Music and the Spoken Word* broadcasts, Mack is the director who makes the big decisions. During his tenure as director, Mack has continued to refine the sound, flexibility, accessibility, and professionalism of the Mormon Tabernacle Choir.

Mack is also an active composer, arranger, guest conductor, and choral clinician throughout the United States and abroad. In addition to the many compositions and arrangements he has written for the Mormon Tabernacle Choir and Orchestra at Temple Square, his works are performed and recorded by choral organizations throughout the world, including the choirs of King's College and St. John's College in Cambridge, England, and the choruses of the Chicago, San Francisco, Cleveland, and Dallas symphony orchestras. He is one of only a few American composers whose works have been presented twice at the annual "Festival of Nine Lessons and Carols" from King's College, broadcast worldwide on Christmas Eve. His *Requiem*, composed in 2007 as part of the rededication concerts of the Salt Lake Tabernacle, has been performed many times throughout the United States and abroad since its premier. Artists such as Renée Fleming, Frederica von Stade, Deborah Voight, Bryn Terfel, The King's Singers, Brian Stokes Mitchell, and narrators Walter Cronkite, David McCullough, Michael York, Jane Seymour, and Tom Brokaw have performed his works.

Mack is a consummate musician who writes, teaches, performs, accompanies, and "enjoys having a foot, as it were, in both the private, solitary world of composing and the more public, collaborative world of conducting."[4] His gifts come from dedication, hard work, and a humble, humane willingness to share the talents God has given him. For Mack, his career is not about accolades, recognition, or standing ovations. It is all about lifting and inspiring people through the beauty of music.

1   "Mack Wilberg: Director," Singers.com, http://www.singers.com/choral/director/Mack-Wilberg/; see also http://www.mormontabernaclechoir.org/about/mack-wilberg?lang=eng.
2   Interview with Mack Wilberg.
3   Ibid.
4   Elliott S. Jones, "A Survey of the Choral Arrangements of Mack Wilberg and Musical Analyses of Representative Arrangements," PhD dissertation, University of Miami, Aug. 2000, 14.

ERNEST L. WILKINSON
Dedication

Courtesy, of L. Tom Perry
Special Collections, Harold B.
Lee Library, Brigham Young
University, Provo, UT.

WHEN ERNEST L. WILKINSON WAS appointed the seventh president of Brigham Young University in 1951, there were six buildings on campus, 4,004 enrolled students, 244 full-time faculty members, and 37 academic departments located in five colleges. In 1971 at the end of his twenty-year tenure, there were more than 200 buildings on campus, 25,000 enrolled students, 900 full-time faculty members, and 71 academic departments in 13 colleges. Such unprecedented growth at Brigham Young University is an indication of Ernest's work ethic. Though often spoken of as a blunt and impatient man, Ernest shrugged off such comments by stating, "If I sometimes offend people it is not because I want to, but because I am determined to get something done."[1]

Ernest LeRoy Wilkinson, son of Robert Wilkinson and Cecilia Anderson, was born May 4, 1899, in Ogden, Utah. Though he was born into a loving family, the neighborhood in which he grew to manhood was less than ideal. It was known as the notorious "Hell's Half Acre" because of the many times police turned a blind eye to bootlegging and other illegal activities. It took self-discipline, the influence of a strong mother, and a decision to attend Weber Stake Academy for him to overcome a rough childhood.[2]

At the academy, Ernest applied himself to his studies and excelled in extracurricular activities. He gained recognition by becoming a champion debater, editor of the school paper, student body president, and valedictorian of his class.[3] Many years later, Ernest expressed gratitude "to my mother, to my Heavenly Father, and the profound influence of a church school[.] I acknowledge my blessings. What could have been a life of iniquity has become one of opportunity and happiness."[4]

In 1918, at the height of a flu pandemic that swept the nation, Ernest entered Brigham Young University with the Student Army Training Corps. Unfortunately, he was one of the first in the corps to be stricken with the deadly flu. While receiving a priesthood blessing to help him overcome the effects of the flu, Ernest pled with the Lord to spare his life. "I promised my Heavenly Father," recalled Ernest, "that if he would spare my life, I would serve [BYU] if ever the opportunity presented itself. Little did I realize that about 30 years later I would be appointed president of Brigham Young University, and that my office would consist of the room where I was restored to health."[5]

Ernest enrolled as a student at Brigham Young University in 1919. He held prestigious student and academic leadership positions before graduating in 1921 and beginning his career as an English teacher in Provo, where he met Alice Ludlow. After a long courtship, they were married in the Salt Lake Temple in 1923. They were blessed with three sons and two daughters.

Ernest attended law school at George Washington University. In 1926 he graduated *summa cum laude* from law school. A year later he received a Doctor of Juridical Science from Harvard Law.[6] Ernest taught law for a few years at the University of California and then at the New Jersey Law School. He left teaching to join a law firm in New York before opening a successful private law practice in Washington, DC. One highlight of his legal career was representing the Ute Indian Tribes in their case against the United States government (*Confederated Bands of Ute Indians v. United States*). The Ute Indians wanted money for tribal lands the federal government had taken from them years earlier. After sixteen years of legal maneuvers, the case was decided in favor of the tribes, who were awarded $32 million in remuneration costs. A direct result of this case was the passage of the Indian Claims Commission Act, which allowed other tribes to seek similar claims against the federal government.[7]

In 1951, after accepting an invitation from President George Albert Smith to be president of Brigham Young University, Ernest loaded his family's possessions in a car and drove to Provo. Because of his earlier commitment to serve BYU if given the opportunity, Ernest refused to accept a salary during the first thirteen years of his presidency. He considered his presidency as personal missionary service.[8] Ernest viewed his greatest achievement at the university to be the establishment of campus LDS wards and stakes. When he first arrived at the university, there was one LDS branch on campus. When he resigned his presidency in 1971, there were ten stakes and ninety-eight campus wards.[9] His successor, Dallin H. Oaks, expressed admiration for Ernest: "There is hardly any aspect of [the] university that does not bear the imprint of Ernest L. Wilkinson."[10]

Ernest died of a heart attack in April 1978, leaving a lasting legacy as a hardworking educator, lawyer, and an efficient and faithful servant of the Lord.[11]

1   Danae Friel, "Ernest Wilkinson, University Builder," *BYU Magazine*, Fall 1999, http://magazine.byu.edu/?act=view&a=207.

2   Ernest L. Wilkinson, *Earnestly Yours*, ed. Edwin J. Butterworth and David H. Yarn (Salt Lake City: Deseret Book, 1971), ix, 5–7.

3   Wilkinson, 5–8; "Register of the Ernest L. Wilkinson, 1899–1978, Papers, 1917-1978," June 2002, L. Tom Perry Special Collections, Brigham Young University, 7.

4   Wilkinson, 8.

5   Friel, 2–3.

6   Wilkinson, ix.

7   Friel, 2.

8   Ibid.

9   Ernest L. Wilkinson Papers, 8–9.

10 Friel, 1.

11 Ernest L. Wilkinson Papers, 9.

JOSEPH B. WIRTHLIN
Honoring Parents

Photo © Intellectual Reserve, Inc.

"I KNEW I WAS CLOSE to the goal line, but I didn't know how close," Joseph Wirthlin said of a conference championship football game. "Although I was pinned at the bottom of the pile [of defenders], I reached my fingers forward a couple of inches and I could feel it. The goal line was two inches away. At that moment I was tempted to push the ball forward. I could have done it. And when the refs finally pulled the players off the pile, I would have been a hero. No one would have ever known. I had dreamed of this moment from the time I was a boy. And it was right there within my reach. But then I remembered the words of my mother. 'Joseph,' she had often said to me, 'do what is right, no matter the consequence. Do what is right and things will turn out OK.' I wanted so desperately to score that touchdown. But more than being a hero in the eyes of my friends, I wanted to be a hero in the eyes of my mother. And so I left the ball where it was—two inches from the goal line. I didn't know it at the time, but this was a defining experience. Had I moved the ball, I could have been a champion for a moment, but the reward of temporary glory would have carried with it too steep and too lasting a price. . . . I knew I must do what is right."[1] Such was the steadfast integrity and quiet goodness of Joseph B. Wirthlin, an Apostle of the Lord Jesus Christ.

Joseph Bitner Wirthlin, son of Joseph L. Wirthlin and Madeline Bitner, was born June 11, 1917, in Salt Lake City, Utah. Joseph's father served in the Presiding Bishopric of the Church for twenty-three years, first as a counselor to Bishop LeGrand Richards and then as Presiding Bishop from 1952 to 1961. Decades later, when Joseph was called to the Quorum of the Twelve Apostles, he spoke gratefully of his parents: "I pay tribute to my beloved earthly father, who taught me humility, diligence, honesty, trustworthiness, . . . and reverence and honor for God's chosen servants . . . [and] to my mother . . . for life itself, and then for the great lessons she taught me."[2] From his parents, Joseph learned compassion and service, the value of hard work, and to face all aspects of life with the attitude "come what may, and love it."[3]

Joseph earned the rank of Eagle Scout in the Boy Scouts of America. He enjoyed Scouting, singing, and especially sports. In high school, Joseph lettered in football, basketball, and track. He was a standout high school quarterback and played halfback on the University of Utah football team. Joseph gave up his senior year of football in 1936 to serve a mission to Germany, Austria, and Switzerland.

On his mission, Joseph told his companion what he hoped to find in a wife. "I didn't know her name, but I had in my mind the type of person she would be—one who lived the gospel and who was strong spiritually. I even described her to my companion—that she would be five foot five, that she would have blue eyes, and that she would have blonde hair." When his mission ended in 1939, Joseph returned to the United States to continue his education at the University of Utah. "I remember hearing someone mention a name: Elisa Rogers, a young woman who was in charge of a university dance at the Hotel Utah," Joseph said. "I decided I ought to meet her. I remember the first time I saw her. As a favor for a friend of mine, I had gone to her home to pick up her sister. Elisa opened the door, and I stared. There she was, beautiful, five foot five, blue eyes, blonde hair."[4] Joseph married Elisa on May 26, 1941, in the Salt Lake Temple and they became the parents of eight children. For sixty-five years, Joseph and Elisa shared what Joseph called "a perfect marriage." Joseph never left the house without kissing Elisa good-bye, and he would call often throughout the day to check on her.[5]

Joseph graduated from the University of Utah with a bachelor's degree in business and began working for his father in the family food processing and purveying business.[6] Joseph eventually took over the family business and expanded its production, and he became a prominent business leader in Salt Lake City.

During these busy and productive years, Joseph was also a leader in the Church. From 1955 to 1964 he served as bishop of the Bonneville Ward in Salt Lake City. The day he was released from serving as a bishop, Joseph was called to serve on the stake high council. Shortly thereafter, he was called to be a counselor to Russell M. Nelson in the Salt Lake Bonneville Stake. In 1971 he was again called to be a counselor to Russell M. Nelson, this time in the general presidency of the Sunday School. Joseph served in that capacity until 1975, when he was called to be an Assistant to the Quorum of the Twelve. He was the last man to be called to that position.

His call to the Quorum of the Twelve Apostles came shortly after his call to serve in the Presidency of the Seventy on October 3, 1986. President Thomas S. Monson said of his service in the Twelve, "It has been my opportunity to work closely with Joseph B. Wirthlin for many years. He personifies the description given by the Savior of Nathanael—'an Israelite indeed, in whom is no guile' (John 1:47). . . . He cares not for personal acclaim, desiring only to please His Heavenly Father and those who preside over the Church."[7]

On December 1, 2008, Joseph died of natural causes at his home in Salt Lake City. He was buried in the Salt Lake City cemetery next to his beloved wife, Elisa, who preceded him in death two years earlier. Following his internment, an endowed scholarship to benefit the Ute football program at the University of Utah was named in his honor. On January 2, 2009, when the Utes won the Sugar Bowl, all of the Utah players wore a commemorative sticker on their helmets with the initials JBW in Joseph's honor.[8]

1   Joseph B. Wirthlin, "Life's Lessons Learned," *Ensign*, May 2007, 46.

2   Don L. Searle, "Elder Joseph B. Wirthlin: Finding Happiness Serving the Lord," *Ensign*, Dec. 1986, 9.

3   Joseph B. Wirthlin, "Come What May, and Love It," *Ensign*, Nov. 2008, 26.

4   Joseph B. Wirthlin, "Lessons Learned in the Journey of Life," *Ensign*, Dec. 2000, 7.

5   "Elder Joseph B. Wirthlin: Committed to the Kingdom," *Ensign*, Feb. 2009.

6   Searle, 10.

7   Ibid., 13.

8   Lee Benson, "About Utah: Elder Wirthlin's Goodness Now a Legacy at U," *Deseret News*, Jan. 16, 2009, http://www.deseretnews.com/article/705277921/ Elder-Wirthlins-goodness-now-a-legacy-at-U.html?pg=1.

WILFORD WOODRUFF
Deliverance

Courtesy of the Church
Archives, The Church of Jesus
Christ of Latter-day Saints.

WILFORD'S CHILDHOOD WAS MARRED BY several accidents, including being bitten by a dog in the last stages of rabies and falling into a pot of scalding water. In his words, "I have been numbered with those who are apparently the marked victims of misfortunes. It has seemed to me at times as though some invisible power were watching my footsteps in search of an opportunity to destroy my life." In pondering the severity of the mishaps, he wrote, "The repeated deliverances from all these remarkable dangers I ascribe to the mercies of my Heavenly Father."[1]

Wilford Woodruff, son of Aphek Woodruff and Beulah Thompson, was born March 1, 1807, in Farmington, Connecticut. While religious subjects occupied his mind at an early age, Wilford did not profess a particular religion until age twenty-three. However, he read the scriptures and participated in "earnest prayer before God day and night as far as I could." Wilford recalled, "I had pleaded with the Lord many hours in the forest, among the rocks, and in the fields, and in the mill—often at midnight for light and truth and for His Spirit to guide me in the way of salvation."

That guidance came in the winter of 1833 as he learned of the restored gospel as preached by Zera Pulsipher. "I believed all that he said," Wilford wrote. "The spirit bore witness of its truth." When he began to read the Book of Mormon, "the spirit bore witness that the record which it contained was true." On December 31, 1833, he was baptized by Zera Pulsipher. "The snow was about three feet deep, the day was cold, and the water was mixed with ice and snow, yet I did not feel the cold," he recalled.[2]

Not long thereafter, Wilford made his way to Kirtland, Ohio, where on April 25, 1834, he met the Prophet Joseph Smith. When the Zion's Camp march began a week or so later, he joined the camp and marched to Missouri. From Missouri he went on a mission to the southern states. This was followed by a mission to the eastern states to share the gospel with family and friends. On this mission he organized an LDS branch at Fox Island before receiving word that he had been appointed to the Quorum of the Twelve Apostles. He was ordained an Apostle on April 26, 1839, at Far West, Missouri.

Wilford was called to serve a mission to England, but poor health threatened to prevent him from fulfilling that mission. Observing Wilford's feeble condition, Joseph Smith remarked, "Well, Brother Woodruff . . . you have started upon your mission." "Yes," Wilford said, "but I feel and look more like a subject for the dissecting room than a missionary." Joseph replied, "What did you say that for? Get up, and go along; all will be right with you." Wilford proceeded on the mission and voyaged across the Atlantic Ocean to reach British shores. About three months after arriving in England, he had baptized hundreds of people at the Benbow farm in Herefordshire. This was the beginning of his successful labor, which enabled Wilford to "bring into the Church, through the blessings of God, over eighteen hundred souls during eight months."[3]

In 1844 an opportunity for missionary service to the eastern states came again. Joseph admonished, "Brother Woodruff, I want you to go, and if you do not you will die." While Wilford was serving in the East, the Prophet was martyred. Sorrowing over the tragedy, Wilford Woodruff and Brigham Young called upon Sister Vose in Boston. Wilford wrote, "Brother Young took the bed and I the armchair, and then we veiled our faces and gave vent to our grief. Until now I had not shed a tear since the death of the Prophet. My soul had been nerved up like steel."[4]

By the end of August 1844, Wilford had returned to Nauvoo and was making preparations to leave for yet another mission to England. Among his preparations was a visit to the widows of the martyrs, Emma Smith and Mary Fielding Smith. Emma gave him a piece of oak for a staff, taken from Joseph's coffin. Mary gave him locks of hair from the heads of Joseph, Hyrum, Samuel, and Don Carlos Smith. Wilford then obtained strands of hair from members of the Quorum of the Twelve Apostles and placed the locks "in the knob of my staff as a relic of those noble men, the master spirits of the nineteenth century."[5]

As president of the British Mission, Wilford preached the gospel and published the good news. When he returned to the States, the Saints had begun their exodus from Nauvoo to Iowa Territory. He joined them in their temporary encampments in Iowa and helped organize a company to cross the plains to the Rockies.

For the remaining decades of his life, Wilford played a vital role in the frontier settlements of the West. However, his main assignment for two decades was to accompany Brigham Young, who told him, "Some day . . . I shall look to you for my journal." Wilford wrote a journal for sixty-three years and a history of the leading men in the Church. In referring to his writings, Wilford wrote, "I seem to be a marked victim of the adversary. I can find but one reason for this: the devil knew if I got into the Church of Jesus Christ of Latter-day Saints, I would write the history of that Church and leave on record the works and teachings of the prophets, of the apostles and elders."[6]

In 1877 Wilford gave the dedicatory prayer for the St. George Temple and at the close of the services was appointed to preside over the temple. In 1879 persecution against plural marriage caused Wilford to go into exile. He wrote, "For the first time in my life I have had to flee from my enemies for the gospel's sake. . . . They are trying to arrest me for obeying the law of God in reference to Plural Marriage." At the death of President John Taylor in 1887, Wilford became the leader of the Church. "It is a position I have never looked for," he wrote. "I pray God . . . to give me grace equal to my day."[7]

His were difficult days as persecution against Church leaders raged. However, on October 6, 1890, Wilford presented a manifesto ending plural marriage to assembled Saints in the Tabernacle. "I want to say to all Israel that the step which I have taken in issuing this Manifesto has not been done without earnest prayer before the Lord," he said.[8]

During Wilford's presidency many other noteworthy events occurred—the dedication of the Salt Lake Temple, the granting of general amnesty to Church members who had practiced plural marriage, and the granting of statehood for Utah. At the celebration of his ninetieth birthday, a banner with the words "We honor the man so honored of God" epitomized the life of the prophet.

As Wilford neared the end of his life, he summarized his journals and concluded that from 1834 to 1895 he had traveled 172,369 miles; held 7,555 meetings; attended 75 semiannual general conferences of the Church and 344 quarterly conferences; preached 3,526 discourses; established 77 preaching places in missions; organized 51 branches; received 18,977 letters; written 11,519 letters; assisted in confirming 8,952 Saints; labored 603 days in the Endowment House; and traveled through England, Scotland, Wales, six islands of the sea, 23 states, and five U.S. Territories in the cause of righteousness.[9]

At Wilford's bedside in San Francisco on September 2, 1898, was his counselor, George Q. Cannon. Cannon wrote of Wilford's last moments: "I arose about 6 o'clock. The nurse told me [Wilford] had been sleeping in the same position all the time. I took hold of his wrist, felt his pulse and I could feel that it was very faint. While I stood there it grew fainter and fainter until it faded entirely."[10] Wilford's remains were conveyed from San Francisco to Salt Lake City by rail.

1   Matthias F. Cowley, *Wilford Woodruff, History of His Life and Labors* (Salt Lake City: Bookcraft, 1964), 5, 11.
2   Cowley, 18, 33, 34, 35.
3   Ibid., 109, 119.
4   Ibid., 204, 208.
5   Ibid., 228.
6   Ibid., 346–347, 477.
7   Ibid., 506, 560.
8   Ibid., 570.
9   Andrew Jenson, *LDS Biographical Encyclopedia*, 1:26.
10 Cowley, 621.

BRIGHAM YOUNG
Determination

Copy print of daguerreotype
courtesy of LDS Church
Archives. Attributed to Marsena
Cannon ca 1853–1854.

FEW MEN OF THE NINETEENTH CENTURY match the caliber and dogged determination of Brigham Young. From humble beginnings in an obscure village in Vermont, he rose to the applause of thinking men; but more important, he grew in favor with God. Although some might contend that the laborious toils of farm labor and unwelcome poverty dominated his early years, the unwavering search for eternal truth permeated his thoughts.

Brigham Young, son of John Young and Abigail Howe Reading, was born June 1, 1801, in Whittingham, Vermont. Reading the Book of Mormon, listening to missionaries, and baptism brought answers to Brigham's search for truth: "When I saw a man without eloquence, or talents for public speaking, who could only say, 'I know, by the power of the Holy Ghost, that the Book of Mormon is true, that Joseph Smith is a Prophet of the Lord,' the Holy Ghost proceeding from that individual illuminated my understanding, and light, glory, and immortality were before me."[1]

Anxious to learn more about his new religion, Brigham journeyed to Kirtland, Ohio, to meet the Prophet Joseph Smith. "When I went to Kirtland, I had not a coat in the world," he said. "Neither had I a shoe to my feet, and I had to borrow a pair of pants and a pair of boots."[2] Of his initial meeting with Joseph, he recalled, "Here my joy was full at the privilege of shaking the hand of the Prophet of God, and receiving the sure testimony, by the spirit of prophecy, that he was all that any man could believe him to be as a true Prophet."[3]

On February 14, 1835, Brigham Young was ordained a member of the Quorum of the Twelve Apostles. As an Apostle, he was zealous in defense of the Prophet. One evening in Kirtland, after overhearing a man loudly rail against Joseph Smith, Brigham reacted: "I put my pants and shoes on, took my cowhide, went out and, laying hold of him, jerked him around and assured him that if he did not stop his noise and let the people enjoy their sleep without interruption, I would cowhide him on the spot, for we had the Lord's Prophet right here and we did not want the Devil's prophet yelling around the streets."[4]

The darkest day of Brigham's life was June 27, 1844, the day of the martyrdom of Joseph Smith. He wrote, "Spent the day in Boston with Brother Woodruff. . . . In the evening, while sitting in the depot waiting I felt a heavy depression of spirit, and was so melancholy I could not converse with any degree of pleasure. . . . I could not assign any reason for my peculiar feelings."[5] Twelve days later he learned of the tragic deaths of Joseph and his brother Hyrum. "The first thing I thought of was whether Joseph had taken the keys of the kingdom with him from the earth," wrote Brigham. "Bringing my hand down on my knee, I said, 'The keys of the kingdom are right here with the Church.'"[6]

With renewed conviction, Brigham returned to Nauvoo, where he resolutely declared to the Saints, "The Twelve are appointed by the finger of God. . . . an independent body who have the keys of the priesthood—the keys of the kingdom of God to deliver to all the world."[7] The authority of the Twelve was challenged on August 8, 1844, by Sidney Rigdon. With characteristic resolution and steadfastness, Brigham met the challenge. He seemed to appear to an assembled multitude like the Prophet Joseph Smith in physical stature and in speech. William C. Staines wrote, "I thought it was he . . . and so did thousands who heard it."[8]

Determined to carry forward the Lord's plans, Brigham encouraged the completion of the Nauvoo Temple. "We want to build the Temple in this place," he said, "if we have to build it as the Jews built the walls of the Temple in Jerusalem, with a sword in one hand and the trowel in the other."[9] Yet as the temple neared completion, threatened violence became unrestrained and a forced exodus was imminent. In February 1846 Brigham advised the Saints to flee from Illinois to safety in Iowa. Thousands responded and fled from the comforts of Nauvoo to the rigors of Iowa's wilderness. Their sacrifice and suffering, from the loess hills of Iowa to the barren plains of Nebraska and the rigors of the Rockies, are without parallel in historic migrations. To Brigham, their migration was an answer to prayer, for the Lord led His people to the right place—"a goodly land."[10]

In December 1847 Brigham was sustained as President of The Church of Jesus Christ of Latter-day Saints, fulfilling the prophecy given by Joseph Smith many years before in Kirtland that "the time will come when Brigham Young will preside over this church."[11] Brigham served faithfully in that capacity for more than thirty years. During those years, he oversaw the settlement of more than 350 communities in the West. When asked if he intended to settle more valleys, he said, "Why certainly we expect to fill the next valley and then the next, and the next, and so on. . . . We intend to hold our own here, and also penetrate the north and the south, the east and the west, there to make others and to raise the ensign of truth. . . . We will continue to grow, to increase and spread abroad, and the powers of earth and hell combined cannot hinder it."[12]

Brigham died at 4 p.m. on August 29, 1877, in Salt Lake City, after calling "Joseph, Joseph, Joseph." He advised that at his interment there should be "no crying or mourning with anyone as I have done my work faithfully and in good faith."[13]

1   *Journal of Discourses*, 1:90.
2   *Journal of Discourses*, 2:128.
3   B. H. Roberts, *Comprehensive History of the Church*, 1:289.
4   Leonard J. Arrington and Davis Bitton, *The Mormon Experience: A History of the Latter-day Saints* (New York: Vintage Books, 1979), 67.
5   Preston Nibley, *Brigham Young: The Man and His Work* (Salt Lake City: Deseret Book Co., 1970), 53.
6   James R. Clark, comp., *Messages of the First Presidency*, 6 vols. (Salt Lake City: Bookcraft, 1965–1975), 1:233.
7   *History of the Church*, 7:233.
8   As cited in Francis M. Gibbons, *Brigham Young: Modern Moses, Prophet of God* (Salt Lake City: Deseret Book, 1981), 104.
9   *History of the Church*, 7:256.

10   Brigham Young to Charles C. Rich, August 2, 1847, as cited in Leonard J.
      Arrington, *Charles C. Rich: Mormon General and Western Frontiersman* (Provo,
      Utah: Brigham Young University Press, 1974), 118.
11   Roberts, 1:289.
12   *Journal of Discourses*, 18:355, 356.
13   As cited in Nibley, 537.

STEVE YOUNG

Grit

Courtesy of the Church History
Library, The Church of Jesus
Christ of Latter-day Saints.

STEVE YOUNG HAS BEEN ONE of the top quarterbacks and one of the highest-paid players in the National Football League (NFL). Biographer Dick Harmon said of him, "Steve Young is a very self-effacing person. He goes out of his way to make his importance, his accomplishments, and his virtues appear as nothing. If you know Steve Young, you will take note that he is not a self-promoter and does not blow his own horn." Steve's definition of success is "to dream and strive for those dreams. To enjoy victory and grow stronger with defeat. To live life to the fullest and fill other lives with joy."[1]

Jon Steven Young, son of LeGrande Young and Sherry Steed, was born October 11, 1961, in Salt Lake City, Utah. By age six, he and his family had moved to Greenwich, Connecticut, where, "compared to the national average, the Youngs' house was in an affluent area. In Greenwich terms, their neighborhood was strictly middle-class."[2] Of his growing up in Connecticut, Steve said, "I used to think there were only four Mormons in the world—me, my parents and Brigham Young."[3]

Steve's father was the first to recognize that his son had "amazing coordination" and would one day compete in sports.[4] His father liked to tell Steve, "If you don't want to be part of the team, then go play golf or tennis." Steve said of his father, "He was big on playing your part. He made me stick with things."[5] Steve turned out to be an "all-American boy." He was a top-notch student and athlete, he was "blessed with good looks, and he had an ability to make everybody feel comfortable." In addition, the "National High School Athletic Coaches Association named [him] an honorable mention high school all-American."[6]

When the time came for Steve to select a college, coaches from Virginia, Syracuse, Cornell, and North Carolina came knocking at his door with "gift-wrapped offers."[7] Steve rejected their offers because his dream was to play with the Brigham Young University Cougar football team. When BYU's head coach LaVell Edwards came with an offer, Steve signed it. Harmon wrote, "If Edwards had only known then what he knew today, he would have had the Mormon Tabernacle Choir and a red carpet out for Steve Young."[8] Instead, Steve was nearly overlooked by Coach Edwards because BYU had "one of the most sophisticated passing offenses in the nation."[9] "'LaVell just couldn't fathom a quarterback running as fast as me,' [Steve] remembers. 'It didn't make sense to him.'"[10]

In his freshman year at BYU, Steve telephoned his father and said, "Dad, I've had it with this whole thing. I'm not having fun; I'm not enjoying myself. I think I'm going to quit." His father responded, "Son, you can quit, but you can't come home. I don't live with quitters."[11] Steve stayed and made BYU history. Although he was initially in the shadow of acclaimed quarterbacks like Jim McMahon, Steve soon outdistanced them all. For example, "as the BYU starter his junior year, he completed 230 of 367 passes (a whopping 62 percent) for 3,507 yards while running for 407 more. He was responsible for 28 BYU touchdowns that year."[12]

By the time his college football career ended, Steve had led the BYU Cougars to a "11–1 record, a national ranking, a bowl victory, and a conference championship. He set an NCAA record for pass completion percentage in a season (1983, 306 of 429, 71.3 percent)" and was a runner-up in the Heisman Trophy voting.[13] All this was accomplished while Steve maintained a 3.4 GPA with a double major in international relations and finance.

Within weeks of graduating from BYU at age twenty-two, Steve became known as the "forty-million-dollar man" because he signed a $40 million contract to play football with the Los Angeles Express. "I almost fainted that day," Steve said. "I remember talking to Channel 5 in

Los Angeles and I had to hold on to the rail. I was overwhelmed. It was unbelievable."[14]

The 1985 football season was difficult for Steve. Losing games and facing the financial instability of the Los Angeles Express caused him much distress. He "finished his USFL career with a very average sixteen touchdown passes and twenty-two interceptions. He completed only 54 percent of his passes and did not look like the superstar people expected from a $40 million man. . . . As it turned out, the USFL died a quick death and never flipped an opening kickoff coin again."[15]

Steve played for the Tampa Bay Buccaneers from 1985 to 1986 before joining the San Francisco 49ers from 1987 to 1999 and becoming the backup quarterback to Joe Montana. Of Montana, Steve said, "I played with the best to ever play the game."

Steve's abilities and reputation increased as he went on to be named Most Valuable Player of the NFL in 1992 and 1994 and a member of the Pro Football Hall of Fame.

When he retired, he had a 96.8 percent passing rate, the highest rating among NFL quarterbacks who had made at least fifteen hundred passing attempts. Harmon wrote of Steve's football career as being a "tale of ups and downs, disappointments and triumphs." Yet throughout his journey of professional successes and setbacks, Steve remained hopeful and determined: "Nobody but you should define what and who you are or what you can do. Having heroes and setting goals are important. And never lose sight of the horizon where tomorrow starts at the ending of today."[16]

1 Dick Harmon, *Steve Young: Staying in the Pocket* (Salt Lake City: Black Moon Publishing, 1995), xi, 23.
2 Laury Livsey, *The Steve Young Story* (Rocklin, CA: Prima Publishing, 1996), 12.
3 Harmon, 14.
4 Livsey, 13.
5 Harmon, 15.
6 Livsey, 24, 31.
7 Ibid., 30.
8 Harmon, 28.
9 Livsey, 38.
10 Harmon, 31.
11 Livsey, 48.
12 Harmon, 35.
13 Ibid., 50.

14 Ibid., 58.
15 Ibid., 78, 80.
16 Ibid., 86, 7, 174.

ABOUT *the* AUTHORS

Lloyd D. Newell

Lloyd D. Newell holds an MA in communications and a PhD in marriage, family, and human development from Brigham Young University, where he is a professor.

The author of more than a dozen books, he has addressed audiences in forty-six states and fifteen countries through his seminars and other speaking engagements. Since 1990, he has served as announcer and writer for the Mormon Tabernacle Choir broadcast, *Music and the Spoken Word*.

He and his wife, Karmel, are the parents of four.

SUSAN EASTON BLACK

DR. SUSAN EASTON BLACK JOINED THE faculty of Brigham Young University in 1978, where she is a professor of Church history and doctrine. She is also past associate dean of General Education and Honors and director of Church History in the Religious Studies Center.

The recipient of numerous academic awards, she received the Karl G. Maeser Distinguished Faculty Lecturer Award in 2000, the highest award given a professor on the BYU Provo campus. Dr. Black has authored, edited, and compiled more than 100 books and 250 articles.

She and her husband, George Durrant, are currently serving a mission in St. George, Utah.

MARY JANE WOODGER

Dʀ. Mᴀʀʏ Jᴀɴᴇ Wᴏᴏᴅɢᴇʀ ɪs a professor of Church history and doctrine at Brigham Young University. After obtaining a master of education degree at Utah State University, she received from BYU a doctor of education degree in educational leadership, with a minor in Church history and doctrine. She was honored by Kappa Omicron Nu with the Award of Excellence for her dissertation research on the educational ideals of President David O. McKay.

She is the author of several books and has also authored numerous articles on doctrinal, historical, and educational subjects that have appeared in various academic journals and religious publications. Dr. Woodger received the Best Article of the Year Award from the Utah Historical Society and has received the Brigham Young University Faculty Women's Association Teaching Award.